As I opened my computer and scanned *Position Yourself for Healing*, I yearned to have the book in my hands so I could take notes and highlight things we will incorporate in our ministry of healing and deliverance. The first part of the book gives a necessary foundation for receiving and/or ministering healing. Part II, *Eliminating Blockages*, reveals powerful truths to help those seeking healing and those ministering healing so they can remove every obstacle hindering the healing they seek. I wholeheartedly recommend Barbara De Simon and her newest book!

Dr. Douglas Carr
www.dcfreedomministry.com

Barbara's book, *Position Yourself for Healing*, fully demonstrates God's desire and grace upon our lives to take us into healing and wholeness. Regardless of the difficult situations of life we have been through, God is able to take every intended curse and turn it into a wonderful blessing. This book will help you to find the place to hope again, even in the midst of any negative situation. Read, enjoy, and receive the healing power of the Lord in your life that leads into victory and freedom.

Faith Marie Baczko, Author, Speaker, and President
Headstone Ministries

ENDORSEMENTS

Without a doubt, Barbara De Simon has written a treasure with this book, and released a tremendous gift to us as she clarifies the absoluteness of God's healing love both from a biblical perspective as well from her personal experiences of walking out the reality of healing and restoration in her own life.

I am excited, along with her (as she writes in her Foreword), about "how your life will change as you apply the strategies in this book. So, without delay, let's discover how we can get into the flow of God's mercy, power, and grace over EVERY aspect of our being— spirit, soul, and body, and not miss a thing God has for us in this life."

Simply put, if we take them seriously, Barbara's insights on eliminating blockages will prove to be invaluable in maturing us as people of the Kingdom.

Mary Audrey Raycroft
Teaching Pastor, Catch the Fire, Toronto, Ontario
Author, Itinerant Speaker and Founder of Releasers of Life Equipping Ministry

· · · · ·•••••●••••••· · · ·

I know and respect Barbara De Simon. She has published several books I have written and has been a valuable help to me. Barbara is stirred by the love and compassion of Jesus. She wants others to see Jesus as active in their lives as He has been in hers. *Position Yourself for Healing* is born out of her love for God, gratefulness for what He has done for her, and compassion for those who need His touch.

A powerful truth is highlighted through the Gospels and the book of Acts. Love and compassion are the hinge upon which the door of miracles hang. When Jesus and His followers saw people in distress, their compassion stirred them to partner with the Father in doing what He was doing and speaking what He was speaking. Such compassion, mixed with faith, led to outstanding healings: the blind received their sight, the deaf heard, the lame walked, the woman bent over by a spirit of infirmity immediately felt her spine straighten. Another woman had spent years and all her money on physicians without getting better. Jesus' love and compassion stirred faith and she received healing. Simon Peter's mother-in-law was healed so quickly she got up and prepared a meal for her guests. Lepers were cleansed, a boy was delivered of a deaf and mute spirit, and the man with a legion of demons, who no one had been able to help was set free. Miracles abound on the hinge of compassion!

It is the love and compassion of Jesus that stirs Barbara to minister to the sick, release freedom to captives, and bind up the wounds of the broken hearted. It is compassion that moved her to write this book and make it available to those who want to do what Jesus did, and even greater things than these, because He has gone to the Father.

On occasion, Jesus and His followers were so moved by compassion for mourners, they raised their dead to life—a mother's son, Dorcas whose friends gathered in her house and mourned her passing, and Mary and Martha's brother, Lazarus. The shortest verse of the Bible simply says, "Jesus wept" (John 11:36). Perhaps He wept not only from the grief He shared with Mary and Martha, but because He was calling Lazarus back to this world, knowing Lazarus would face persecution from the religious and would die again. I wonder if Jesus reflected on how He personally left the splendour of heaven when He entered this sin-sick world. Lazarus, like Jesus, was persecuted by those who had a form of religion but tried to squelch the power thereof. It is rumored that Lazarus never smiled again after being raised from the dead.

POSITION
Yourself
FOR HEALING

Finding the Sweet Spot Where
Healing Becomes Reality

SECOND EDITION

BARBARA DE SIMON

Cover design by Barbara De Simon

ISBN: 978-1-7774720-8-5

POSTION

Yourself

FOR

HEALING

DEDICATION

It is with a grateful heart that I dedicate this book to my late parents, Ella May and Victor Faulkner. I honor you and thank you for who you were—always doing the best you knew how. Thank you for teaching me Who my Heavenly Father was and still is; it has been the bedrock of my life and has enabled me to stand firm and never waver in the truth that God is love and God is good. Praise to His name! The Lord is ALWAYS for me, not against me. His will and purposes are always for my benefit. Thank you, mom and dad. Rest in peace with Jesus.

TABLE OF CONTENTS

AUTHOR'S FOREWORD

I can't think of any better way to begin this labour of love than with the following scripture:

> If I could speak all the languages of earth and of angels, but didn't love others, I would only be a noisy gong or a clanging cymbal. If I had the gift of prophecy, and if I understood all of God's secret plans and possessed all knowledge, and if I had such faith that I could move mountains, but didn't love others, I would be nothing. If I gave everything I have to the poor and even sacrificed my body, I could boast about it; but if I didn't love others, I would have gained nothing. Love is patient and kind. Love is not jealous or boastful or proud or rude. It does not demand its own way. It is not irritable, and it keeps no record of being wronged. It does not rejoice about injustice but rejoices whenever the truth wins out. Love never gives up, never loses faith, is always hopeful, and endures through every circumstance. Prophecy and speaking in unknown languages and special knowledge will become useless. But love will last forever! Now our knowledge is partial and incomplete, and even the gift of prophecy reveals only part of the whole picture! But when the time of perfection comes, these partial things will become useless. When I was a child, I spoke and thought and reasoned as a child. But when I grew up, I put away childish things. Now we see things imperfectly, like puzzling reflections in a mirror, but then we will see everything with perfect clarity. All that I know now is partial and incomplete, but then I will know everything completely, just as God now knows me completely. Three things will last forever—faith, hope, and love—and the greatest of these is love. (1 Corinthians 13 NLT)

This says it all, doesn't it? Although we are able to prophecy and speak in tongues, it is only in part and although they are both valuable, it is more important to love—to begin with love, to love through, and to end with love being at the forefront of our mind and heart. With love being the goal, let us put childish things away and grow up in the Lord and in His truth, accepting His revelation according to the Holy Spirit.

In these days of confusion and tolerance, it is crucial to know what love is and what it is not. In the world, love seems to require the acceptance of *all* things and *all* behaviors and has an expectation of agreement from everyone, on every matter. If I don't agree with someone, it is seen as hate. But this is not a biblical understanding of love. Although love is patient, kind, and does not dishonor others, it also rejoices with the truth and will protect others no matter the cost.

If I saw that a person was about to cross the street in front of a speeding car, I would intervene. I would stop them! Obviously, it wouldn't be love for me to just stand by as they get hit by a car! If a woman is about to exit a public restroom with toilet paper stuck to the bottom of her shoe, I stop her and tell her! Even if it's a stranger. It might embarrass her *for a moment*, but it's much better than the ongoing humiliation she would suffer if I ignored it.

In the same way, if I experience breakthrough in my life and the Lord reveals a key that others can also use, it is not love for me to keep it to myself. And if the Lord puts a word on my heart that could bring healing to someone, I'm going to share it, gently, for redemptive purposes, even if there is a possibility it won't be received. My ego or feelings are of no consequence when it comes to someone else's wellbeing. I would rather speak and be rejected than not speak at all.

Ephesians 4:11-16 tells us that Christ has given the church, apostles, prophets, evangelists, pastors, and teachers to equip God's people to do the work of the Kingdom and to build up the body of Christ until we ALL come into unity of the faith and of the knowledge of Jesus, being made perfect, growing up into the fullness of Christ. This is accomplished by speaking the truth in love, not by speaking easy words, comfortable words or words that tickle the ears, but *truth in love*. Truth can be hard to hear, but love speaks it anyway. Love is not always ooey, gooey, dripping with sentiment, but can be tough at times, necessary, but also life giving and redemptive. Speaking "in love" isn't about the tone of our voice, it is about having love in our heart for the person we are speaking with (thank you to Dr. Bernardine Daniels for that nugget of truth).

So often when a person speaks truth, it can come from a place of annoyance or judgement, but this is when we need to be silent. It is not for us to speak truth when our heart is not right. Only when our heart is full of love for an individual should we speak; only then are our words seasoned the right way, in the power of God and able to bring about transformation.

All the challenges addressed in this book I have had to work through with God. I am no stranger to adversity in various forms and I am still a work in progress, but I am submitted to the One Who redeems it all—who makes beautiful, new things out of broken pieces. I don't write this book because I'm perfect or have all the answers. I write this book because God has put a love for people in my heart and a passion to see the fullness of Christ's resurrection power made manifest in my life and the lives of others. If my Lord Jesus suffered for it, by golly, I'm going to lay hold of it—with force if I must.

Having said that, here's our first, tough love, truth bomb: As true followers and disciples of Christ, when we don't experience *all* Christ died to give us, fulfilling the days ordained for us on this earth, the deficit is not on God's end. The deficit is on our end, *possibly* in our life, *perhaps* in our heart, or our mind, but *definitely* at minimum in this world. When that happens, we must *contend* for what is rightfully ours. How we contend is the subject matter of this book.

Have you ever just tolerated something like a physical or emotional issue that just kind of wore you down, until finally, one day, you rose up and said, "enough is enough?"

I felt like Eeyore from Winnie the Pooh—always with a dark cloud over my head, never really feeling successful and always sensing unfortunate events coming my way. I knew these feelings were not in line with who I was as a daughter of God, and I had prayed and dealt with what I knew was tied to it, but finally one day, as this gloom persisted, I kind of snapped (in a good way). I finally decided I wasn't going to tolerate it anymore and I allowed myself to express the deep exasperation I felt about it, in prayer with God.

With this familiar darkness hovering, I began to make my way to the clinic for blood work. Again, I was getting blood drawn for a cholesterol test and I wasn't happy about it. The doctor just wouldn't let up. I had no other markers for potential heart problems. My blood pressure was fine. I didn't smoke. But I was in my fifties and my family history was riddled with red flags. So, there I was again. All the numbers indicated high cholesterol despite what I did with my diet and exercise, and I was fed up with the doctor's pressure to take medication.

As I drove, I prayed with fervour. I prayed loudly, fully persuaded of my words and in full agreement with them. First, I praised God for Who He was and is, and I declared the finished work of Christ on my behalf. I declared who I am in Jesus, and I let the devil know his time was up. I commanded all curses to be broken and all familiar spirits to leave me alone, in Jesus' name. I got my sword out and I fought the good fight with the truth, clearing the atmosphere around me. What happened next changed me. What happened next shifted my entire life; the presence of the Lord God Almighty fell in my car like I've never experienced before.

I pulled over to park by the curb as the Glory of God fell and hung in the air, thick like honey. I was grateful the Lord waited until I was almost parked as I literally became afraid to move. I was frozen. Hands out, head bowed, hot tears leaking from my eyes, my mouth whispering prayers in a heavenly language, taking Him in. Loving Him. Loving Him, loving me. Completely overtaken by His goodness and kind of in shock as I had never experienced His presence with such intensity. It turns out, when we take a bold stand for Jesus—for all He died to give us—for righteousness and for ourselves to live in God's fullness, heaven manifests in the here and now and we're never the same. From that day forward, I never felt that dark cloud looming over me again. All praise and glory to our saviour and best friend, Jesus.

So, I begin *Position Yourself for Healing* in a posture of love and in the love of Christ before you, and I encourage you to reject any and all false guilt and condemnation that might want to come against you as you read (it is not coming from me or my words). There is no condemnation in my heart or my intent with this book, only love, encouragement, and exhortation to enter into a full gospel according to the scriptures and God's heart for you. There's work to do in this world. Every disciple of Jesus has a job to do, out of their own deep well of love with Jesus, and we must be healthy enough, emotionally, and physically to fulfill it.

In a world where evil exists and thrives, we *must contend* for heaven to manifest in our midst and in our body. It is not a road of passivity or timidity. It is a road of standing and then standing some more, just as Ephesians 6:10-18 outlines, as we submit to God and resist evil. Our battle is not against flesh and blood but against evil rulers and unseen powers in the earthly realm and atmosphere. We don't fight for victory, we fight *from* victory, enforcing the truth and the reality of it in our lives.

I'm excited about how your life will change as you apply the strategies in this book. So, without further delay, let's discover how we can get into the flow of God's mercy, power, and grace over *every* aspect of our being, spirit, soul, and body, and not miss a thing God has for us in this life. Let's take a deep dive together!

INTRODUCTION

I think all who pick up this book would agree that healing is important, and healing, in some form or another this side of heaven is something most people are seeking, for different reasons. Wanting long life and a better quality of life is universal but the *why* behind it can vary. Some want to be available for their family, some want to be comfortable, pain-free and enjoy life, and some know they have been called by God to fulfill a mission here on this earth.

To expand these thoughts even further, let's remember that we are a three-part being, created by God in His image. We are primarily a spirit-being. We have a soul which is our mind, will, and emotions and we live in an earthly tent which is our physical body. Many people, when thinking about healing, only see the need in our physical parts, but in fact, we all have the need for divine healing in every part of who we are.

We, as descendants of Adam and Eve, need healing in all three aspects of our being. We need spiritual healing due to the fall of Adam and Eve. Their rebellion caused us all to die in spirit and so we need to be re-born by the Spirit of God to be alive to God and in relationship with Him again. We need healing in our soul (mind, will and emotions) in order to be at peace and live a life free of emotional and mental breakdown. Lastly, we need healing in our body so we can live out our days on this earth being able to move and physically be where we need to be without confinement.

Now more than ever, in our world of artificial this and artificial that, lab-grown and over-processed food sources, fear, anxiety, stress and trauma, our health on every front is being threatened. We contend with health issues that hold us hostage and sometimes cut the number of our days short. We pray for healing, but the experience of it for ourselves and others is elusive and difficult to obtain. Sometimes we win, but other times we lose. I have been on both sides of the contention. I have prayed for myself and been healed, AND I have prayed for myself and NOT been healed. . . yet. I have prayed for others and seen healing. I have also prayed for others and NOT seen healing—at least how I had hoped.

When praying for healing, my intent, and I think with most Christians who pray for healing, is for a person to be healed *on the earth* so they will stay with us longer. There are times when this is realized and we celebrate, but there are other times when it's not realized, and it can be heart-breaking. We don't understand how a merciful and gracious God *seems* to not come through for us and we feel disillusioned for a time. However, if we are willing to see things from a higher perspective, indeed from God's perspective, things look a whole lot different.

You know that expression, "You can't see the forest for the trees?" This expression describes moments when we can actually be blinded to the broader perspective of a situation because we are too close to the details; we are so invested in *our* desired outcome of a situation that we can't see the bigger picture. God sees the bigger picture and His desire is for us to see it too. So, He invites us up into our heavenly position with Him[1] to see through His eyes.

I used to hate it when I heard people say this. I used to think it was unbelief speaking and perhaps it's hard for you to hear too. The truth is, the God-perspective is, the best and fullest form of healing is found on the other side. The greatest healing is found by crossing over and being home with Jesus and just because the person you've prayed for transitioned to heaven, doesn't mean they weren't healed. They *were* healed! They were *completely* healed, and they are happier in heaven than they ever were on the earth.

If you operate as an intercessory prayer partner, someone who is drawn to come alongside others to pray and declare the truth of God's Word on their behalf, perhaps you have been tempted to feel

---

[1] "And God raised us up with Christ and seated us with him in the heavenly realms in Christ Jesus," (Ephesians 2:6 NIV).

disappointed because the outcome you wanted didn't come. Perhaps you have struggled to understand why. I think this is very common. First, take your position as a heavenly being sitting in heavenly places with Jesus so you have the right perspective, then ask the Lord to show you what He sees. The Lord loves to give us His understanding.

As we seek His understanding together, the Lord could show you any number of things. God loves it when we come to Him with our questions and broken hearts. He loves to comfort those who are hurting, and He loves it when we choose to love and trust Him through it all.

Our second *tough love, truth bomb* as follows is something to consider when we don't see the healing in others we've been praying for: *praying for someone else is a whole lot different than praying for yourself*. Why? I think several reasons, but one we very often miss is that it's not possible for us to know what the other person *really* wants. Do they *want* to be healed on this earth, or do they want what they see as everlasting relief found in heaven? We think we know what they want. After all, how could they want to leave us? And perhaps they tell us what we want to hear, but we have not lived their life—we have not walked in their shoes. We don't know the pain they carry around in their heart and body from this world.

Sometimes (now don't shoot the messenger), we want physical healing for someone else more than they want it for themselves. *Sometimes* this affects outcomes, but *nothing* is black and white here. We want our loved one healed because we don't want them to leave us, but it is possible that once our loved one gets a glimpse of heaven, they would rather cross over and remain there, rather than be in this world a minute longer. The perspective of the one who is considering the possibility of finally being home with Jesus is a lot different than the perspective of the one about to lose their loved one.

There is a reason why Jesus asked the man at the Pool of Bethesda, "Do you *want* to get well?" (John 5:6b NIV, emphasis added). Sometimes people don't want to be healed here on earth— perhaps because they're weary of this fallen world or a difficult life, or because they just really love Jesus, and heaven is so inviting.

People can have other reasons, sometimes hidden deep, for not wanting to be healed. It is possible, because of their brokenness, that they have a sense of heroism or martyrdom in enduring illness and dying early. And even other times people have become accustomed to their maladies, and their maladies have become part of who they are. Regardless of the reasons, we will not experience healing here on earth if we first do not desire it—no matter who is praying for us.

Of course, these are not the only reasons for not seeing the healing we want in others. There could be other reasons, but we don't always know what they are. God's ways are higher than ours and there are some things we won't understand until we get to heaven. This beautiful relationship we have with God requires faith and trust in Him, believing that in ALL things, God works for the good of those who love Him. What the enemy intends to use to harm, God takes in His hands and says, "NO! She (he) is mine! I will redeem it. I will comfort and restore her (his) heart."

Even though there are still mysteries with God, I do believe, going into the year 2022, we are on the cusp of the greatest outpouring of revelation and glory we have ever seen. (And now at the revision of this book in 2024, we are even closer!) The veil between heaven and earth is getting thinner and we will "see" and understand more about the Kingdom of God than we ever have before. Throughout this decade, many mysteries will be unveiled, and greater breakthrough will be had by many.

Healing. The whole topic is a bit messy. There can be a whole lot of emotion tied up in it, which makes me just want to avoid the conversation all together because I don't want to offend, but the Lord is not letting me. My heart is compelled by love to reach out to you and every reader, with encouragement, truth, tools, and strategies on living your best life under the protection of Christ, free from chronic illness, disease and strife which comes directly from the evil one. Hopefully you will see and receive that love throughout these pages.

If there is something you can do or pray that will alleviate your own suffering, don't you want to know what it is? Are you surprised by that possibility? Are you thinking, *but isn't my healing all up to God?* If you thought that, you're not alone, but here's the answer: It's actually not. We participate with God in partnership to bring about our own healing and how we participate is the topic of this entire book. So, I implore you, keep reading. Push past your inclination to be offended. Push past your religious rebuttals and allow the Holy Spirit to whisper to you. You could find a key that will unlock the healing and divine health you've been looking for.

Welcome to *Position Yourself for Healing*. I pray this book delivers revelation so powerful, it ushers in a whole new victory and breakthrough in your life and causes you to remain and abide in TRUE life abundant, just as Jesus promised in John 10:10.[2]

Pull up a chair friend; the table is being set. The Cook in the kitchen has been marinating these words for years and the Holy Spirit is all about serving them up in such a way that you can and will receive them. Be healed in Jesus' name!

---

[2] "The thief does not come except to steal, and to kill, and to destroy. I have come that they may have life, and that they may have it more abundantly" (John 10:10 NKJV).

Chapter 1

PASSOVER

This book has been on my heart for many years, ever since I re-released my first book, *Barren No More* in 2016. It has taken me five years to finally get these first words down on paper (or on my computer to be exact), not because it's not important, but because it is. It is extremely important. It is vital to many in this hour so they can experience the victory they need, here and now. Many are called to extraordinary assignments but won't be able to achieve them without healing in their mind and body. There has been much resistance in the spirit to me writing this book. Even now, there are five other things trying to distract me, but I resolve now, to do as the Lord has called.

My book, *Barren No More*, is a book that contains twenty-one steps to inner healing and deliverance but was written for women/couples going through infertility struggles or a delay in childbearing. In it, I give my testimony of healing and breakthrough in bearing children which had much more to do with heart and emotional issues than physical issues, but as we know, the body's health will follow the health of the soul (inner man/heart) so it's possible my body had an issue, I just never had it diagnosed. (See additional resources: The Deepest Well by Dr. Nadine Burke Harris and Scared Sick by Robin Karr-Morse and Meredith S. Wiley.) For biblical references supporting this truth see Proverbs 14:30, Proverbs 15:13, Proverbs 17:22, Proverbs 18:14, Proverbs 4:23, and Proverbs 23:7.

Today, two days post Easter Sunday (Resurrection Day) and Passover 2021, a year when Easter and Passover coincide perfectly, seems like a great time to begin writing this book for two reasons. First, Passover and Easter coinciding is a wonderful picture of the Jewish and Christian faiths coming together. Secondly, Passover illustrates for us God's heart for healing and deliverance in a powerful way.

Passover is one of the Jewish feasts that God commanded the Israelites to celebrate each year. It's a time of remembrance—a time to recall and honor the first Passover, God's great act of deliverance on behalf of Israel's ancestors who were oppressed, enslaved, and held captive in Egypt. Passover is also a strategic time for us to celebrate Jesus as our Passover Lamb—the One Who rescued us and delivered us from slavery to sin and the devil. Let's remember Who God really is on our behalf, bringing to the forefront of our mind the desire of God's heart for all His children to be free, walking in deliverance, divine health, and healing.

After generations of enslavement, the God-ordained time of Israel's deliverance had come. God called Moses to stand in His place and become the deliverer for Israel as he stood before the Glory of God in a bush on fire—yet unconsumed. After some convincing, Moses headed to Egypt to fulfill his mission, but for a time, God hardened Pharoah's heart so that he would not allow the Israelites to leave. Pharoah relentlessly refused to let the Israelites go, lasting through 10 plagues, until his own eldest son was taken. Every first-born son and cattle among Egypt perished and became a sign of God's judgement against the Egyptians (Exodus 4-12) for their mistreatment of God's people.

In a great foreshadowing of Jesus' mandate, the Lord provided a way out and a great deliverance for His people through the blood of a spotless lamb applied to the door frames of the Israelites' homes. The spirit of death which visited every household that fateful night, passed over those who had dipped the hyssop branch and created a blood barrier—a blood streaked, blood dripping down, entryway.

The blood marked their homes. The blood sealed their doors shut to the spirit of death just as now, the blood of Jesus, our spotless Lamb and our Heavenly Father's first-born Son, seals our doors shut to death as well. Indeed, the blood of Jesus still works, *completely* delivering us from early and eternal death, *when we apply it to every* part of our lives.

The Israelites needed divinely inspired direction, not their own good ideas. And so do we.

For Israel's deliverance to occur, God's people needed a prophet to hear God's voice and specific direction on how to proceed. They needed God's Word in that hour, not their own good ideas or soulish musings. They needed Moses, who was able to communicate with God and who was willing to be obedient to God's call on His life. We too need to hear God's voice to know His heart and direction for our own healing and deliverance.

After 430 years, God's hand moved and the time of Israel's oppression in Egypt came to an end. Amidst the details of their mass exodus, the heart of our God and Healer is revealed. Not only were the Israelites set free from slavery—back-breaking work and mistreatment, they were also enabled to plunder Egypt causing them to leave with articles of clothing and objects made of silver and gold. The fear of God fell on the Egyptians and whatever the Israelites asked for, they were willing to give. After the first-born of all the Egyptians died, they must have been very eager to see the Israelites go! Additionally, God promised to keep the Israelites in good health as they submitted to His ways:

There the Lord issued a ruling and instruction for them and put them to the test, He said, 'If you listen carefully to the LORD your God and do what is right in his eyes, if you pay attention to his commands and keep all his decrees, I will not bring on you any of the diseases I brought on the Egyptians, for I am the LORD, who heals you. (Exodus 15:25b–26 NIV)

Through forty years in the wilderness, the Israelites' clothes did not wear out and their feet did not swell (Deut. 8:4 NIV). The Lord God fed them with Manna from heaven and met all their needs. It was God's heart to take care of His children in every way, from the top of their heads to the tip of their toes.

God wants us to intersect His Glory, so we can be well in every way.

Unfortunately, the Israelites rebelled against God and yes, God allowed them to feel the consequences of their disobedience, but His heart was and is always for restoration, deliverance, and healing. We see it all throughout the Exodus story.

God wants us to intersect His Glory, His healing stream, so we can be well and healed in every way. God wants us to hear His direction and instruction and heed His Word to experience the manifestation of *all* Jesus died to give us. God has done His part. He has accomplished all He needed to, to heal us *completely*. Jesus hung on the cross and with His last breath said, "It is finished." Jesus' job of destroying the works of the devil, atoning for our sin, bearing away our sickness and disease, restoring us to the Father, graciously granting to us His health and righteousness was finished and DONE.[3] He needed to do nothing more. The power of sin and death and *everything tied to it*—sickness, weakness and disease was broken. These things no longer have any hold on us (born-again lovers and followers of Jesus), and no longer have any authority in our lives. Romans 8:1-2 says:

---

[3] Colossians 2:13-15, 1 John 3:5&8, 2 Cor. 5:21, 1 Peter 2:24

Therefore, there is now no condemnation for those who are in Christ Jesus, because through Christ Jesus the law of the Spirit who gives life has set you free from the law of sin and death. (NIV)

This verse tells us we are no longer bound to the law which caused us to live in sin, to be dead to God and to remain in a perpetual state of dying, but we have been set free and are now bound to a different law—the law of the Spirit Who gives life. Now, we are empowered to live holy and righteous[4] as we continually receive renewing life from the Spirit, bringing about healing in every aspect of our being. Romans 8:11 says:

> The Spirit of God, who raised Jesus from the dead, lives in you. And just as God raised Christ Jesus from the dead, he will give life to your mortal bodies by this same Spirit living within you. (NLT)

We are empowered by the Spirit to live holy lives, free from sin.

This is the absolute truth, however, living it and experiencing it takes our surrender and our participation. We are called to put to death the misdeeds of the flesh and live by the Spirit: "For if you live according to the flesh, you will die; but *if by the Spirit you* put to death the misdeeds of the body, you will *live*" (Romans 8:13 NIV, emphasis added). "You will live" indicates life abundant, not just a beating heart, but emphatically living true life, actively with *full* vigour and health.[5]

Jesus makes all things new (Rev. 21:5), but this is *mostly* a process in our lives and not an instantaneous event at our re-birth. When we are born-again, we are re-born *immediately* in spirit, in fact God's Spirit comes to dwell within us, but our soul and body are not *immediately* regenerated or healed. Our soul and body are healed over time *as we submit* to the Lord and invite the Holy Spirit to

---

[4] "By his divine power, God has given us everything we need for living a godly life" (2 Peter 1:3 NLT).

[5] https://www.blueletterbible.org/lexicon/g2198/kjv/tr/0-1/

overtake every aspect of our being. Perhaps a person's re-birth experience is so powerful that their soul is transformed in great measure at the same time, but we can't assume it happens that way for everyone. Our complete transformation is a work of the Holy Spirit, and the Lord will re-new us according to His purposes and in His time as we submit to Him.

It is a glorious thing to be renewed by the Lord. As we are willing to allow it, by being in the Spirit and willfully submitting our soul and body to the Spirit, God will encounter us, touch our wounded places, and heal our emotions. He may even give you direction on things to change in the natural to bring about healing in your body. He may instantaneously heal your body, or He may heal you over time as you submit to His direction. Your body may heal simply as a wonderful side effect of having your mind, emotions and heart healed. Either way, Jesus is interested in healing *every part* of you, including your broken heart, weary soul and your weakened or sick body—after all, He did create each part of you with perfect intentions and He wants to see each part of you come back to that same wholeness.

> *Jesus wants to heal every part of who we are—spirit, soul, and body.*

Just as God completely liberated the Israelites from all oppression connected to Egypt, so He has provided for our complete liberation from our Egypt, including freedom from sin, sickness, disease, and death (unto hell) through Jesus Christ. Jesus stepped into our world with all its chaos, oppression, and sin, and allowed the weight of all our pain, suffering, illness, disease, and death to fall on Him. Anything we could possibly suffer in this world He suffered and took upon Himself.[6] Despite the crushing weight of it all, He emerged victorious offering new life to all who are willing to partake. We can enter in to that same new life with Christ when we

---

[6] "This High Priest of ours understands our weaknesses, for he faced all of the same testings we do, yet he did not sin" (Hebrews 4:15 NLT).

completely surrender our lives to Him and give Him control, dying to ourselves, our wants, our will, and our desires.

If you're asking, "If Jesus took death upon Himself, why are we still experiencing it?" First, I would say, we're not. We aren't experiencing death. Disciples of Christ don't experience death; they experience transition, from one reality to another. We will never taste death which is hell. Even though our flesh and blood, our earthly *tent*, shuts down and ceases to function, our inner man, *who we really are*, goes from this world straight to heaven, with Christ, where we will immediately be present with Him in our heavenly body. I am not suggesting that in this world we will live forever. No. Our earthly bodies are temporal and will pass away. In this world we are subject to time, so our bodies age, but it is the will of God for us to age gracefully and fulfill the days He has ordained for us on this earth.

It is the will of God for us to age gracefully and fulfill our days on the earth.

Laying hold of these truths and believing them with all our heart is our first step to seeing them manifest in our lives. If we're unsure, we will miss out. Consider James 1:5-8:

> But if any of you lacks wisdom, let him ask of God, who gives to all generously and without reproach, and it will be given to him. But he must ask in faith *without any doubting*, for the one who doubts is like the surf of the sea, driven and tossed by the wind. For that person ought not to expect that he will receive anything from the Lord, being a double-minded man, unstable in all his ways. (NASB, emphasis added)

These verses speak about asking the Lord for wisdom but can be applied to asking the Lord for anything. Asking in faith looks like being fully persuaded that you will receive what you ask for. It is believing *without* even a hint of doubt. Doubt and faith do not mix; in fact, doubt nullifies faith. Jesus said in Matthew 21:21-22:

> I tell you the truth, if you have faith *and don't doubt*, you can do things like this and much more. You can even say to this mountain, 'May you be lifted up and thrown into the sea,' and it will happen. You can pray for anything, and if you have faith, you will receive it. (NLT, emphasis added)

So many people believe God *can* heal but they aren't convinced He's *willing*. Unfortunately, this is enough doubt to cause us to be double-minded, not receiving anything from the Lord. This is why no one is healed when we add the tag line, "If it be your will," at the end of our prayer for healing. Do not be in doubt over whether it is God's will to heal you. God's Word is clear! We have already been healed by His stripes[7] (the wounds inflicted on Jesus' body), but we must *completely* believe it to experience it.

In Matthew 8, a man with leprosy came to Jesus worshipping Him and saying, "Lord, if You are willing, You can make me clean" (Matthew 8:2 NKJV), and Jesus said, "*I am willing*; be cleansed" (Matthew 8:3 NKJV, emphasis added). The Spirit of Jesus is more than willing to heal you too, my friend. He is no respecter of persons. In fact, Jesus has already done it. Believe it. Know it, and it will manifest.

Passover was not just for the Israelites. Passover is also for us, the Gentiles, and followers of Jesus Christ. Jesus is our Passover Lamb, and His blood still works on our behalf as we apply it to our life, soul, body, and every point of entry.

Dip the hyssop branch in the blood friend. Apply it to the gateways of your life. Plead the blood, declare your innocence in Christ, and watch as healing comes like a wave of refreshment and renewal, crashing through your pain, grief, illness, and everything trying to hold you back. Believe it! Put your faith behind it and you will see it.

---

[7] "—by whose stripes you were healed" (1 Peter 2:24 NKJV).

Chapter 2

OUT OF THE BOX

The healing power of God shows up in unlikely places—amid a crowd *imparted* to an inconspicuous woman who had been bleeding for twelve straight years (Mark 5:25-34), a meeting between Jesus and a Greek woman as she fell at His feet believing in faith that all her daughter needed were crumbs from His table (Mark 7:24-30), a cobblestone street in Israel as Healing Evangelist Todd White ministered to a man who was Muslim,[8] and even a small fishing cottage in northern Ontario as my pre-Christian father successfully positioned himself in the love and mercy of God.

There my father sat on the couch in that cottage—Bible open. Me, young, impressionable, maybe six years old or so, taking it all in. I don't remember anything else from that trip, except for the horror of that massive fishing hook pierced straight through my father's thumb, sticking out front to back. Eyes wide, I wasn't sure how he would survive such a thing, but after a few days on that couch, praying and reading, he calmly removed that hook from his own

---

[8] Darren Wilson, *Father of Lights* (WP Films), DVD.

thumb without incident. Perhaps you don't think that's a big deal, but to me, it was a miracle.

I wonder if you're catching my point. Did you notice? Jesus healed many *before* His crucifixion and resurrection. A woman was healed simply by touching Jesus' garment without His prior knowledge or consent, as power was drawn out of Him by her desperation, expectation, and faith—or simply put, the cry of her heart. Jesus healed the daughter of a *Greek* woman after He very outwardly stated He had come first and primarily for the Jews. She could have taken offense, but she chose to remain humble and faithful, *shifting the compassion of God in her favor*. The healing power of God worked for a Muslim man, and my father who didn't yet believe in the divinity of Jesus.[9]

> God uses healing to demonstrate His love and mercy to pre-believers.

For years I was under the false thinking that one must first be a follower of Christ to be healed. This simply is not true. Being a Christian is not a pre-requisite for the mercy of God and healing. In the Bible, Jesus healed many who were not yet His followers. In fact, healing was used as a demonstration to many, for the truth of Jesus' identity and the love of God. The Holy Spirit will still do this today. Romans 5:8 says, "But God demonstrates His own love toward us, in that while we were still sinners, Christ died for us" (NKJV). While we were still sinning, still rejecting Him, Christ gave us His all—everything, including healing and His very life. Romans 5:8 could very well say, *while we were still sinners, Christ made healing available to us,* as it is prophesied in Isaiah 53:5 and re-iterated in 1 Peter 2:24, ". . .by His wounds you have been healed" (NIV). While we were still sinners, Christ took the scourging in His own body, so we could be healed in ours.

Healing is indeed part of the redemption package Jesus died, rose again, and ascended for. Jesus Christ is our Savior, Healer, and

---

[9] "For in Christ all the fullness of the Deity lives in bodily form..." (Colossians 2:9 NIV).

Deliverer, providing for us complete restoration of spirit, soul, and body. Just in case you're not convinced, here's Isaiah 53:4, "However, it was our sicknesses that He Himself bore, And our pains that He carried; Yet we ourselves assumed that He had been afflicted, Struck down by God, and humiliated" (NASB). Also, Psalm 103:2-5 makes it clear as follows:

> Bless the Lord, O my soul, And forget none of His benefits; Who pardons all your iniquities, Who heals all your diseases; Who redeems your life from the pit, Who crowns you with lovingkindness and compassion; Who satisfies your years with good things, So that your youth is renewed like the eagle. (NASB)

Second Corinthians 5:19 says that God reconciles us to Himself through Christ and in the process does *not count our sins against us*. Jesus, as demonstrated with the woman caught in adultery (John 8:1-11), does not condemn us, but sets us free through His love, compassion, and healing.[10] It's the kindness of God that leads us to repentance,[11] not a pointing finger, judgement, or anger. Likewise, we should not hold anyone's sin against them nor look down on them, but we are to love people and be like Jesus to them regardless of their beliefs and/or actions. The mercy of God, healing, forgiveness, reconciliation, and eternal life are available to all to accept as His gift. The Lord in His kindness woos us to Himself, through the Holy Spirit, longing and waiting for us to turn to Him— finally surrendering our lives to His Lordship in repentance.

> The Lord isn't really being slow about his promise, as some people think. No, he is being patient for your sake. He does not want anyone to be destroyed, but wants everyone to repent. (2 Peter 3:9 NLT)

---

[10] "For God did not send His Son into the world to condemn the world, but that the world through Him might be saved" (John 3:17 NKJV).

[11] "...not knowing that the goodness of God leads you to repentance" (Romans 2:4 NKJV)?

Although throughout these pages I present keys on how to co-operate with God to access healing for yourself, I am in no way saying, "One must jump through all these hoops to be healed." God is sovereign and He, in His mercy, can cause His love and healing to break through to whomever He chooses, whenever He chooses. Perhaps the love of God will suddenly cause a miracle to happen in your body as you sleep in your bed. Perhaps healing will manifest when you least expect it, however if it doesn't, the keys found in this book may help you access it.

There is a river flowing from the throne of God, full of His healing oil and it falls from heaven to earth like a waterfall. Positioning yourself under that waterfall and in that river is vital and may require an adjustment of some sort—a heart shift, an attitude change, a fresh surrender, a deeper surrender, a look up or a bow down, a new stirring of faith through study

Position yourself under the waterfall of heaven.

and worship, perhaps even a bold declaration that will break oppression and perhaps shift the very trajectory of your life. Only God knows our best move, but He is more than willing, in fact, He is eager to tell us what that is. All we need to do is listen and hear what the Spirit is saying with a humble heart.

··········●··········

The healing power of God has shown up in my own life numerous times, but most recently, quietly in my bedroom as I pled the blood of Jesus over my digestive system, all the way from the top to the bottom, as per the Lord's instruction.

For roughly six years, I have suffered with severe indigestion, regurgitation, and acid reflux daily. I juggled different diet changes, medications and strategies trying to alleviate the problem, gaining only VERY short-term relief, but a few weeks ago, as I drove home from church, praying for a friend, the Lord downloaded a word of knowledge. I saw in my mind's eye a young boy, crouched and cowering in a corner, afraid and trying to protect himself from the rage spewing against him and I heard in my spirit the word, *terror*. As the pictures were coming, I also understood that terror had taken up residence in that young boy's digestive tract and the Lord said to me, "Plead the blood of Jesus over his digestive tract to heal the damage it has caused."

After I received the word, I resolved to connect with my friend as soon as I could, but I also realized that that same word also applied to me. Just last year, I met with a mentor and pastor, Dr. Douglas Carr,[12] for a deliverance appointment, and he identified a spirit of terror in me that had come through abuse. He dealt with it, and I was delivered, so I knew that part was taken care of, but we didn't connect the dots to digestive issues. So, when I recently received the direction from God, I believed Him, and I prayed, pleading the blood of Jesus over every part of my digestive system, declaring the healing power of the blood over any damage caused by the spirit of terror, seeing in my mind's eye the coating of my esophagus, stomach, and intestines with that precious red flow.

I felt the shift immediately. I went through a few days of physical cleansing but was free from indigestion and reflux almost immediately. Now, months later, I am still free from chronic digestive upset. Praise God! The same miracle could happen for anyone willing to exercise their free-will to be delivered from terror and whatever may have opened the door to it (abuse, watching horror movies, or any event or circumstance that caused severe fear). As I contemplated my healing afterward, I realized that I hadn't even "asked" God to heal me as typically we might, and the Lord said to me, "You don't need to. Healing is already yours. Just take it."

· · · · · · • • • • ● • • • • • • • · · · ·

---

[12] Dr. Carr's website is www.dcfreedomministry.com where his resources can be purchased, and upcoming seminars are posted.

Healing flowed quite easily in the New Testament. Lepers were touched and made clean. Even some, including Lazarus, were raised from the dead. The Bible says that ALL *who came to Jesus* were healed. Consider the following passages:

> So the news about Him spread throughout all Syria; and they brought to Him ALL who were sick, those suffering with various diseases and pains, those under the power of demons, and epileptics, paralytics; and He healed them. (Matt. 4:24 AMP, emphasis added)

> When evening came, they brought to Him many who were under the power of demons; and He cast out the *evil* spirits with a word, and restored to health ALL who were sick [exhibiting His authority as Messiah], so that He fulfilled what was spoken by the prophet Isaiah: "HE HIMSELF TOOK OUR INFIRMITIES [upon Himself] AND CARRIED AWAY OUR DISEASES." (Matt. 8:16-17 AMP, emphasis added)

> Being aware of this, Jesus left there. Many followed Him, and He healed ALL of them [who were sick], and warned them not to tell [publicly] who He was. (Matt. 12:15-16 AMP, emphasis added)

> And when the men of that place recognized Him, they sent *word* throughout all the surrounding district and brought to Him ALL who were sick; and they begged Him to let them merely touch the fringe of His robe; and ALL who touched it were perfectly restored. (Matt. 14:35-36 AMP, emphasis added)

We see the word *all* several times in these verses. But does that mean that everyone who was ill was healed? No, it doesn't. It does *not* mean that every sick person was healed, but it does mean Jesus healed all *who came to Him—all who were hungry for it and all who sought Him out.* He never turned anyone away or said, "Oh sorry, you're going to have to stick this one out. My Father is trying to teach you something." No. Never. He had compassion on everyone that came to Him. Jesus said in John 10:10, "The thief comes only to steal and kill and destroy; I have come that they may have life, and have it to the full" (NIV). Unfortunately, not everyone believed in the miracles He was doing. Not everyone was willing to put faith in Him. Not everyone could receive nor wanted to and not everyone was open to the truth of Who Jesus was.

Jesus healed a paralyzed man at the pool of Bethesda and His question to the man was, "Do you want to get well" (John 5:6b, NIV)? Seems like a silly question, but apparently it needed to be asked. Why? Perhaps he was used to his condition and wasn't completely motivated to live differently—perhaps he didn't like change—or perhaps Jesus was just trying to stir his faith and expectation. Many others were there by the pool paralyzed, unable to move, but Jesus didn't heal them nor did any of them seek Him for healing. It seems

Do you want to get well? Are you willing to do what it takes?

the Father sent Jesus to the pool for the one—the one who was chosen by God to play a part in His great story of redemption in that moment, early on in Jesus' ministry.

In addition, there was a time and place where Jesus *couldn't* do miracles. He healed *a few* but not everyone and He was limited to what He could do.[13] That place was His hometown of Nazareth. It wasn't that Jesus didn't *want* to do miracles, he *couldn't*. Have you ever heard of Jesus not being *able* to do something? It seems heretical, doesn't it. What was it that *seemed* to make the power of God impotent in that place? According to Matthew 13:57, the people took offense at Jesus. They could not believe that Jesus, the

---

[13] Mark 6:5, "And He could not do any miracle there except that He laid His hands on a few sick people and healed them" (NASB).

carpenter, the boy that grew up in their own town, could do such things.

> ...And they were [deeply] offended by Him [and their disapproval blinded them to the fact that He was anointed by God as the Messiah]. Jesus said to them, "A prophet is not without honor (respect) except in his hometown and among his relatives and in his own household. And he COULD NOT do a miracle there at all [because of their unbelief] except that He laid His hands on a FEW sick people and healed them. (Mark 6:3-5 AMP, emphasis added)

What did they struggle to have faith in? Or more accurately, Who? They had no trouble having faith in God. They doubted Jesus. They doubted that such miracles could come through, in their perception, just a man, and additionally the hands of someone they *thought* they knew. They had already made their minds up about who Jesus was and He wasn't the One sent by God to be their Messiah. In their eyes, He was not the Son of God. He was just one of the runny-nosed kids from the neighborhood who grew up and came back spouting lofty words, full of pride. They were stuck in their minds on their own fleshly opinions and not able to see the truth.

Offense and unbelief cause us to miss out on miracles and healing.

Many times, Jesus revealed that faith and belief, made healing possible. He said, "Your faith has made you well" (Luke 17:19 NIV), "Daughter, your faith has healed you" (Mark 5:34 NIV), "Go,' said Jesus [to Bartimaeus], 'your faith has healed you" (Mark 10:52a NIV, brackets mine), "Go! Let it be done just as you believed it would" (Matthew 8:13 NIV), and "According to your faith let it be done to you" (Matthew 9:29 NIV). Faith is the currency of heaven; it will give you access to all heaven offers, however, faith must be joined with action and not mixed with doubt.

How does healing come? We can't *physically* see Jesus, track Him down and ask Him to heal us like they did in the Bible, so how does

Jesus heal us now? He heals us through the Holy Spirit, which is in fact the same way He healed those in the Bible. The healing power Jesus possessed *while on the earth* was the power of the Holy Spirit in and on Him.

Jesus' ministry began after His baptism in the Jordan and after His time of testing in the wilderness. Through this time, the Holy Spirit came upon Jesus and remained, filling Him, clothing Him, and empowering Him for ministry on earth. Yes, Jesus Christ is God and always has been God (John 1:1-3), but the scriptures are clear that Jesus willingly set His own divinity aside while on earth.

When Jesus was here, He functioned like that of a man only. Jesus did not heal in His own power, but in the power of the Holy Spirit. We get this understanding from the following passages: First, Jesus' baptism from Luke 3:21-22:

> One day when the crowds were being baptized, Jesus himself was baptized. As he was praying, the heavens opened, and the Holy Spirit, in bodily form, descended on him like a dove. And a voice from heaven said, "You are my dearly loved Son, and you bring me great joy. (NLT)

Then right after, in Luke 4:1&2:

> Then Jesus, FULL OF THE HOLY SPIRIT, returned from the Jordan River. He was led by the Spirit in the wilderness, where he was tempted by the devil for forty days. (NLT, emphasis added)

After His time of testing in the wilderness, the Bible says:

> Then Jesus returned IN THE POWER OF THE SPIRIT to Galilee, and news of Him went out through all the surrounding region. (Luke 4:14 NKJV, emphasis added)

Jesus was baptized, filled with the Holy Spirit, and *then* empowered by the Holy Spirit after His time of temptation. In John 17:5 just prior to His crucifixion, Jesus prayed, "And now, Father, glorify me in your presence with the glory I had with you before the world began" (NIV). Philippians 2:5-8 gives us this great summary:

In your relationships with one another, have the same mindset as Christ Jesus: Who, being in very nature God, did not consider equality with God something to be used to his own advantage; rather, *he made himself nothing by taking the very nature of a servant, being made in human likeness. And being found in appearance as a man, he humbled himself* by becoming obedient to death—even death on a cross! (NIV, emphasis added)

The Holy Spirit is the Spirit of God and the presence of God on the earth. He is the One that connects us to Heaven. In John 16:7, Jesus says, "But very truly I tell you, it is for your good that I am going away. Unless I go away, the Advocate [Holy Spirit] will not come to you; but if I go, I will send him to you" (NIV, brackets mine). It is better for us to have the Holy Spirit Who is Spirit and accessible everywhere, unlike Jesus Who existed on earth as a limited physical person. The Holy Spirit even lives inside us. He's that close!

God's power to heal already lives in your body.

"But the Advocate, Holy Spirit, whom the Father will send in my name, will teach you all things and will remind you of everything I have said to you" (John 14:26 NIV). "And if the Spirit of him who raised Jesus from the dead is living in you, he who raised Christ from the dead will also give life to your mortal bodies because of his Spirit who lives in you" (Romans 8:11 NIV). God's power to heal already lives in your body, so if you haven't been healed yet, ask Father God to give you more of His Spirit. Ask Him to fill you continually!

Have you ever tried to top up your gas tank in your car when it was already full? No, neither have I. That would be dumb! Gas would spill all over the ground. Our gas tanks were designed to only hold so much. Have you ever over-filled your coffee cup? Absolutely. It's important to get as much goodness in the cup as possible! Right? The problem is though, if you don't drink it black, you may need to dump a bit out to get the cream in it. What am I getting at? Well, just as a gas tank and a coffee mug can only hold so much, it's possible we also have a maximum capacity. Perhaps if we want more of the Holy Spirit living inside us, we may have to first release some other things to create space for Him to occupy. Something to think about.

· · · · · · ●●●●●●● ● ●●●●●●●● · · · · ·

Is it possible to be healed in a church service, conference, or revival meeting? Is it possible to be healed as a healing evangelist or pastor lays hands on you and prays? Is it possible to be healed as the elders of the church anoint you with oil and pray the prayer of faith? Is it possible to be healed when you respond to an altar call and receive prayer from a lay minister? Yes, yes, yes, and yes! All of it, YES! Absolutely, many healings have taken place in these situations and circumstances. I

The power of God is not confined to a church building, nor is it saved for those who you feel are more spiritual.

have received great emotional healing by responding to altar calls at different churches as well as engaging with the Spirit during worship. Indeed, I would say if you're in need of healing, make it a priority to get to special services and church gatherings as much as you can. However, just as these scenarios can bring healing, so it is just as possible for you to be healed in your own home as you seek the Lord in your own private space and time, within your very own intimate relationship with Christ. Now that is good news!

The love, goodness and power of God is not confined to church buildings, nor is it kept for the spiritual elite, those who you *thought* were more spiritual or holy than you or those who hold an office or have a title. Healing is not a one-time action of God nor something He does. Healing is Who He is. It is part of His character and nature. When you encounter the presence of God, you also encounter healing power.

How can you experience and encounter God's healing power right at home? Well, if you're asking that question, you've picked up the right book! Packed within the next two hundred or so pages, you will receive incredible insight on how to put yourself right smack dab in the middle of the very goodness of God pouring out from His heart to you, which, without a doubt includes the healing of your spirit, soul, and body.

Never doubt that the power of God heals. All we need to do is get into position to receive. Remember the woman with the issue of blood from Mark 5:24-34? She had been bleeding for twelve straight years! She would have been anemic and so very weak, but despite that, she roused herself and ventured out from her home—her safe place—and into a crowd to find Jesus. She just knew if she could only touch the tassel of His garment, she would be healed.

Rouse yourself and get into position to receive.

In that day, the woman with the issue of blood was seen as "unclean," and no one would have wanted to be near her. She would have been ostracized and rejected, probably living on the outskirts of town. It took great effort and fortitude for her to find Jesus. She pressed through a crowd, pressed through her own insecurities, pushed beyond the opinions of others as well as religious and social boundaries. She was not supposed to be there, but she went anyway. She did not let the expectations of others limit her. She was *bold* and *desperate*, so she went after her healing.

Only after relentlessly pursuing Jesus despite the obstacles in front of her, being in His presence and touching the edge of His garment, her bleeding stopped, and she was made whole. Her position to receive healing was *out of her comfort zone*, past all she thought she knew, past everything she had been taught in the synagogue. Her position for being healed was *at the feet of Jesus*. Have you ever wondered how she got through the crowd? Surely if someone had seen her, there would have been a riot. No, she got through the crowd undetected and unseen—maybe even on her hands and knees, crawling and scraping her way past everyone.

What about you beloved? Do you want to be healed? Are you willing to do whatever it takes to receive? Healing does not very often come when we are passive, nor does it come when we aren't willing to get *up close and personal* with the Spirit of God. As believers, we are invited into an intimate relationship with God— to get *up close and personal* with Him. It's important to remember that relationships are a two-way street, and they must be built, developed, and nurtured to be maintained. In every relationship, we have a responsibility to do our part.

Getting close with God takes a push through the natural realm, our flesh and carnality, false boundaries and sometimes our comfort zone to touch heaven—to enter into the sound and manifestation of healing.

Jesus taught us to pray in Matthew 6:10, "Your Kingdom come. Your will be done, On earth as it is in heaven."

Have you ever thought about what heaven is like? Revelation 21:4 says, "and He will wipe away every tear from their eyes; and there will no longer be any death; there will no longer be any mourning, or crying, or pain; the first things have passed away" (NASB). If there's no death, mourning, crying or pain in heaven, I think it's safe to say there's no sickness, illness, disease, virus, infection, condition, malformity, dysfunction, disability, exceptionality, weakness, or infirmity at all. And Jesus instructed us to call the Kingdom of God into the earth realm and to declare God's perfect will which is in heaven to be done right here on earth as we pray: "Your kingdom come. Your will be done, On earth as it is in heaven" (Matthew 6:10 NASB). If Jesus told us to pray it, it must be possible! It *is* possible to experience God's perfect heavenly will right now. Jesus didn't tell us to ask for it. He told us to declare it! "Your will be done, on earth as it is in heaven," is not a question. It's a statement! It is a statement and declaration made in faith.

Are you ready to believe with everything in you that it is indeed God's will for you to be healed? Are you ready to press through? Are you ready to go beyond yourself, beyond your own understanding and beyond your natural state into the supernatural? If so, let's dive into deep waters and unpack more truth from the Holy Spirit.

Chapter 3

GOING BACK TO GO FORWARD

Have you ever been confused about God and His heart for humanity based on the differences between the Old and New Testament? Have you ever felt like God may be schizophrenic—appearing mean and aggressive in the Old, then suddenly soft and forgiving in the New? What's the deal? What happened to God? Did He change or perhaps attend anger management class? All kidding aside, it may help us to understand healing if we understand God and where sickness began in the first place.

I recently had a newly born-again friend, struggling with her health, ask me questions about whether God caused her to be sick to punish her for the years she wandered away from Him. I have a feeling she's not alone in this, so let's nip this misunderstanding in the bud before we embark on any further study.

First, it's important to point out that there is a huge difference in how God's people were able to relate to God and experience Him in the Old Testament and the New. In the Old Testament, people experienced a lot of judgement from God because of their sin, but in the New Testament, God forged a new covenant of grace with them and us through Jesus because He wanted His mercy and love to win. Thankfully, when we are surrendered to Christ and living our lives "in Christ" or "in the Spirit," Jesus fulfills the requirements of the law (all the commandments to be righteous) on our behalf. Even in the Old Testament, God wanted to be merciful. He wanted to bless His people and have a love relationship with them but couldn't because of their weaknesses and inability to be holy before Him.

God personifies perfectly in His character absolute love, holiness, and righteousness. He always does what's right and good. There is not one ounce of bad or evil in Him. If we think that God is bad in any way, we are misunderstanding Him. Yes, there are times in the Old Testament when we see the judgement of God causing people to be ill and die, but it is not because God is evil and wants to hurt people. These instances come out of another attribute of His character which is linked to righteousness and that is His desire for justice. While God is fully and completely love, He is also fully and completely just. He simply cannot let injustice and sin go unpunished. If He did, He would not be a good Judge. There must be a consequence for sin. Romans 6:23 says, the wages of sin is death.

God personifies perfectly in His character absolute love, holiness, and righteousness.

Before Jesus and His new covenant of grace, God gave the people His instructions on how to come into His love and blessing. He gave them the ten commandments and He gave them the *law* on what to do and not to do. God gave Israel *all* His instructions outlined in detail, a lot of which is found in the book of Deuteronomy. Over and over, you will see that the Lord says, "If you do this... then it will go well with you" (see Deuteronomy 28:1-14 as an example). He also clearly warns the people of what will happen if they don't obey Him (see Deuteronomy 28:15-68). Again, not because He is mean, but because He is a holy God and must be a good and righteous Judge. Second Chronicles 7:13-14 is a great example:

> When I shut up the heavens so that there is no rain, or command locusts to devour the land or send a plague among my people, if my people, who are called by my name, will humble themselves and pray and seek my face and turn from their wicked ways, then I will hear from heaven, and I will forgive their sin and will heal their land. (NIV)

God wanted to be merciful so He tells the people how they can access healing: humble yourself, pray, seek My face, and turn from your wicked ways (repent).

When people had trouble in the Old Testament, it was a consequence to their actions, rather than a mean vengeful God acting out against them. He told Adam and Eve, eat from all the trees of the garden except for one, for if you do, you will die. God simply told them, "This is how it is. If you eat of this tree, you will die" (paraphrased).

God created the heavens and the earth. He set up and put into motion all the laws of nature *and* all the spiritual laws, like sowing and reaping, that would affect all the people of the earth. God knew that if Adam and Eve ate from the tree of the knowledge of good and evil, their understanding would be opened to evil, and they would know things they were not created to know nor could handle, so He warned them. Unfortunately, Eve was deceived by the snake in the garden and believed the lie that God was withholding something good from them. Eve ate the forbidden fruit and shared it with Adam, after which they both reaped the consequences of their disobedience to God. They died, spiritually, just as God told them they would, and that same "fall" became the doorway through which all sickness and disease entered. (Note: Dying spiritually means you become dead to and separated from God.)

Even in the Old Testament, God desired relationship with His people. God walked in the garden with Adam and Eve, but because of their disobedience, God had to banish them from the garden and was forced to strip them of privileges and blessing. It wasn't what God wanted, but something He had to do because He is a holy and righteous judge, and because He knew how best to protect Adam and Eve. God knew that if He allowed Adam and Eve to remain in the Garden, they would partake of the Tree of Life in their fallen state and remain "fallen" forever (Gen. 3-22-23). Unfortunately, all throughout the Old Testament we see the same disobedience to God that Adam and Eve began. We see a pattern of dishonor, idol worship, and failing to follow God's laws and ordinances.

If a parent warns their child, "Don't touch the stove or you will be burned," and the child touches the stove, do we blame the parent for the child's inevitable suffering? Do we think, *what a mean parent*? No. The parent warned the child and did everything in his/her power to lead the child so they wouldn't suffer, but the child used his/her own free-will and made a bad choice. Now the child suffers with a nasty burn to no fault of the parent. But, to illustrate for you the heart of God in this example, let's imagine for a moment that the child who is burned acknowledges his/her disobedience and repents. The earthly parent has no ability to ease the child's suffering beyond natural remedies, but because God is above all natural laws, His mercy can provide relief. If a disobedient child humbles himself/herself, prays, seeks the Lord with all his/her heart, and turns away from sin, God in His mercy, love and compassion could and very likely would, ease the pain of that burn and cause that burn to heal at a supernatural rate, far faster than it would have in the natural. This is God. This is how God's heart responds to humility, and repentance (a turning away from sin and a willing change of mind, heart, and attitude). You might even say, humility and repentance UNLOCKS the healing power of God that is available to all who believe.

God's heart has always been for His people, always preferring to be compassionate and merciful, to the point that He was willing to sacrifice His very own Son (Who was willing to submit to His Father's will). God in His timing, implemented His plan of salvation, making a way for mankind to live at peace with Him and experience complete freedom from sin and its affects. God made a way to, in effect, cancel the "fall" (the original sin of Adam and Eve) and empower us to live holy in Jesus through the Spirit.

In the OT, they were instructed to slaughter animals for the remission of sin. In the NT, Jesus became the last and ultimate sacrifice for sin. His blood paid the price for the sin of the whole world making it no longer necessary to kill anything else. Jesus was that ultimate sacrifice on our behalf because He was a man, yet he was sinless, and perfect. He had no sin of His own, making Him capable to carry the sin of others.

God's heart has always been for His people, always preferring to be compassionate and merciful.

We used to be slaves to sin. We see it all through the OT. People could not be righteous on their own. Now, God has given us Jesus, Who has taken all our sin away and paid the price to fulfill the justice of God. God's justice has been met through the death of Jesus, which means He no longer has to impute His justice on us. Jesus fulfills all the requirements of the law on our behalf. His righteousness has become our righteousness. We stand before God the Father forgiven and righteous, not because of anything we've done but because of what Jesus has done on our behalf. Once we accept that gift, we have the responsibility to live out that righteousness as the Spirit enables us. Philippians 2:12-13 says:

> Therefore, my dear friends, as you have always obeyed— not only in my presence, but now much more in my absence—continue to work out your salvation with fear and trembling, for it is God who works in you to will and to act in order to fulfill his good purpose. (NIV)

God has also given us His Spirit to live inside us and He gives us the empowerment and ability to choose not to sin (2 Peter 1:3). But even when we slip up, God forgives us when we confess to Him. When our hearts are right, meaning we have given our heart to Christ, we love the Lord God with all our heart, and it is truly our hearts desire to be His child and to please Him, we stand in the mercy of God, which means we do NOT get what we deserve and the grace of God, which means we get what we don't deserve. Now that God's justice has been met through Jesus, He is free to express His love and compassion to us as He has always wanted. We are truly free to be His children and for Him to be our God and our most gracious Heavenly Father.

We stand in the mercy of God. We do not get what we deserve.

Have you ever heard the term double jeopardy? There is a clause in the 5th Amendment to the Constitution of the United States called the Double Jeopardy Clause. It prohibits anyone from being prosecuted (doing time or paying the price) twice for the same crime.[14] Well, Jesus paid the price for our crime/sin. The wages of sin is death and Jesus has already died that death on our behalf. Double jeopardy is not allowed. Our sin does not need to be paid for twice! Whatever we have confessed and received forgiveness for, is under the blood of Jesus and we no longer need to suffer consequences for that sin. If the accuser (the devil) is still accusing you of something you've already confessed and ceased, tell him to get lost, in Jesus' name. The devil is a liar and a deceiver. Confession and repentance activate God's forgiveness and pays your debt in full.

The thinking that God is punishing us for our past by putting sickness and disease on us can come from a misunderstanding of the Old Testament and the character of God, but also from an old worldly mindset that has not yet been renewed by the Word. Those

---

[14] https://www.law.cornell.edu/wex/double_jeopardy

who have not yet surrendered their lives to God are still experiencing consequences of sin, but those who God has called to be His, who have surrendered all, are now welcomed to live in the reality of His mercy, grace, and healing. However, it takes a renewing of our mind and prayer to experience it. Mercy and grace can be very foreign to us as we have spent many years living in the world doing things as the world does, trying to earn our way. Our minds must be renewed, out of a worldly mindset into a heavenly one. We must have a revelation of God's mercy and grace and shed our old way of thinking to experience it.

Sometimes, the renewing of our mind takes time. We may not fully grasp all God has done for us nor understand every benefit that is ours (Psalm 103). Unfortunately, this lack of revelation can hold us in a pattern of worldly thinking giving curses and illness an opportunity to continue to operate in

Choosing to believe the truth of the Word over your circumstances will bear much fruit.

our lives. It is therefore very important to renew our mind by reading the New Testament, asking God for understanding and revelation and believing the Word above all else, even when we don't yet see the manifestation of it. Choosing to believe the truth of the Word of God over your circumstances will bear much fruit. Romans 12:2, "And do not be conformed to this world, but be transformed by the renewing of your mind, that you may prove what *is* that good and acceptable and perfect will of God" (NKJV).

Some of the churches in the New Testament struggled to remain in the truth of the revelation of the Gospel. They seemed to keep sliding back to old thinking and old ways, but the apostles encouraged them to not be deceived again nor return to a yoke of slavery in their minds (Galatians 5:1). In other words, the churches were admonished to not go back to the law but remain in faith and the new covenant. The apostles warned them that if they went back to the old way of thinking, trying to be righteous on their own, they would come under the curse of the law once again. To reiterate, here's Romans 12:2 again but in the New Living Translation: "Don't copy the behavior and customs of this world, but let God transform you into a new person by changing the way you think. Then you will learn to know God's will for you, which is good and pleasing and perfect" (NLT).

It can be even more difficult for some. Some have been taught their whole lives, sometimes by strict parenting methods, disappointments, and difficulties in life, that they will be punished harshly for bad behavior. Some have been trained by trauma and may have learned some of the following distorted beliefs:

- No one gets anything for free.
- "Get out of jail free" cards don't exist.
- Nothing will ever be handed to them on a "silver platter."
- There's no special treatment.
- Everything must be earned.
- Life is not fair.
- They don't measure up.
- They must look after themselves because no one else will.

Indeed, life in this world has been immensely difficult for some. Open arms, acceptance, and unconditional love can be completely foreign—some can't seem to wrap their minds around it at all. It takes a revelation from God and cataclysmic shift in their thinking to see it and accept it to be true *for themselves*. The good news is that God wants that for everyone—even you, possibly more than you want it. So, hang in there! Revelation of His goodness will come as you are obedient to reading and studying God's Word. The Word will break through, and strongholds of old thinking patterns will be broken by the power of the Spirit as we *submit to* and *choose to believe* His Word, despite your circumstances.

Allow me to share with you a few passages from Proverbs that speak about wisdom, understanding and God's (your Father's) instruction. Notice how according to these passages, your Father's

Words and instruction will bring long life, protection, prosperity, and divine health to your body:

> My son, if you accept my words and store up my commands within you, turning your ear to wisdom and applying your heart to understanding—indeed, if you call out for insight and cry aloud for understanding, and if you look for it as for silver and search for it as for hidden treasure, then you will understand the fear of the LORD and find the knowledge of God. For the LORD gives wisdom; from his mouth come knowledge and understanding. He holds success in store for the upright, he is a shield to those whose walk is blameless, for he guards the course of the just and protects the way of his faithful ones. (Proverbs 2:1-8 NIV)

> My son, do not forget my teaching, but keep my commands in your heart, for they will prolong your life many years and bring you peace and prosperity. Let love and faithfulness never leave you; bind them around your neck, write them on the tablet of your heart. Then you will win favor and a good name in the sight of God and man. Trust in the LORD with all your heart and lean not on your own understanding; in all your ways submit to him, and he will make your paths straight. Do not be wise in your own eyes; fear the LORD and shun evil. This will bring health to your body and nourishment to your bones. (Proverbs 3:1-8 NIV)

> My child, listen to me and do as I say, and you will have a long, good life. I will teach you wisdom's ways and lead you in straight paths. When you walk, you won't be held back; when you run, you won't stumble. Take hold of my instructions; don't let them go. Guard them, for they are the key to life. (Proverbs 4:10-13 NLT)

> My child, pay attention to what I say. Listen carefully to my words. Don't lose sight of them. Let them penetrate deep into your heart, for they bring life to those who find them, and healing to their whole body. (Proverbs 4:20-22 NLT)

Friends, you can't get any plainer than that. All of God's instruction, His wisdom, knowledge and understanding is for our well-being and good. One of the best things we can do is "take" God's Word everyday by reading it over ourselves, just like we would take medicine. God's Word is healing to our body, mind, and emotions. You can find a list of healing scriptures in Appendix A. Read them over yourself repeatedly and believe them with all your heart.

Chapter 4

FOUNDATIONS

We all know that building on a firm foundation is vital to the stability and integrity of any structure. In fact, a home that is not built on a firm foundation would not be inhabitable very long and possibly even dangerous to live in. Jesus uses this analogy in Matthew 7:24-27, as He teaches on the importance of obedience to His Word:

> Anyone who listens to my teaching and follows it is wise, like a person who builds a house on solid rock. Though the rain comes in torrents and the floodwaters rise and the winds beat against that house, it won't collapse because it is built on bedrock. But anyone who hears my teaching and doesn't obey it is foolish, like a person who builds a house on sand. When the rains and floods come and the winds beat against that house, it will collapse with a mighty crash. (Matthew 7:24-27 NLT)

Jesus and our relationship with Him is our firm foundation for abundant life. There are three elements that are needed to establish our relationship with Jesus and keep it strong, so we can receive healing. They are, an *authentic transformation* of the heart resulting in salvation, a filling *and* baptism in the Holy Spirit, and being able to hear and follow the voice of the Lord in obedience.

To recap just a little before getting into our foundation in Christ, I want to establish again that it is quite possible for healing to suddenly manifest for someone who is not yet a believer in Jesus, especially when a minister is used by God to intercede (stand between/represent) and *demonstrate* God's love as he/she shares the Gospel. God in His goodness sometimes just suddenly gives someone who's wayward, a *taste* of His mercy, with the purpose of showing them Who He *truly* is. This happened *many* times in the Bible (one example is in Acts 3:2-8) and is described by the scripture found in Mark 16:20 by the words, "the LORD worked with them (the New Testament apostles) and confirmed his word by the signs that accompanied it" (NIV, brackets mine).

> *The Holy Spirit can instantly soften a heart with one word of knowledge.*

Street healings happen with current-day healing evangelists like Todd White, and many others who are serving in obscurity every day. They share Jesus on the streets in their everyday lives and God backs them up with words of knowledge, words of wisdom and miraculous healings. A pre-believer can very often receive healing like this because they are open, child-like, and soft-hearted. But even if they are not, the Holy Spirit can instantly soften their heart with one word of knowledge through the mouth of the evangelist. One supernatural Word spoken right to the heart can suddenly open a person's eyes to the reality and truth of God and His love for them, bringing revelation and healing to many issues.

A believer *can* suddenly receive healing in their body anytime anywhere as well, but it doesn't happen because God suddenly makes a choice to heal them or decides in that moment to have mercy on them. This would imply that there was a moment prior when God was withholding mercy and healing, which does not line up with scripture. Psalm 84:11 says, "For the LORD God is our sun and our shield. He gives us grace and glory. The LORD will withhold no good thing from those who do what is right" (NLT). Additionally, Romans 8:32, "He who did not spare his own Son, but gave him up for us all—how will he not also, along with him, graciously give us all things" (NIV)? The *only* thing God would withhold from us would be things that we're not ready for but healing certainly doesn't fit in that category. God is a good, good Father with wisdom beyond us.

As I said earlier, God has already made the choice to invite *all* who trust in Him to be healed. God's mercy has been made complete for the believer and it has already been imputed to them in fullness. A believer is suddenly healed usually because *they* have boldly and persistently reached out in faith to grab it or something they've done, believed, or prayed in repentance has suddenly positioned them in agreement with God, causing

> *God's mercy is imputed to the believer in fullness at the moment of decision.*

everything demonic to flee and healing to manifest. An area where they were out of alignment or out of agreement with prior, was put into its rightful place.

It *can* (not always) be difficult for Christians to receive healing and I believe there are three reasons for that. First, once we accept the gift of salvation, we have a responsibility to be obedient to Christ[15] which sometimes is overlooked. Some believers think they can take advantage of grace and not submit to the Spirit, nor grow in holiness. Disobedience, therefore, becomes a barrier to their healing.

The second and third reasons have to do with growing up in mainline denominational churches in North America. Unfortunately, many have done a dis-service to their people in two ways. First,

---

[15]"Jesus replied, 'Anyone who loves me will obey my teaching. My Father will love them, and we will come to them and make our home with them'" (John 14:23 NIV).

many (not all) local churches in main-line denominations have not taught on healing. They have not taught inner healing and deliverance, nor have they taught on the need for it or its benefits. They have not taught a complete Gospel. Many have also not taught their people to hear God's voice,[16] nor how to apprehend the presence of God. They have taught how to get a ticket to heaven which is great. They've taught spiritual disciplines, but they have failed miserably on teaching *Spirit-led* faith. In fact, what *many* mainline churches have taught is religion, which has *in part* developed groups of Pharisees who can be experts at pointing fingers and blame-shifting, arrogant, self-righteous, and judgemental (looking down on others, condemning them)—not like Christ, not spiritual, and certainly not expectant of anything miraculous. I'm sorry if this sounds judgy but it is true. (A discussion on judgements is coming.) I do know of a few churches that have done a *great* job at teaching a full gospel and I'm sure you do too, so please hear me when I say I am not talking about *all* churches. And I'm in Canada, so it could be different in other countries.

Attempting to minister to someone on the streets who has been *churched* can be like running head-long into a brick wall. Often, they can be completely unbelieving in the things of the Spirit and even offended by your ministry. It is wise for street ministers to be sensitive to the Spirit's leading and only minister to those the Spirit leads them to. Most of the time (there's always exceptions) it's better to let *churched* believers seek healing for themselves if they want it and believe for it. They can do this by seeking the Lord, reading the Word, praying, going to healing services and/or a Healing Rooms ministry, and of course using the keys presented in this book.

A lot of what I have learned over my thirty-five years of Spirit-led faith, I have learned from small-group experiences with Spirit-led facilitators, and privately in my own walk with the Holy Spirit. It has

---

[16]"My sheep hear My voice, and I know them, and they follow Me" (John 10:27 NKJV).

also been confirmed by recent church leaders in my life who hear God, are free from religion, and on fire for the Lord. We should not be surprised at how the Holy Spirit, the Spirit of truth, speaks to us making known to us the deep truths of God's Word, as well as giving us direction and a heads-up on what is to come. Remember, Jesus said in John 16:12-14:

> *I have much more to say to you, more than you can now bear.* But when he, the Spirit of truth, comes, he will guide you into ALL the truth. He will not speak on his own; he will speak only what he hears, and he will tell you what is yet to come. He will glorify me because it is from me that he will receive what he will make known to you. (NIV, emphasis added)

Jesus is coming back for a bride, not friends or servants—a bride, who is madly in love with Him.

Hearing the Holy Spirit speak to us is not adding truth to the Bible. It is simply being in relationship with a living God who has a voice and still loves to communicate with us now. Of course, God is not schizophrenic. He does not change in character, so He never speaks anything to us that contradicts His heart or written Word.

Secondly, the church in many main-line denominations have also done a dis-service to people by teaching that a simple prayer recited somehow leads to salvation. The traditional *pray after me* scenario has led some people to a moment where they have recited words without having their heart engaged or have given their mental ascent to the gospel but have not given their heart in love to Jesus. They have not had a revelation of Who Jesus is nor of His love for them, which *may* have led some people to think they are saved, when *perhaps* they really aren't. Remember, Jesus is coming back for a *bride*. He is not coming back for *just* friends or *just* servants, nor those that simply believe in Him. He is coming back for a *bride* who is in *love* with Him. So, as a quick evaluation of your own heart, do you *love* Jesus? Are you in love with Him? Jesus said in John 14:21, "Those who accept my commandments and obey them are the ones who love me. And because they love me, my Father will love them. And I will love them and reveal myself to each of them" (NLT).

A true salvation experience begins with a revelation of one's need, a revelation of one's own sin and brokenness. It continues with a revelation from the Holy Spirit of Jesus and His sacrifice for us personally, then a revelation of the goodness and kindness of God which then causes a person to fall in love with Jesus and on their knees in repentance.[17] A true salvation experience is a change of heart *and* mind causing someone to stop and turn around, changing direction. It causes a person who is unknowingly headed for a cliff, to adjust their course so they turn around and head back to the arms of God. And it's this call back to God, back to love, that instigates and perpetuates a change in desires, through the Spirit, which leads to a change in behavior. Holiness is *not* an act of the human will. It is *not* striving and pulling up your bootstraps, *trying* to do better. It is a change of heart and transformation of the soul initiated and perpetuated by the Holy Spirit, *as we yield to Him*.

> *The fruit of a true salvation experience is a change of heart and mind that causes a person to stop and turn around.*

Let's be real about our walk with God, Christian. Are you *really* a *follower* of Christ? Have you *really surrendered* your life, every bit of it, even your will, to Jesus? A Christian is a *follower* of Christ which means they watch what Jesus does, and by the empowering of the Holy Spirit, they imitate Him. They think how Christ thinks. They say what Christ says. To some degree, they are "little Christs." They may not do it perfectly yet, but their desire is to get there. They are grieved by their sin and how they fall short, and they live

---

[17] "... the goodness of God leads you to repentance" (Romans 2:4b NKJV)?

a life of repentance when they do. They *love* Jesus with all their heart. They don't just believe in Him (even the devil believes in Him). Born-again believers *love* Him. They sacrifice for Him. They give things up to *do* His Word. They live a life of service, and they are obedient to Christ. They long to be with Him.

Love for, trust in, and surrender to Jesus is a huge part of the foundation that we must have to experience relationship and intimacy with God, to encounter His presence, and to receive healing. Don't settle for less my friend. Seek the Holy Spirit and ask Him to bring you *all* the way in. Surrender your life afresh today. I pray the Holy Spirit captures your heart through these words. It is *not* His desire for you or anyone else to perish[18] nor to live one more day without His *discernable, abiding* presence.

> Baptism in the Holy Spirit will cause your spiritual senses to awaken so you can hear His voice.

In addition to an authentic conversion and full surrender to the work and Word of Christ, a second experience as outlined in the New Testament called the baptism of the Holy Spirit[19] is crucial for a firm foundation, for numerous reasons. Being baptized in the Holy Spirit will cause your spiritual senses to awaken, giving you the potential to discern in the Spirit. As you exercise your spiritual senses, they will develop, and you will gain wisdom and understanding from God's perspective being able to "distinguish between what is morally good and what is evil" (Hebrews 5:14b AMP). You will read your Bible and get it. You will grow in your ability to recognize God's voice and discern His presence. And you

---

[18] "In the same way, it is not my heavenly Father's will that even one of these little ones should perish" (Matthew 18:14 NLT).

[19] "I baptize with water those who repent of their sins and turn to God. But someone is coming soon who is greater than I am—so much greater that I'm not worthy even to be his slave and carry his sandals. He will baptize you with the Holy Spirit and with fire" (Matthew 3:11 NLT).

will be empowered to overcome temptation and any other nonsense the devil throws at you.

As you yield to the Holy Spirit, you will experience a deeper prayer life. You will hear the Holy Spirit direct you on how to pray and what to pray, so you are praying God's heart and not your own soulish desires. As you continue to yield, you can even begin to experience a new prayer language which is private and intimate between you and God. Best of all, you will begin to feel the love of God like never before and you will go from a Christian life that is just theory to a wonderful life of *experiencing* God. God will come alive to you! This is the beauty of being baptized in the Holy Spirit and it pains me to know so many Christians miss out because their church or denomination chooses to ignore it.

> *Do you trust God enough to give His Spirit the reigns of your life? If not, healing of the heart must come first.*

What does it mean to be *baptized* in the Holy Spirit? I would suggest to you that it means being fully immersed in, saturated by, inside and out, and completely filled to overflowing with the Holy Spirit and His power. Once we're baptized and filled, it is then our job to yield to Him and give Him control.

This I think is the sticking point for some people. They see giving control over to the Spirit as not having control over themselves. This is a misunderstanding; it's not one or the other. God never overrides our free will. We always have the choice to yield or not to yield in any given moment. God is good. God has our *best* interest at heart. He never forces Himself on us and He never forces us to do anything we don't want to do. He may nudge us out of our comfort zones, and want us to obey, but the final choice is always ours. He knows our heart completely and He is so very patient with us. It really comes down to trust. Do we trust God enough to give His Spirit the reigns of our life? If not, there is likely a heart issue standing in the way, which will also unfortunately block the manifestation of healing.

John the Baptist said in Matthew 3:11, "I indeed baptize you with water unto repentance, but He who is coming after me is mightier than I, whose sandals I am not worthy to carry. He will baptize you with the Holy Spirit and fire" (NKJV). We know from this passage that Jesus is the One to baptize us with the Holy Spirit. It is worthy to note also that the Holy Spirit was imparted to the disciples twice—once with an emphasis on internal awakening and once with the addition of external equipping and empowerment. *Baptism* in the Holy Spirit causes one to not only be filled but to "wear" the Holy Spirit on the outside, equipped with Godly fire, passion, and power. The two instances of the disciples receiving the Holy Spirit are as follows:

1. John 20:19-22. After Jesus' resurrection, Jesus appeared to his disciples showing them his pierced hands and side. He commissioned them and *breathed* on them saying, "Receive the Holy Spirit." Jesus breathed on them with the intent of imparting the Holy Spirit to them internally. As Jesus breathed out, they breathed IN what Jesus released—the Holy Spirit. This impartation represents what happens for believers at their salvation experience—the *infilling* of the Spirit.

2. Acts 1:5. The second instance of impartation happened at Pentecost and represents the *baptism* of the Holy Spirit. Jesus gave the apostles instruction to remain in Jerusalem and wait for the "gift" His Father promised: "For John baptized with water, but in a few days you will be *baptized* with the Holy Spirit" (Acts 1:5 NIV, emphasis added). The apostles waited in Jerusalem for the Holy Spirit to come, as they were instructed. In due time, the Holy Spirit came spontaneously just as Jesus said He would: "Suddenly a sound like the blowing of a violent wind came from heaven and filled the whole house where they were sitting. They saw what seemed to be tongues of fire that separated and came to *rest on* each of them. All of them were

filled with the Holy Spirit and began to speak in other tongues as the Spirit enabled them" (Acts 2:2-4 NIV, emphasis added).

The baptism in the Holy Spirit can happen spontaneously as you believe, surrender, open your heart to Him, and ask to be filled *and* empowered. It can happen as you read these words right now or as an anointed leader imparts the Spirit to you by the laying on of hands, or as you listen to the Word being preached at church, in your car and even at home.

We see Jesus being spontaneously baptized in the Holy Spirit right after His water baptism in Matthew 3:16, "After his baptism, as Jesus came up out of the water, the heavens were opened, and he saw the Spirit of God descending like a dove and settling *on him*" (NLT, emphasis added). We see new believers being baptized in the Holy Spirit spontaneously as they listen to Peter share the Gospel in Acts 10:44 and we see others being baptized in the Holy Spirit with the laying on of hands in Acts 8:17 and Acts 19:6.

God is Spirit and to worship Him, we must worship in Spirit and in truth.

The Holy Spirit is not just for certain denominations. He is for everyone, and we need Him to connect to God. God is Spirit and in order to worship God, we must worship in Spirit.[20] If we want to approach the throne of grace in our time of need, we can only do so in the Spirit.[21] Obviously, the throne of God is not in the natural, it is in the spiritual realm. If we want to receive healing, we must also do so in the Spirit. Partnering with the Holy Spirit is not an option, if we want to function as a Christian who is alive, aware,

---

[20] "God is Spirit, so those who worship him must worship in spirit and in truth" (John 4:24 NLT).

[21] "So let us come boldly to the throne of our gracious God. There we will receive his mercy, and we will find grace to help us when we need it most" (Hebrews 4:16 NLT).

walking in the things of God, hearing His voice, and receiving healing.

Robert Boyd Munger has written a very well-known devotional booklet called, *My Heart: Christ's Home*. You may have heard of it. This devotional introduces readers to what it means to surrender every aspect of their lives to the control of Christ by comparing our heart to a home. I've actually not read it in its entirety, but I love the idea. Using this comparison, imagine that salvation (repenting, believing, confessing, and surrendering), is like inviting Christ into our home, through the front door.

The front door is the entrance way, and the Lord has come in. He has brought life and light back into our home, but where does He reside? Does He just stay in the foyer or is He welcomed into *every* room? Is He restricted to the formal living room

Honoring the Holy Spirit is just as important as honoring Jesus and Father, God.

where things are in order or is He free to roam—to open closets and cupboards and look under the bed? Is He treated like a guest or like He belongs there? Is He treated like part of the family or is He treated properly—like He's the head of the house—like He's in charge?

Perhaps Jesus is honored well, given access to every room, and received as the authority figure in the home, but what about the Holy Spirit? The Holy Spirit is not synonymous with Jesus; they are two separate members of the Godhead with different assignments, functions, and roles in our lives. So, do we invite the Holy Spirit in and honor Him the same way we honor Jesus, as we should?

Here's what I fear happens in denominations that don't believe in the *baptism* of the Holy Spirit: they open the door, and the Holy Spirit comes in, but they immediately stuff Him into the front hall closet, not permitting Him to move, fill the house nor do any of what He desires to do—such as heal, comfort, transform and communicate truth.

POSITION YOURSELF FOR HEALING BY BARBARA DE SIMON

Unfortunately, some Christians don't trust the supernatural demonstrations of God through the Holy Spirit as it feels strange, out of control, and they can't understand it with their natural minds. It offends their flesh. However, we all must allow our mind and experience to be governed by the Spirit, not the flesh. Romans 8:6-8 says the following:

> The mind governed by the flesh is death, but the mind governed by the Spirit is life and peace. The mind governed by the flesh is hostile to God; it does not submit to God's law, nor can it do so. Those who are in the realm of the flesh cannot please God. (NIV)

God's presence is perfect love and perfect love always casts out fear.

Friends, to experience the supernatural love of God, we are going to have to be willing to experience His supernatural Spirit. We should not be afraid to let the Holy Spirit do what He wants to do. He wants to bless us outrageously and heal us on the inside and out.

I have had some of the most profound, amazing healing experiences flat on my back, on the floor, completely overtaken by the power of God, as the Holy Spirit has ministered to me through visions on the screen of my imagination. He has taken me back to some very painful and traumatic experiences and brought me through them again amidst His presence, completely changing my memory of them. The only reason it was possible for God to do this for me was because I was willing to submit to Him. I was willing to give the Holy Spirit control.

If you have been fearful or prideful or not honoring of the Holy Spirit, repent and ask God to forgive you. Then, open your heart to receive and simply ask God for His gift of the Spirit. Do not be shy. Jesus tells us in Luke 11 to ask for the Holy Spirit and to keep on asking.

And so I tell you, keep on asking, and you will receive what you ask for. Keep on seeking, and you will find. Keep on knocking, and the door will be opened to you. For everyone who asks, receives. Everyone who seeks, finds. And to everyone who knocks, the door will be opened. You fathers—if your children ask for a fish, do you give them a snake instead? Of if they ask for an egg, do you give them a scorpion? Of course not! So if you sinful people know how to give good gifts to your children, how much more will your heavenly Father give the Holy Spirit to those who ask him. (Luke 11:9-13 NLT)

We can even ask repeatedly. In fact, I would encourage every believer to continually ask for more of the Holy Spirit. You will find that as you serve the Lord pouring out to others, you will need to be replenished with His power and presence.

Hearing the voice of God is the third element of our relationship, which is vital for our foundation. How can we have a relationship with anyone without hearing their voice and being able to talk with them? Jesus declares in the parable of the sheep in John 10 that He is the gate, and He is the good Shepherd who sacrifices His life for the sheep. He also says His sheep know His voice and follow it.

I tell you the truth, anyone who sneaks over the wall of a sheepfold, rather than going through the gate, must surely be a thief and a robber! But the one who enters through the gate is the shepherd of the sheep. The gatekeeper opens the gate for him, and the sheep recognize his voice and come to him. He calls his own sheep by name and leads them out. After he has gathered his own flock, he walks ahead of them, and they follow him because they know his voice. They won't follow a stranger; they will run from him because they don't know his voice. . . I am the good shepherd; I know my own sheep, and they know me, just as my Father knows me and I know the Father. So I sacrifice my life for the sheep. I have other sheep too, that are not in this sheepfold. I must bring them also. They will listen to my voice, and there will be one flock with one shepherd. (John 10:1-5, 14-16 NLT)

We absolutely have the ability, through the Spirit, to recognize the voice of Jesus our Lord and to be directed by Him. We hear His voice in different ways, but *primarily* through reading His Word, the Bible.

Have you ever noticed that as you read the Bible, occasionally a certain passage, verse, phrase, or word will jump out at you or be highlighted—a portion of what you are reading penetrates your heart with power and reverberates in your inner being? This is an indication that God is bringing that portion of His Word to your attention and is speaking it to you in that moment. You may not be able to identify what's happening, but if you pay close attention, you may notice that it feels like a vibration in your spirit. This is because God's voice is adding sound to the written Words you are reading. The written Word becomes the spoken Word. At this moment, His Word comes alive with power, changing and healing as it defies natural laws, exposing what needs to be exposed, cutting, and dividing what is soulish from what is spirit. Hebrews 4 puts it this way:

> For the word of God is alive and powerful. It is sharper than the sharpest two-edged sword, cutting between soul and spirit, between joint and marrow. It exposes our innermost thoughts and desires. Nothing in all creation is hidden from God. Everything is naked and exposed before his eyes, and he is the one to whom we are accountable. (Hebrews 4:12-13 NLT)

Of course, the whole of the written Word is God's Word and is alive, but it is the portion that God wants you to hear in the moment that will pierce you when you need it. And you will just know in your spirit, *there's power on that Word FOR ME right now and I need to receive it, BELIEVE IT, and step into it, to experience the benefits flowing from it.*

Did you know that God created the world simply by speaking? He did not need to hire an architect, or contractor to build anything. He did not need any raw materials. He simply spoke, and it was. "And God said, 'Let there be light'; and there was light" (Genesis 1:3 AMP). The sound of His voice creates. The sound of His voice establishes exactly what He says.

It is incredible what I noticed just the other day in Matthew 14:22-32. Let me share it with you. Jesus sent His disciples out in the boat ahead of Him while He dismissed the crowd that had been listening to Him speak. Later, shortly before dawn, Jesus went out to them walking on the water. Initially the disciples were afraid and thought He was a ghost, but Jesus called out to them, calming their fear.

Read the Word of God expecting to hear a Word that will cause your healing to manifest.

Peter, the zealous bold one, said to Jesus, "Lord, if it's really you, *tell me to come to you*, walking on the water" (Matthew 14:28 NLT, emphasis added). "'Yes, come.' Jesus said. So, Peter went over the side of the boat and walked on the water toward Jesus" (Matthew 14:29 NLT). I never thought of this too much before, but *Peter asked Jesus to command him to come out on the water* BEFORE he attempted it. He waited for the Word from Jesus. Why? Why not just get out of the boat and go? Well, Peter understood that he needed the Word of the Lord before he could experience supernatural things that defy earthly laws. Peter does not take anything for granted nor does he presume anything. And neither should we. Jesus is the One Who has authority over the natural realm, not us. The natural laws submit to Jesus and His Word. If we need something in the natural realm to shift, we need the Word from Jesus to do it.

The Word of the Lord creates, empowers, releases, and overcomes every earthly limitation. Therefore, we need to read healing scriptures over ourselves. Something we read is going to catch the breath of God, cut through our issue and bring healing. Having said that, I believe also, that just as Peter asked the Lord to command him to come out on the water, we are invited to ask Jesus to command our healing.

Seeking the Lord in the secret place is vital to hearing Him speak a Word of healing. When I say, "secret place," I mean in a private place and way, so you and the Lord can be together intimately to share your hearts together. Don't just make time to pray quickly in the morning as you dress or drive the car or perhaps when you're doing chores. Seek the Lord INTENTIONALLY, behind closed doors, with NO DISTRACTIONS, and give Him your time. Prioritize a time when you can be set apart to hear Him. Only one Word from Him can create your miracle healing.

Prayer is supposed to be a dialogue, not a monologue.

In summary, READ the Word and HEAR the Word. When a portion of scripture resonates in your heart, read it over repeatedly and read it aloud. Sit with it. Chew on it. Receive it. Believe it. If there is something you need to do to activate it, do it!

Another common way God speaks to us is through prayer. Did you know that prayer is supposed to be a two-way conversation? Prayer was never meant to be a monologue but a dialogue. Why is that important for healing? Well, a few pages back, I mentioned that disobedience can become a barrier or blockage to healing. I also mentioned that one could have a "heart issue" if they aren't willing to trust the Holy Spirit which can also block healing. This "heart issue" could be fear or it could be pride; either one will stop healing from manifesting. Here is the thing though. . . God wants you healed! And He is more than willing to tell you what is keeping your healing from manifesting. All we need to do is ask Him. Obviously, we then need to be open to hear His voice, discern what God is saying and be obedient.

I've always loved King David's prayer in Psalm 139:23, "Search me, O God, and know my heart; test me and know my anxious thoughts.

Point out anything in me that offends you and lead me along the path of everlasting life" (NLT).

Jesus was excellent at hearing His Father's voice. We see this in operation as He healed various individuals using different actions and words. Throughout the Gospels, Jesus did not use any "cookie cutter" healing methods. Instead, He listened to His Father and His Father told Him what to do. Jesus' actions dealt with *everything* that stood against a person's wellbeing—everything in his soul and body operating together to cause illness.

Some people Jesus touched. Some He didn't touch, and some touched Him. A few He had to deliver from evil spirits.[22] A few He anointed with His spit; one he mixed with dirt[23] and one He had to remove from the town and pray for twice.[24]

Jesus did not use "cookie cutter" healing methods. He heard His Father's voice and obeyed.

The man whose eyes were anointed with spit mixed with dirt, in John 9:1-7, was told to go wash in the pool of Siloam which means "sent," after which he was healed. Not every blind person who was healed had to do that—just him (that we know of). It follows then that there must have been purpose for the washing in that particular pool. Perhaps it had to do with washing away an old identity and ushering in a new one. With every splash of the water, he exercised his faith as he carried out this divinely appointed prophetic act, choosing to believe, accept, declare, and establish his new identity as a "sent" one.

The blind man from John 9 was born blind and Jesus specifically says in John 9:3, "It was not because of his sins or his parents' sins," Jesus answered. "This happened so the power of God could be seen in him" (NLT). However, this is not a blanket statement for all

---

[22] Luke 13:10-17

[23] John 9:1-7

[24] Mark 8:22-26

people who were blind or ill as Jesus also said to the man who was healed at the pool in John 5:14, "Now you are well; so stop sinning, or something even worse may happen to you" (NLT). There are different reasons for people to be ill and we must seek the Lord to know what those are.

Another healing I will emphasis is found in Mark 2:1-12. Here we see a man who was paralyzed being carried by four of his friends, trying to get close to Jesus as He preached in the home where He was staying. The home became so packed with visitors, no one else could even get in the door. As a result, the men got on the roof, opened it, and lowered the man down on his cot in front of Jesus. The man's friends wanted him healed physically, but Jesus' VERY FIRST words to the man are, "My child, your sins are forgiven" (Mark 2:5 NLT). Why? He didn't say this to the other people He healed. It's possible He said this to stir up the scribes that were there and to illustrate a point, but I believe, it was something else.

Regret is a fruit of worldly sorrow and will hold you captive. Godly sorrow sets you free.

After reading Matthew's account of the same healing in Matthew 9, I believe the paralytic was vexed in his soul with grief and regret over his sin. Part of Matthew 9:2 says, "Son, BE OF GOOD CHEER; your sins are forgiven you" (NKJV, emphasis added). That precious man needed to be cheered up and relieved of his regret before his body could be healed. Second Corinthians 7:10 says, "Godly sorrow brings repentance that leads to salvation and leaves no regret, but worldly sorrow brings death" (NIV). Friends of God, don't hang on to regret. Let it go. Don't be stuck in worldly sorrow which leads to hopelessness, illness, and death, but let Godly sorrow bring you to repentance and lead you all the way out. God says you are forgiven, so receive it and forgive yourself. Make the declaration over yourself, "I am forgiven." And I say to you, "Your sins are remitted, paid for and cancelled."

One time I went to a conference with a friend to a nearby city. We shared a hotel room and as I sat on the bed, criss-cross apple sauce, I felt the familiar sting in my left hip as my muscles and/or tendons refused to co-operate. I persevered singing a song that I had come to love, called "You Are My King (Amazing Love).[25] Perhaps you know it. It goes like this:

> "I'm forgiven because you were forsaken.
> I'm accepted. You were condemned.
> I'm alive and well. Your Spirit is within me.
> Because you died and rose again.

> Chorus: Amazing love, how can it be?
> That you my King would die for me.
> Amazing love, I know it's true.
> It's my joy to honor you. (x2)
> In all I do, I honor you.

> YOU are my King.
> You are MY King.
> Jesus, You are my King.
> Jesus, You are MY King.[26]

As I sat on that bed, singing, and declaring that I was forgiven, suddenly the sting in my hip vanished. The pain was gone, and flexibility was restored. God's healing manifested in my body according to my confession of forgiveness.

God speaks. He's alive and He has a voice. He is speaking to us ALL the time. Sometimes He speaks through the pages of the Bible and in prayer. Other times He speaks through different things like dreams, books, and songs. Even other times He speaks through people—particularly when you're listening to a sermon online or when someone anointed prays for you or gives you a prophetic

---

[25] https://www.youtube.com/watch?v=C3E6ia8E74U

[26] Written by Billy James Foote. 1999 worshiptogether.com Songs (ASCAP) (admin. by EMI CMG Publishing).

word. In addition, you may find God speaks to you through social media or even a billboard!

You may be asking, "How do I know if God is speaking to me when I read a billboard?" That's a good question. It's a little out of the box, isn't it? You will know it's God when it grabs your attention, convicts you, won't leave you alone, and perhaps confirms something you've already been thinking or praying about. Over time, you will begin to recognize His voice, how it makes you feel, and other signs that come with it.

I'll never forget the first time I heard the voice of God in my spirit as I prayed. The Lord answered a question I had asked Him, responding with a clear Word of direction. It just about blew my mind.

I was standing at the sink washing dishes and I had just had a healing experience in the car on the way home from Toronto. As a passenger on a three-hour ride, there was a lot of time to think. Without even realizing it, God guided my thoughts as He opened my eyes to a hurtful event from my teen years and He led me to forgive someone who had stolen my innocence.

After the car ride as I stood at the sink, I had a new sense of peace. The anxiety, hate and emotional pain I had felt previously was gone and I was so thankful. I asked the Lord directly, "What do you want me to do with this now?" and immediately I heard God say in my thoughts, "Join the youth group." I was stunned. Becoming an adult sponsor for high schoolers was not even on my radar. It wasn't something I had thought about before. However, I did what God told me to do and I loved it. I became an adult sponsor for the youth group at our church and it stretched me, caused me to grow and use my spiritual gifts to bless others. It was exactly where God wanted me to be at that time in my life.

One final way I will mention that God speaks is through dreams. This is a whole teaching by itself, but I will say this:

- Everyone has dreams whether we remember them or not.

- Not every dream is from God.
- Dreams from God are vivid and seem very real.
- God speaks in dreams through symbols and what they mean biblically and/or to you.
- Keep a journal by your bedside to journal your dream as soon as you wake up before you forget.
- God dreams can be extremely helpful to you in life as they can contain direct messages from God.
- The Holy Spirit will give you the interpretation of the dream if you ask Him.
- Talking your dream out sometimes gives you clues as to what it means.
- It is biblical.[27] Daniel and Joseph both interpreted God's messages in dreams.

Several years ago, my daughter was at college and at the end of the school year, as she was getting off the campus bus, she slipped and hit the back of her head on the step. We thought she was fine until she went back to school a few months later and began having severe headaches and difficulty with her memory. She finished the semester, took a break from college, and came home to rest and heal.

Shortly after she returned home, as I sought the Lord on her behalf, I had a dream:

> I was at a college campus in the campus bookstore, and I was in line, waiting to buy a scarf. The scarf was white and on the scarf were two handprints with the words, "They will lift you up." When I reached the cashier, the cashier didn't know how to cash out that particular item, so I helped her out by cashing myself out on the bookstore's register.

---

[27] "For God speaks again and again, though people do not recognize it. He speaks in dreams, in visions of the night, when deep sleep falls on people as they lie in their beds" (Job 33:14-15 NLT).

I knew the Lord was speaking to me. I was at a college campus, so it was obviously referring to my daughter. She was the only one in the family at college. I was purchasing a scarf that was white which speaks of covering and purity. MY purchasing the scarf was confirmation that I had successfully partnered with God to activate His covering over me and my children. As Jessica's mother, the one in authority over her, my covering translated to her covering. Most powerfully though, the inscription on the scarf pointed me to the Word, Psalm 91:11-12:

> For he will command his angels concerning you to guard you in all your ways; *they will lift you up in their hands*, so that you will not strike your foot against a stone (or your head against a step). (NIV, brackets and emphasis mine)

Pay attention to your dreams. The healing Word we need very often comes this way.

The next morning as I contemplated the dream and read the scripture, I realized by the Spirit in that moment, that God was actually changing history. As I caught revelation of His breath and voice on that Word from Psalm 91, I saw in my mind's eye, angels slipping their hands underneath my daughter's head as it hit the step, protecting her from the impact. From that moment on, she no longer had severe headaches due to a concussion or problems with her memory. (For more information about how God speaks in dreams, look for resources by Barbie Breathitt or James Goll.)

These are the foundations of connecting with God: an authentic salvation experience of heart transformation, baptism in the Holy Spirit, and hearing His voice followed by obedient action. All three set you up to begin and grow a vibrant, intimate relationship with God, through Jesus and the Holy Spirit. They also set you up to be healed in every way. If you are convicted that you don't have all three of these elements, simply follow the Spirit and re-dedicate your life to Jesus as He leads you. This may look like:

- Surrendering to Jesus afresh and accepting Him again (or for the first time) as your Savior AND Lord.

- Asking God to fill you with the Holy Spirit and new life.

- Asking Jesus to baptize you IN the Holy Spirit to clothe you in His power so you can live for Him, be a witness wherever you go and serve Him well.

- Getting to know God and His heart by reading His Word.

- Memorizing verses that are special to you.

- Praying and expecting to hear God's voice and asking the Lord to help you.

- Giving the Holy Spirit an opportunity to speak to you by asking Him direct questions. Start simple.

- Spending time with God and attuning your ear to the sound of His voice.

- Allowing the Holy Spirit to pray through you however that looks and sounds.

- Being open to praying in tongues—a heavenly language between you and God. Learn more from a book by John Bevere called, "The Holy Spirit: An introduction."

- Praying in tongues often.

- Joining a church fellowship that teaches biblical principles and a FULL gospel including the Holy Spirit and the activation of all His gifts from 1 Corinthians 12:7-11 in our lives.

Notes

Chapter 5

AUTHORITY

When we are sick or burdened with an ongoing illness, one of the most beneficial things we can do for ourselves is to seek the Lord and ask Him *why* we are experiencing that illness. God wants us well, knows the solution to every problem and is more than happy to tell us what it is.

Most illnesses and diseases do not manifest in our body without a root cause in our heart or our soul which is where our mind, emotions and will reside. Our body is an outward expression of our inner selves. All three parts of us are integrated. Our body does not operate by itself, independent of our spirit and soul. We are a FULLY integrated three-part being, made in the image of God. Just as God the Father, God the Son and God the Spirit are all in unity and agreement with one another, so we are too. Our spirit, soul, and body work together. They agree with one another. (If we have anger in our soul, it will leak into our body.)

Listen to Proverbs 4:23, "Guard your heart above all else, for it determines the course of your life" (NLT) or the New King James Version, "Keep your heart with all diligence, For out of it spring the issues of life." *Heart* in these verses is referring to our inner man or our soul.

Proverbs 23:6-7 tells us about a miser who may say with his mouth, "Eat and drink!" even though in his heart he's resentful about what it's costing him to share his food. His words do not reflect the truth in his heart; he speaks falsehoods. Proverbs 23:7 tells us, "For as he thinks in his heart, *so is he*" (NKJV, emphasis added). In other words, it is what's in his heart that determines who he really is, not his empty, insincere words. The scripture goes on in verse 8 to tell us that if we do eat the miser's food, we will end up vomiting out the morsels we've consumed because we've eaten his food without his blessing. These verses *bring home* for us the importance of the spiritual heart/soul condition on our overall health.

> *The condition of our heart or inner man is the greatest determining factor to health.*

Of course, some extreme negative environmental factors (like living with black mould or air pollution) can affect the health of our body, but *often* they are not the *sole* cause of disease. There are bad habits such as eating poorly or not exercising that can contribute to disease, but again may not be the *sole* causing factor. I would also point out here that eating poorly and not taking care of oneself are behaviors that are rooted in deeper things—perhaps depression which very often is a spiritual attack on the mind, or it can be a soul wound (sometimes more than one) that is perpetuating poor self-esteem, self-hate, loneliness, discouragement, and/or hopelessness. Over-eating or eating a lot of foods high in sugar are coping mechanisms—one way people try to cope with emotional pain and wounds in the soul.

Some medical doctors and therapists have *begun* to recognize the truth that disease is *greatly* caused by things like adversity in childhood, chronic fear and anxiety, lingering stress, trauma, and repressed emotions.[28] But many doctors do not. Unfortunately, these factors are not frequently seen as causative nor addressed in the medical field. Many doctors even cringe at the suggestion. Nonetheless, it doesn't make it any less true. Generational iniquity (genetics as the world sees it) can also play a role in disease but that will be addressed in a later chapter.

If there is a soul-wound or repressed emotions that are contributing to your ill health, the Lord is more than happy to show you what those are. We are also more than able to exercise our free-will to repent and come out of agreement with any issue the Lord shows us. For instance, if God shows you that low self-esteem is a problem for you, it would be beneficial to ask the Lord where it came from. Where did you learn that you weren't good enough? When did you begin to accept that as truth? The Holy Spirit will show you and when He does, simply:

- Agree with God. (For example, you might pray: "Yes Lord, that happened, and it hurt me deeply," or, "Yes Lord, I believed the lie that I was worthless because of that rejection.")
- Repent for accepting the lies regarding your worth.
- Forgive anyone who hurt you or treated you unfairly.
- Forgive yourself and receive God's forgiveness and cleansing.
- Forgive anyone who hasn't celebrated you as they should (a mom, dad, sibling, spouse, friend).
- Ask God to cleanse every wound that was created.
- Recognize the truth of who you are in God's eyes (read Psalm 139 to find out).
- Come out of agreement with and *renounce* self-hate, self-rejection, self-deprecation, and self-pity.

---

[28] See resources like *The Deepest Well* by Dr. Nadine Burke Harris, *Scared Sick* by Robin Karr-Morse with Meredith S. Wiley and *When the Body Says No* by Gabor Maté M.D.

- Bind every spirit identified above (spirit of self-hate, spirit of self-rejection etc.) and command them to leave you. Breathe them out.
- Thank God for how He made you and decide from this moment forward to celebrate God's creation—to celebrate you.
- Receive God's love for you.

You are God's unique and glorious creation—His work of art. Just as we don't appreciate criticism of our artwork, criticizing ourselves is not honoring to God. It is possible that there are deep wounds contributing to this, in which case, I would recommend seeing a pastor, prayer minister, or counselor to help you sort through it. It is vital to not let these wounds and emotions fester in our heart. A wound that is not cleansed and treated becomes infected, causing us great harm, even manifesting into illness and disease.

Being critical toward ourselves and not seeing ourselves through eyes of love is sin.

What am I talking about when I say, "wound?" I'm talking about any mark left on your soul from something or someone who has hurt you. It could be the results of a long-term destructive habit that has undermined your wellness, a pattern of negative self-talk, the results of a bad choice, or it could be something someone has done to you, said to you, or said about you.

One time in prayer I was enjoying feeling the presence of God with me and "beholding" Him as best I could. In the Spirit, I was looking intently at His being, His heart, His countenance, using my godly imagination in the Spirit trying to "see" Him and suddenly I realized, as I beheld Him, He was also beholding me. It startled me a bit and it caused me to quickly look away. I was uncomfortable with Him looking so intently at *me*—seeing everything, seeing my imperfections and wrinkles and whatever else I felt insecure about. I had to do some repenting that day and come into an understanding that in His eyes, I am beautiful just the way I am, and He loves me completely and perfectly. In fact, He doesn't even see my imperfections. I had to come *into* agreement with God about who I was as His masterpiece and *out* of agreement with every negative narrative I had learned since childhood.

I once started to read a book by Beth Moore entitled, "Get Out of that Pit." I don't believe I finished it, but I really liked the analogy she used about being in a pit emotionally. Wounds in our soul can cause us to be in a pit and we must get out to be free and to walk in divine health.

Sometimes we are in a pit because we jumped in (perhaps through sin of our own choosing). Sometimes we are in a pit because we accidentally fell in and sometimes, we are in a pit because we were pushed in. The good news is, we *can* get out of every single one, no matter how we got there. We are never just stuck. If we will partner with God, acknowledge we are in the pit and *truly desire to get out*, Jesus will reach down and pull us out—*every* time. Don't ever think that we can just clean that pit up, put some paint on the walls, add some nice furniture, and it becomes a descent place to live. A pit will always be a dirty, old pit, no matter how you try to dress it up. There will always be mud to deal with. There will always be unnecessary misery in our lives if we choose to stay in the pit.[29] Make it very clear to God that your desire is to get out.

> *Decorating a pit does not make a pit any less damaging to our hearts.*

We may have gone through some tough stuff in life. We may have been rejected and even betrayed by loved ones, but even though we have suffered injustice, we are NOT to remain victims. We are NOT to just sit in our pits and think that we better just get used to being there because we can't undo what someone has done. No, we can't erase the past, but we can change our perspective of it.

---

[29] Beth Moore, *Get Out of That Pit* (Nashville: Thomas Nelson, 2007). Print.

We can choose to believe that it doesn't have to control us or hold us captive. We can choose to understand that it was a bad choice somebody else made that had more to do with their own pain than anything to do with us. We can choose to forgive our oppressor and not allow that wound to hold us captive.

This is the power we have as a human being. We have the capacity to choose our response to every action and every circumstance of life and with Christ, we have even greater power and even authority over our own mind, soul, and wounds.

In Paul's second letter to the Corinthians, he confronts the Corinthian church and boldly explains in chapter 10 that even though they (the Apostles) were in the world, their warfare was not waged in the earth realm. He says, "we do not wage battle according to the flesh, for the weapons of our warfare are not of the flesh, but divinely powerful" (2 Cor. 10:3-4 NASB). Those weapons Paul referred to are the spiritual weapons of God including divine authority, the fellowship and power of the Spirit, the Word of God (spoken/prophetic and written/Bible), our confession or testimony, the name of Jesus, the blood of Jesus, praying in tongues, praise and worship, and more. Paul then continues to tell the Corinthians that in their prayers, the Apostles were taking authority over and destroying every high and lofty argument and thought pattern raised up against the knowledge of God. He even tells them that they (the Apostles) were taking every thought plaguing the minds of the Corinthians captive and making them obedient to Christ (2 Cor. 10:5).

Our weapons are not of this world, but they are certainly powerful and effective.

This is the same warfare that we must wage, against any prideful arguments in our own mind against the truth, any lies the devil has sown into our heart which we have believed and any thought that enters our mind which is contrary to God, including any thought that is for instance, lustful, slanderous, fearful, anxious, critical, bitter, prideful, vengeful, full of grumbling and complaining, ungrateful, argumentative, contentious, not loving, not peaceful and not joyful. We must capture every thought in our mind and make sure it lines up with God.

Did you know that we can control our own thinking? If you didn't, you do now! Stop just allowing your mind to wander away into ungodliness. Take authority over your mind and demand holiness there. Repent for thinking in an ungodly way. Controlling your thoughts will bear tremendous fruit. You will find that controlling your thoughts will produce controlled emotions and stable moods. It may even begin to lead you out of mental health issues like depression and others.

Taking every thought captive will bear much fruit and greatly improve mental health.

One day I was driving to the local pregnancy center where I was volunteering. I was very upset about a ministry venture I had attempted that afternoon, which in the natural appeared as having failed. Random accusing thoughts about being a failure plagued my mind as hot tears streamed down my face in droves. *I need to get it together*, I thought, *I can't show up and work like this*, but no matter how hard I tried, I could not seem to make myself stop crying. Immediately, the Holy Spirit helped me realize that my thoughts were the root of my emotional breakdown, and He led me to take authority over them. I put my hand on my head and said, "In Jesus' name, every voice that is not God, I command it to shut up right now!" Instantly, I mean INSTANTLY, like a switch had been flipped, the tears that had been coming fast and furious before, in the blink of an eye, just simply stopped. One second, I had no control over my emotions and the next, I was as cool as a cucumber. I was stunned that my state had changed so drastically, so quickly. Only the power of God has that effect.

Ephesians 6:10-12 says:

> A final word: Be strong in the Lord and in his mighty power. Put on all of God's armor so that you will be able to stand firm against all strategies of the devil. For we are not fighting against flesh-and-blood enemies, but against evil rulers and authorities of the unseen world, against mighty powers in this dark world, and against evil spirits in the heavenly places. (NLT)

From this scripture we learn there are dark spirits, "evil rulers and authorities," "mighty powers," and "evil spirits" that war against us. They want us to stay in our pits. They want us to be in fear, frustration, discouragement and to give up; they want us to be contentious with one another, to be in strife, and to argue against the truth.

You have been given the power to be an overcomer in every situation, but you must open your mouth to exercise it.

While reading this book, perhaps you have had thoughts in your mind, telling you, *there's no use, I've tried everything, it's hopeless, I'll never get well*, even perhaps, *this author is nuts; she's speaking heresy*. These thoughts are not your thoughts! And they certainly are not from God! Those thoughts are evil spirits trying to control the narrative in your mind and your circumstances. We must recognize their source and deal with them. Put your hand on your head and take authority over those thoughts right now! Pray and declare, "In the name of Jesus, I reject and renounce every lie and every evil thought, and I repent for entertaining them. I now bind and take authority over every prideful, evil, and lying thought in my mind, and I command them to be silent NOW! I muzzle every evil spirit and break its power over me, in Jesus' name." This is praying in the authority Jesus gave us.

Jesus said in Luke 10:19, "I have given you authority to trample on snakes and scorpions and to overcome ALL the power of the enemy; *nothing will harm you*" (NIV, emphasis added). Now, exercise your authority in Christ for yourself. You have been given the ability to be an *overcomer* in *every* situation! Jesus paid dearly to give you authority and power over the enemy, so use it—don't let it go to waste.

Now, as we continue to build on this knowledge, don't be overwhelmed. This may be new to some but remember how big our God is. He created the universe, and He tells the sun when to shine and the moon when to appear. He draws the line in the sand for the waters and says, "This far and no further." He names the stars, and He knows the number of hairs on your head. He is with you, and He is for you. His eye is on you, and He never forgets about you. "For the eyes of the LORD run to and fro throughout the whole earth, to show Himself strong on behalf of those whose heart is loyal to Him" (2 Chronicles 16:9 NKJV). He sees you and He loves you with an everlasting love. With those reminders at the forefront of your mind, let's continue.

The Lord is ready and willing to show Himself strong on your behalf.

In addition to evil spirits putting thoughts into our mind, evil spirits can also attach themselves to our soul when given the opportunity (through repetitive sin, wrong heart attitudes or iniquity) and cause illness. This is illustrated well in Luke 13:10-13 as follows:

> Now Jesus was teaching in one of the synagogues on the Sabbath. And there was a woman who for eighteen years had had an illness caused by a spirit (demon). She was bent double and could not straighten up at all. When Jesus saw her, He called her over and said to her, "Woman, you are released from your illness." Then He laid His hands on her; and immediately she stood erect again and she began glorifying and praising God. (AMP)

Now, let's be wise and understanding. Just because in this passage of scripture, the evil spirit caused a problem with the woman's spine, *does not* mean every person with a spinal issue is demonized nor does it mean this is the only illness a demon can cause. Let's not get religious! Let's not create any rules or patterns out of this but realize we need to be discerning about the root cause of illness.

This discussion, unfortunately, may cause disagreements, as many Christians assume that evil spirits cannot be in them nor cause illness. This is not true. While it is true, a Christian cannot be *possessed* by evil spirits, as possession is about ownership and every Christian is *owned* by Christ. However, a Christian can be demonized, which can be understood as being *oppressed* of soul. *Oppression* means, *subject to harsh or authoritarian treatment, burdened with cruel or unjust impositions or restraints, and subjected to a burdensome or harsh exercise of authority or power.*[30] I think you're beginning to get the picture. When we are *oppressed* by demons, the enemy is successfully exercising his power over us, influencing us in our thoughts, moods, emotions, words, choices, and behaviors and *attempting* to control us.

A Christian cannot be possessed, but he/she can be oppressed of soul.

Remember our discussion from before. When we are saved, our spirits are immediately re-created and made brand new, but our souls are not. Our soul is healed over time in a process, so parts of our soul can still be unhealed. This is the area where demons can be attached, causing us to be in bondage.

Sometimes a word picture or illustration can help us understand difficult concepts. Let's consider the following illustration to help us understand how we can be or become *oppressed* by demons: Imagine you lease a car.[31] You don't own the car; it belongs to

---

[30] Various online dictionaries

[31] Thanks to Dr. Bernardine Daniels for introducing this illustration.

someone else, but it's on loan to you. You can drive the car anywhere you want and use it for whatever purpose you want. You can also open the passenger door to anyone. You can invite whomever you wish into your car and allow them to ride with you for however long you want. Imagine also, that certain *less-desirable* passengers, like demons, get to ride with you *by default*, even if you don't want them to, based on things like repeated sinful actions not repented for, un-healed emotional wounds, long-held wrong beliefs, deep hatred and/or bitterness, etc. These *less-desirable* passengers don't have to get out of the car until YOU stop giving them access and YOU tell them to get out. YOU oversee that car on loan to you. You're responsible to take care of it properly. The *owner* of the car is *not* responsible to control who rides with you—that is your job. I will say that again. The *owner* of the car is *not* responsible to control who rides with you!!! That is your job. You have been given dominion or the control over it.

> *Demons ride along with us like passengers when we open the door through sin.*

Do you see the parallel? The Lord has given us free-will and the choice to live however we wish. We have personal autonomy, and the Spirit of God does not over-ride our choices. God will try to lead us His way, but the final choice is ours. Having choices is good, but we also need to realize that we will experience the consequences of those choices. Demons may ride along with us accordingly, whether we want them to or not. It is possible to allow the Holy Spirit to drive our car but getting to that point of *complete* surrender and perfect discernment is a process and we spend many years driving our car with the Holy Spirit in the back seat, allowing *less-desirable* passengers to ride along with us.

To give you an example of someone in the Bible who was still in bondage in their soul, even after being saved and baptized, consider the man named Simon in Acts 8 who had been practicing magic in Samaria. Philip had gone down to Samaria preaching the gospel, performing miracles, and delivering people from unclean spirits. All the people who heard Philip paid attention to what he was saying, and many believed and were baptized, including Simon the sorcerer. Verse 13 says, "Now even Simon himself believed; and after being baptized, he continued on with Philip, and as he observed signs and great miracles taking place, he was repeatedly amazed" (NASB). We see in verses 14-22 that Peter and John came to assist Philip for the purpose of imparting the Holy Spirit to the people through the laying on of hands and when Simon witnessed it, he offered the apostles money if they would give him the same power and authority. The apostles, of course, rebuked him. Peter said to Simon:

> "May your money be destroyed along with you, because you thought you could buy the [free] gift of God with money! You have no part or share in this matter, because your heart (motive, purpose) is not right before God. So repent of this wickedness of yours, and pray to the Lord that, if possible, this thought of your heart may be forgiven you. *For I see that you are provoked by bitterness and bound by sin.* But Simon answered, "Pray to the Lord for me both of you, so that nothing of what you have said will come upon me." (Acts 8:20-24 AMP)

We are not told what happened with Simon after this incident. We don't know how the apostles prayed for Simon, but we know from this encounter that even after Simon believed and was baptized, he was still bound by sin and needed ministry. I would suggest to you that Simon needed deliverance from demons that were bound (tied) to his soul due to the witchcraft and sorcery he had been engaged in.

Demons can be bound to our soul through many things—word curses spoken over us repeatedly, trauma, abuse, wounds, repetitive sin, and generational iniquity are just a few common examples. But don't fret! Never should we be afraid of them, be embarrassed about it, or feel condemned. Evil spirits are easily dealt with! They just need to be discerned and cast out.

Remember, we are not dealing with a situation, like that from the 1973 movie, *The Exorcist*. No Christian is possessed. No one's head is spinning around! Hollywood has done a great job of freaking people out and sowing fear into hearts around this issue, but casting demons out of a Christian can be very simple and does not have to be dramatic. We can even do this for ourselves when we close the points of entry demons have used (through repentance and renunciation), as well as understand who we are in Christ and the authority Jesus has given us over the devil.

The full truth of what Jesus accomplished on the cross for us is so much more than a ticket to heaven when we pass from this earth. We *must* understand how Jesus has transformed our identity completely and purchased us as His very own possession. When we believe and surrender to Christ, we belong to Him, and we become a brand-new spiritual creation. Second Corinthians 5:17 says, "Therefore, if anyone is in Christ, he is a new creation; old things have passed away; behold, all things have become new" (NKJV).

When a person has surrendered to Christ and is open to ministry, demons are easily dealt with.

Understand that *in Spirit*, we have not been renovated or upgraded. No! We have been completely recreated *in Spirit* and reborn as a child of God—born of God with a completely new *spiritual identity* as a son or daughter of God. All things have passed away, and all things have become new. Ephesians 2:4-7 says:

> But because of his great love for us, God, who is rich in mercy, made us alive with Christ even when we were dead in transgressions—it is by grace you have been saved. And God raised us up with Christ and *seated us with him in the heavenly realms* in Christ Jesus, in order that in the coming ages he might show the incomparable riches of his grace,

expressed in his kindness to us in Christ Jesus. (emphasis added)

Our spiritual identity is now found *in* Christ Jesus. Think about what it means to be *in* something. It means you are *inside of* something, which means you are *contained by it*—you are *surrounded by it* on all sides and if we are in Christ, we must be where He is!! We are seated in Heavenly places with Him, far above all principalities and evil spirits. Physically we live in this natural world, but spiritually we have been given citizenship in heaven, a victorious position far above the devil and a heavenly perspective to see things with the wisdom of God.

According to the Word of God, in Christ, spiritually we are:

- The salt of the earth (Matt. 5:13).
- The light of the world (Matt. 5:14).
- Children of God (John 1:12).
- Part of the true vine, a channel of Christ's life (John 15:1&5).
- Chosen and appointed by Christ (John 15:16).
- Slaves to righteousness (Romans 6:18).
- Joint heirs with Christ, sharing His inheritance (Romans 8:17).
- The dwelling place of God (1 Cor.3:16, 6:19).
- United with the Lord and one Spirit with Him (1 Cor. 6:17).
- Members of Christ's body (1 Cor.12:27, Eph. 5:30).
- Saints (1 Cor. 1:2, Eph. 1:1, Phil. 1:1, Col. 1:2).
- God's workmanship (Eph. 2:10).
- Righteous and holy (Eph. 4:24).
- Hidden with Christ in God (Col. 3:3).
- Chosen of God, holy and dearly loved (Col. 3:12, 1 Thess. 1:4).
- A son of light (1 Thess. 5:5).

- A holy partaker of a heavenly calling (Heb. 3:1).
- God's living stones, being built up in Christ as a spiritual house (1 Peter 2:5).
- Members of a chosen race, a royal priesthood, and a people for God's own possession (1 Peter 2:9-10).
- Enemies of the devil (1 Peter 5:8).
- Born of God and protected from the devil (1 John 5:18).

All these statements are true of us *when* we surrender to Christ. In and of ourselves, we are nothing, but with Christ and in Christ, we are everything—only because of Him and His Spirit living in us. God plus nothing equals everything. We do not add anything to God, but God adds *everything* to us. We may not walk in our new identity perfectly, but that's where grace comes in. God has given us everything up front but then teaches us how to walk it out in this world. Spiritually, we are already perfected; naturally, we are not. We are in process.

> *The devil is a fallen angel and was created by God. In no way is he as powerful as God— not even close.*

Finally, let's remember that the devil is a fallen angel who was created by God; *no* creation is *ever* greater or even on parr with its creator. God is the supreme creator and is far above any other spiritual power, including the devil. Jesus has triumphed over the devil, disarmed the false powers and authorities, and made a public spectacle of them all.[32]

In the Bible, when kings went to war and won, the triumphant king would parade his defeated foe through the streets in humiliation, dragging the enemy's body behind his chariot. Spiritually speaking, Jesus, our *triumphant King* did this same thing to the devil and all

---

[32] "In this way, he disarmed the spiritual rulers and authorities. He shamed them publicly by his victory over them on the cross" (Colossians 2:15 NLT).

his cohorts. This same Jesus lives in us in Spirit, giving us that same victory!

If you're still having difficulty understanding or believing for your authority over the devil, please pick up and read, *Victory Over the Darkness,* by Neil T. Anderson. It will lead you to all the truth from God's Word that you need to stand in Christ. There is never any need for Spirit-filled, Spirit-baptized, born-again believers to be afraid of the devil. In fact, in Christ, *you* are a threat to him. A demon may try to intimidate us but all we need to do is:

1. Repent for whatever the Holy Spirit convicts us of.
2. Renounce wrong motives, thoughts, attitudes, behaviors, and associations.
3. Bind the demons with our words as led by the Holy Spirit.
4. Declare the demons ineffective and powerless over us because of the blood of Jesus and Who our Father is.
5. In faith and confidence, tell them to get out and leave us RIGHT NOW! Breathe them out in faith.
6. Ask Father to send the Holy Spirit to fill us afresh.

There will be prayers throughout this book that will give you specific words to pray. Also Dr. Douglas E. Carr has some great resources that will give you specific direction on how to identify and deal with demons. His first book, *Free Indeed,* is a great overview and his new book, *Breaking Patterns of Perversity: Freedom from Iniquity,* will help you be free from iniquity (and associated spirits) passed on through the generations of your family (more on that later). All his books can be purchased from Amazon. If you are unsure of your status as a born-again believer, or feel nervous about casting out demons, ask the Lord to lead you to someone who can help.

It goes without saying that in order to cast out demons, one must pray in faith and authority. It is also true that when we pray for healing in our body, our prayers are more effective when we again, pray in faith and authority. Praying for what we already have or begging God to heal us, is *not* praying in faith.

Have you ever prayed and asked God to be with you? I've done it many times, but God's Word has already told us that He will never leave us or forsake us.[33] We would do well to believe what God has already said and pray from a place of belief and faith. Even if we don't *feel* God with us, He *is* there. So, it would be better to pray, "Lord, thank You that You are always with me; You have promised it in Your Word, and I believe it. Help me to sense Your presence. Help me to sense Your love and Your comfort. Open my spiritual senses, God, to Who You are, in Jesus' name."

Similarly, God has already done everything necessary to make healing available to us—we just need to access it. So, don't pray, "Lord, please heal me." Pray, "Thank You, God for healing me, spirit, soul, and body. Your Word says that by Your wounds, I AM healed,[34] and I choose to believe Your Word with every

> *Asking the Lord for what you've already been given according to the Word, is a lack of faith and could be unbelief at work.*

fibre of my being. I renounce unbelief and I ask You, Lord, to root it out and rid me of it. I pray, God, that Your Spirit, by whose power Christ was raised, would cause every cell in my body to line up with the truth and be made whole and brought back to life. I open myself up to You completely right now; I command my soul to open to the Holy Spirit now and I give You, Holy Spirit, access to every part of me. I ask Lord, that every truth in heaven would be made manifest in my body, right now, in Jesus' name." We can even take

---

[33] "I will never leave you nor forsake you" (Joshua 1:5 NIV). "God has said, "Never will I leave you; never will I forsake you." So we say with confidence, "The Lord is my helper; I will not be afraid. What can mere mortals to do me" (Hebrews 13:5-6 NIV)?

[34] "He himself bore our sins" in his body on the cross, so that we might die to sins and live for righteousness; "by his wounds you have been healed" (1 Peter 2:24 NIV). Also Isaiah 53:5

our faith and authority further and begin to *govern* our natural circumstances and our physical health through binding, loosing, commanding, and making declarations into the spirit realm.

About ten years ago I started a journey with the Holy Spirit as He began to teach me about praying with authority. As I mentioned earlier, Jesus gave us authority to trample on snakes and scorpions and ALL the power of the enemy (Luke 10:19). In addition, we have been given the keys of the Kingdom according to Matthew 16:19:

> I will give you the keys (authority) of the kingdom of heaven; and whatever you bind [forbid, declare to be improper and unlawful] on earth will have [already] been bound in heaven, and whatever you loose [permit declare lawful] on earth will have [already] been loosed in heaven. (AMP)

The enemy resists our blessings, and we must war in prayer for them to manifest in the earth.

As I sought the Lord, He began to show me that He has already blessed us in the heavenly realms with *every* spiritual blessing[35] and to see them manifest in the natural realm, I had to begin to *command* my blessing and pull them into the earth realm.

He also reminded me of how in Daniel 10:10-14, Daniel had to fast 21 days to receive understanding of a message the Lord gave him. When Daniel finally received his answer, the messenger (angel) of the Lord revealed that he (the messenger) had been resisted in the heavenly realm by the prince of Persia (a demonic entity) and needed help to break through.[36] The moment Daniel prayed, his

---

[35] "All praise to God, the Father of our Lord Jesus Christ, who has blessed us with every spiritual blessing in the heavenly realms because we are united with Christ" (Ephesians 1:3 NLT).

[36] "But for twenty-one days the spirit prince of the kingdom of Persia blocked my way. Then Michael, one of the archangels, came to help me, and I left him there with the spirit prince of the kingdom of Persia" (Daniel 10:13 NLT).

answer was released from heaven, but the angel was engaged in warfare through the heavenlies for twenty-one days. So, it is clear, the enemy resists our blessings, and we need to take authority over that resistance in order to see them manifest. As a result, I began to command my blessings through the heavenlies into the earth realm.

After that, I began reading a book by Dutch Sheets called, *Authority in Prayer*, and I learned even more. You'll have to read the book for yourself to get the humor about the dog, but he begins by asking a thought-provoking question and making an incredible statement: "Who is ruling your world? I'm not referring to the big one, as in planet earth. At least not yet. I'm talking about the world you live in every day, your personal world. I'm speaking of your home, family, job, health, dog—well, okay maybe not your dog. God doesn't intend that any outside force dominate you. He has given you jurisdiction over your life."[37] By page eight, he had my attention.

Dutch continues to tell a story very humorously about how God began to teach him how to govern his life and circumstances. It all began when he was at the airport, on his way to an important speaking engagement, in a very long line of unruly passengers waiting to check in. After some time, Dutch became concerned he might miss his flight, so he began to ask the Lord to intervene. The Lord then informed Dutch that all the chaos happening in the line was all because of him and the demonic resistance to his assignment.

Interestingly enough, after Dutch asked the Lord again to please do something about the situation, the Lord responded, "No, *you* do something about it. Move in the authority I have given you and command the demonic hindrances of your assignment to be ineffective. Declare that you have favor and will get to your

---

[37] Dutch Sheets, *Authority in Prayer: Praying with Power and Purpose* (Minneapolis: Bethany House, 2006) 8-9. Print.

meeting on time."[38] Dutch then wraps up the story by doing as he was told and following every detail of additional instruction God gave him. Dutch ended up experiencing supernatural favor by skipping the line, getting an up-grade to first-class *and* reaching his meeting on time! After reading Dutch's story, I immediately had an opportunity to test what I had been learning—to govern my own circumstances to see change.

My daughter was pitching for her school's softball team, and they were in the playoffs that weekend. Her team had made it all the way to the finals two years in a row, but the year prior they lost to a tough rival school who took great pleasure in speaking all kinds of nasty things against them. They suffered great humiliation after working hard all season.

Angels and demons in the atmosphere are empowered by our words and behaviours.

That Saturday they first played the finals for their division and won. Then they had to face the same team that had previously humiliated them. In the same fashion, they spoke hateful, crude remarks against the girls as they played. I began to recognize that something spiritual was at work.

Our team was not playing well. The oppression around them was affecting them greatly. They missed fly-balls and infield hits that they normally would have easily picked up and thrown out. They continually over-threw the ball; it was a comedy of errors, except no one was laughing. The opposing team seemed to hit the ball unusually well and were making every catch and every throw on target. If you've ever seen the movie, "Angels in the Outfield," it was kind of like that only it was demons who were controlling the game.

---

[38] Sheets, *Authority in Prayer*, 11. Print.

Two thirds of the way through the game, our girls were losing miserably, and I wondered what would happen if I began to govern the circumstances by binding the evil spirits at work, loosing the Holy Spirit over the game, and declaring favor over my daughter and her team. So I did. It took about two minutes for the game to begin to turn and only about one inning for the girls to be totally back on their game! They had a huge come-back and ended up winning the game, *plus* the season, over the *entire* region where we live—*both* city and rural divisions. The girls were over-the-moon. It was such a blessing.

The local newspaper interviewed one of the girls on the opposing team. She said, "It was like our bats just stopped working." Grin. It is noteworthy to say here that I did not pray against the girls on the opposing team. I prayed against the demons in the atmosphere. I simply shifted the atmosphere to dis-empower evil and empower the Holy Spirit through binding and loosing. I used my Kingdom keys just as we are supposed to.

We can lock and unlock angelic activity in the atmosphere with the authority Jesus gave us.

We have the ability to lock and un-lock spiritual activity in the heavenly realm with the authority Christ has given us. We do that by opening our mouth in prayer, making decrees and declarations based on the Word of God into the atmosphere which let demons know what is allowed and what is not. We don't let the devil push us around! We govern the spirits which then leads to governing our circumstances. Remember, the Apostles said in 2 Corinthians 10:3, they did not wage war as the world does and neither do we. We have been given access to spiritual weapons that are mighty and powerful in Christ, and we have been given the fullness of Christ dwelling within us. This is confirmed by Colossians 2:9-10, "For in Christ all the fullness of the Deity lives in bodily form, and in Christ you have been brought to fullness. He is the head over every power and authority" (NIV).

Is it possible to undermine the authority Christ has given us? Have you ever known someone in authority who didn't act the way they should? Have you ever heard of or known a corrupt police officer, an adulterous pastor, or an abusive parent? Did you lose respect for them and as a result see them as less of an authority figure in your life? I'm going to guess that you answered, "yes," to that last question.

When those in authority don't steward their authority well, they undermine themselves and as a result will fail to continue to operate in that authority. We stop listening to the sermons of that adulterous pastor and stop seeking counsel from them, don't we? A corrupt police officer is stripped of his badge and held accountable for his actions. An abusive parent is held accountable by God, and the law if caught, and will likely lose relationship with their adult children.

When we don't steward well the authority Christ gave us, we undermine it, and we end up being hindered in our walk.

What about us? Do we lose our spiritual authority when we don't bridle the flesh, put to death its sinful desires and exercise self-control? Do we undermine our authority in the spirit realm when we continue to live in sin even after we've repented? Yes, we do. We can't pick and choose what areas we want to submit to God in. It's all or nothing. God wants it all and He deserves it all! Doesn't He? He gave us His all and we need to reciprocate with the same devotion.

As we grow spiritually in our faith-walk and gain personal victories, overcoming temptation and destructive heart attitudes, our spiritual power and authority begin to *work* for us in greater and greater measure. Do you remember back in chapter two when we talked about Jesus being baptized? We looked at how Jesus was *filled* with the Holy Spirit at His baptism but was *empowered*[39] (miracle working power/strength/ virtue) by the Holy Spirit *after* He emerged out of the desert having *overcome* the temptations the devil threw at Him.[40] Do you see the difference? Being *filled* and being *empowered* seem to be two different things. With that in mind, here's what I believe the Holy Spirit is saying to us right now:

> "Overcoming activates My power
> and authority in you."

God calls us all to be overcomers with His help! What do you think being an overcomer looks like? To overcome something means to defeat something—to succeed, prevail over, to have the victory, to gain mastery over, to conquer. To be an overcomer means to be someone who stands in victory, who isn't mastered by a thing but has mastery over it. Nothing controls an overcomer except Christ. No habit, no need, no other person controls them.

Is there anything or anyone in your life that you feel controlled by? If so, this is one area the Lord is putting His finger on right now and calling you to deal with. Pray beloved! This could be something that is connected to ill health in your body. Remember, God, Jesus and the Holy Spirit are gentle, and they are NOT into controlling us or overriding our free-will. Only the devil controls. So, if we are feeling controlled in an area, that is the devil at work. We must come out from under that and gain the victory. When we pass the test, just as Jesus passed His tests, we gain ground, and we are activated in more supernatural ability and authority.

There are two different words in the Greek that are translated *power*, in various passages, even though one of them doesn't really mean power. Those words are, *dunamis,* which means *miraculous*

---

[39] The word "power" is translated in Luke 4:14 from the Greek word dunamis which means miracle working power, might, ability, virtue (blueletterbible.org).

[40] "Then Jesus returned in the power of the Spirit to Galilee, and news of Him went out through all the surrounding region" (Luke 4:14 NKJV).

power, ability, and strength, and *exousia*, which more accurately means *authority*. Some passages use *dunamis* and some use *exousia*, but how many of you know, authority is useless unless you've also got the power? You can have power without authority but if you've got supernatural authority, you *must* also have supernatural power to back it up. As well, those with power *and* authority are greater than those with only power. What good is power when you don't have the authority or right to use it?

With that understanding, listen again to Luke 10:19, "Behold, I give you the *authority* to trample on serpents and scorpions, and over all the *power* of the enemy, and nothing shall by any means hurt you" (NKJV). What has Jesus given us? Authority. What does the devil have? Power—but no authority to use it.

> *When we are faithful to persevere and overcome, God knows we can be trusted with His power.*

Also, check out Luke 9:1-2, "Then He called His twelve disciples together and gave them *power and authority* over all demons, and to cure diseases" (NKJV, emphasis added). Then in Luke 10, He sends out seventy others, anointing them with the same power and authority saying to them, "Whatever city you enter, and they receive you, eat such things as are set before you. And heal the sick there, and say to them, 'The kingdom of God has come near to you" (Luke 10:8-9 NKJV). Just as Jesus sent the seventy and anointed them with power and authority, so He has sent us and anointed us (Mark 16:15-18), as we are faithful to overcome.

Lastly, when Jesus told the disciples to wait in Jerusalem for the gift of the Holy Spirit, He said to them, "But you shall receive *power* (dunamis: miraculous power) when the Holy Spirit has come upon you; and you shall be witnesses to Me in Jerusalem, and in all Judea and Samaria, and to the end of the earth" (NKJV, emphasis and brackets mine). It is the baptism of the Holy Spirit that gives us dunamis. And dunamis is the root word of our English word dynamite! The power of God in you works like dynamite to blow up and obliterate anything not of Him!

Have you been baptized in the Holy Spirit? If so, you have the dynamite, miracle working power of the Kingdom of God available to you. Make sure it is activated by being an overcomer and passing the tests God puts on your path. When we are faithful to persevere, letting go of every bad attitude, overcoming temptation, offense, bitterness, and everything that binds, God knows we can be trusted with His power and authority.

If you're not yet baptized in the Holy Spirit, ask Jesus now! Don't wait any longer. Cry out to Him for everything He has for you. "Jesus! Baptize me in the Holy Spirit! Would You cause the very Spirit of God to descend upon me and consume me now! I repent for not submitting nor accepting His baptism but *now* I'm ready! I humble myself under His mighty hand and open myself to His authority and control—in Jesus' name. Holy Spirit, come! Consume me! Possess me now. Amen." And watch what happens. Hear the voice of the Lord. Is there something you must do to align yourself first? If so, do it! If something is causing you to sin, get rid of it! Is your Netflix subscription tripping you up? Get rid of it! Cut it out. Be obedient and open yourself up to God to take control of your desires, your heart, and your behaviors.

Beloved, God's got you. Do you know what "beloved" means? It means, "the one who is loved." Why do I keep calling you "beloved?" Is it because I'm just sappy? Is it just me and my personality? No! It's the Holy Spirit. The Holy Spirit is putting that word in my heart to describe you. To Him, you are His beloved, no matter what. He loves you! YOU are "the loved one" of the Lord. Even though He sees *everything* you don't want anyone to see, He still loves you all the same. Receive Him. Receive all of Him. Don't refuse any gift God has for you. He knows what you need, and He knows how to bless you perfectly.

Notes

Chapter 6

LIVING BY THE SPIRIT

Romans 8 is so rich with truth regarding how to lay hold of healing in our body and see it manifest now. Let's have a look at it:

Therefore, there is now no condemnation for those who are in Christ Jesus, because through Christ Jesus the law of the Spirit who gives life has set you free from the law of sin and death. For what the law was powerless to do because it was weakened by the flesh, God did by sending his own Son in the likeness of sinful flesh to be a sin offering. And so he condemned sin in the flesh, in order that the righteous requirement of the law might be fully met in us, who do not live according to the flesh but according to the Spirit. Those who live according to the flesh have their minds set on what the flesh desires; but those who live in accordance with the Spirit have their minds set on what the Spirit desires. The mind governed by the flesh is death, but the mind governed by the Spirit is life and peace. The mind governed by the flesh is hostile to God; it does not submit to God's law, nor can it do so. Those who are in the realm of the flesh cannot please God. You however, are not in the realm of the flesh but are in the realm of the Spirit, if indeed the Spirit of God lives in you. And if anyone does not have the Spirit of Christ, they do not belong to Christ. But if Christ is in you, then even though your body is subject to death because of sin, the Spirit gives life because of righteousness. And if the Spirit of him who raised Jesus from the dead is living in you, he who raised Christ from the dead will also give life to your mortal bodies because of his Spirit who lives in you. Therefore, brothers and sisters, we have an obligation—but it is not to the flesh, to live according to it. For if you live according to the flesh, you will die; but if by the Spirit you put to death the misdeeds of the body, you will live. (Romans 8:1-13 NIV)

That's a mouthful! But let's pull out some key points.

1. There is a "law" of the Spirit—that is the Holy Spirit, and that LAW states that the Spirit gives Life. Wherever the Holy Spirit is recognized as God and given absolute pre-eminence, there is life. The Holy Spirit and life are inseparable. Just like the law of gravity operates in the natural realm without partiality, so does the *law* of the Spirit operate on behalf of those living by the Spirit, in Christ Jesus.

2. There is also a law of sin and death which is the law of the flesh that states, wherever sin is, death is. Sin and death (or the process of death) are inseparable. Anyone living by the flesh, will experience the *law* of sin and death. It will operate without partiality; it is a law.

3. The Spirit sets us free from the law of sin and death, through Christ Jesus.

4. We will *truly live* when we live by the Holy Spirit within us—by His power, His enabling, and His leading.

5. Living by the Spirit brings *true life* (vitality and health—life according to God's timetable).

6. Living by the flesh brings death (sickness, disease, and early death).

Unfortunately, while living on the earth, there is no delete button for the sinful nature. We still carry it around in our body, but by the Spirit it has been disempowered and crucified with Christ. To reinforce that truth, we also need to, in the power of the Holy Spirit, willfully put to death the misdeeds of the body (stop using our body as an instrument of unrighteousness) and *choose* to live by the Spirit. We need to let our dead "sin nature" *stay* dead, without resurrecting it by our own will and wrong desires.

"Living by the Spirit"—I wonder if we really understand what that looks like. We tend to live by what we see and feel in the natural realm as it is obvious, easy, and right here in front of us. Living by the Spirit takes great intentionality and focus—a choice to sometimes ignore what we see with

Allowing the spiritual realm to take precedence over the natural is a choice.

our natural eyes and allow what we see with our spiritual eyes to become superior. Living by the Spirit is something else—something other.

As a human being, we are primarily spiritual beings. We are spirit. We have a soul where our mind, will and emotions reside, and we live in a body. Our body is like a tent or a house that our inner man lives in. Before we are saved, we are led by our souls and our feelings. After we are saved, the Holy Spirit becomes one with our spirit, giving us renewed inner life. We then need to command our soul to submit to the Spirit and allow the Holy Spirit to lead our lives. Living by the Spirit looks like seeking God's ways, God's heart, and God's perspective on everything—hearing His voice, obeying His direction, submitting our mind and will to His, thinking His thoughts, relying on Him in all of life and allowing His gifts to flow out of us.

Because I am a practical person and I like to use word pictures, imagine you accidently cut in line at the grocery store and someone gets mad and starts yelling at you, even calling you names. What do you do? If you were living by the flesh, you might have a few different responses depending on your personality and past woundedness. You might say, "I'm so sorry" repeatedly, be horribly embarrassed and leave the store in tears, struggling with your self-esteem. You may even have thoughts like, "I'm such an idiot!" Someone else, living by the flesh, might respond with the same aggression, get angry and yell back, shooting a few choice names and expletives, or saying something like, "Calm down!" or "Take it easy! It was an honest mistake," *in defense of yourself*. Either way, both responses are from your own feelings, soul, and flesh.

Expressing compassion and empathy in an atmosphere of hate, is evidence that you're moving in the Spirit.

Contrarily, if you were living by the Spirit as a mature believer, how would you respond? Well, you would respond as if you were Jesus. First, your accuser's words would not penetrate your heart. It wouldn't hurt you or offend you in any way. Why? Because you know it was an honest mistake and you know who you are to God— His beloved son or daughter. You know you are right before God and to you, only God's opinion matters. You live for an audience of One. You might say, "I'm sorry, I didn't realize the line was there. Please forgive me," because you did make a mistake and it would only be right to apologize but, you would also be able to ignore all other rants being spewed at you without reaction or inclination to defend yourself. Additionally, you would have compassion and empathy for the other person and *see* them from God's perspective. Perhaps the Spirit would even show you his/her heart and give you understanding of why he/she is responding the way he/she is. Perhaps the Spirit would show you that he/she is just tired and weary from a long day. The Spirit may even move you to do something for the person to make up for your mistake, but the key is to hear the inner leading of the Spirit of God and be obedient.

Another good example (given that this book is about the healing of illness) is what we do when we get sick. If we're living according to the flesh, we do whatever feels right to our flesh, whatever the world has educated us to do or whatever is easiest. Perhaps we pop a few pills, or we run to the doctor immediately, for a diagnosis. But, if we're living by the Spirit, the first thing we do is pray. We ask God about it. For example:

> "Father God, I have this pain in my side; show me if there is anything in my heart that is giving this pain license to manifest. (Listen for an answer and respond) Cause Your Spirit to flow in my body, God, to bring Your healing power. In the name of Jesus, I rebuke this pain now and command it to go. I do not receive it. It is not part of who I am in Jesus. I have been set free from the law of sin and death by the law of the Spirit of life. I am forgiven and washed clean by the blood of my Savior, Jesus. I am a brand-new creation in Him. By His stripes I AM healed now! ALL PAIN GO NOW, in Jesus' name."

Pray over yourself. If the pain goes, great!! If the pain doesn't go or cease, continue to pray, and ask the Lord to give you wisdom and knowledge on how to proceed. Continue to ask Him what is causing the pain. Wait on Him to answer you. Spend time in worship and pray in tongues to stir up your spirit to hear the Holy Spirit. Ask Him if there is something in your heart at the root of the pain. What happened right before the pain started? Did you get angry at someone? Did you talk badly of someone? Did someone sin against you? Do you need to confront someone who is hurting you or not stewarding their responsibility in your relationship? Ask God if you need to forgive someone. Ask Him if *you* have sinned somehow. Finally, ask Him if you should go to the doctor. (If you're struggling to hear the Lord, there is no shame in going to the doctor but at least pray first and give God an opportunity to speak to you. Ask the Lord to lead the doctor, give the doctor wisdom and to protect you as you go.)

The key here is to seek the Lord *first* for an answer and the doctor second. There is no sin in taking medication or a pain reliever but taking too much can affect your health as well. *Living by the Spirit* is living by the wisdom of God (not worldly wisdom) and allowing the Spirit of God to take control.

In this world, we think more knowledge is what we need so we get this degree and that degree, even going to seminary and letting other people (*sometimes* without the Spirit's lead) tell us how to interpret the Bible, but human or worldly knowledge does not give us true life. It may help us get a job or career but it's not going to give us eternal life or divine health—only the Holy Spirit and the wisdom of God can do that.

> *The Holy Spirit should always be our main source of knowledge, wisdom, and understanding.*

Unfortunately, when we rely on worldly knowledge and wisdom, it can become even more difficult than usual to live by the Spirit because we think we know everything. Thinking that worldly knowledge is the answer and seeking it out like one should seek God is dangerous and can get us entangled with demons of idolatry, humanism, and intellectualism (Matthew 6:33 tells us to seek first the Kingdom of God, not the world). Many Christians live this way. They've given mental assent to the gospel, even received salvation, but they ignore the Holy Spirit and live by their own logic, knowledge, and wisdom rather than God's. Apart from the mercy of God, someone living this way would need to repent and possibly get delivered from demons of humanism, intellectualism, and idolatry to be healed.

The Holy Spirit should *always* be our *main* source of knowledge, wisdom and understanding, especially if it is our desire to live by the Spirit. Don't confuse human wisdom for God's wisdom. Ask the

Lord for discernment to tell the difference and get to know the sound of the Lord's voice to distinguish it from your soul.

God's wisdom is going to sound foolish to your flesh/intellect but it's the opposite that is true. First Corinthians 3:19 tells us that to God, it's the wisdom of this world that is foolish. James 3:17 gives us clues to help recognize the wisdom of God, "But the wisdom from above is first of all pure. It is also peace loving, gentle at all times, and willing to yield to others. It is full of mercy and the fruit of good deeds. It shows no favoritism and is always sincere" (NLT).

· · · · · · · · ● · · · · · · · · · · ·

First Corinthians 12:4-11 advises us of the manifestation gifts given to men by the Holy Spirit. Recognizing and moving in these gifts is part of living by the Spirit.

> There are diversities of gifts, but the same Spirit. There are differences of ministries, but the same Lord. And there are diversities of activities, but it is the same God who works all in all. But the manifestation of the Spirit is given to each one for the profit of all: for to one is given the word of wisdom through the Spirit, to another the word of knowledge through the same Spirit, to another faith by the same Spirit, to another gifts of healing by the same Spirit, to another the working of miracles, to another prophecy, to another discerning of spirits, to another different kinds of tongues, to another the interpretation of tongues. But one and the same Spirit works all these things, distributing to each one individually as He wills. (1 Corinthians 12:4-11 NKJV)

The manifestation gifts are as follows:

1. Word (message) of wisdom
2. Word (message) of knowledge
3. Gift of faith
4. Gift of healing
5. Working of miracles
6. Prophecy

7. Discerning of spirits
8. Different kinds of tongues
9. Interpretation of tongues

Word of Wisdom

A word of wisdom is a supernatural enabling of the Spirit, to hear for yourself and/or deliver to someone else, a word from God that gives you/them Godly wisdom which perhaps addresses a current issue or question in their life. Wisdom is the correct or needed application of knowledge, experience and/or good judgment required for a situation. This wisdom is not from our own knowledge or experience but from God which goes beyond what we would naturally know or be able to communicate.

While Jesus was on the earth, He operated as a man, and needed the Holy Spirit to be effective in ministry.

There are many examples in the Bible of when the Spirit gave a word of wisdom to Jesus and others. For example, when Jesus healed the blind man from Bethsaida, in Mark 8:22-26, Jesus first took him out of the town. Jesus put spit in his eyes and placed His hands on the man, twice. Jesus also made him "look up." Why? Because Jesus looked to His Father on what needed to be done and God told Jesus, by the Spirit, to say, "Look up." (Jesus only ever did what He saw His Father doing and only ever said what His Father was saying.) Jesus received words of wisdom on how to heal every person that He healed, and each action and word was significant, meant to address the issues at the root of the illness.

Remember, Jesus, even though He was with the Father from the beginning of time, divine in every respect, He came to earth as a man only and He ministered on the earth through the empowering of the Holy Spirit. He had to submit completely to the Holy Spirit and operate in the gifts of the Holy Spirit to be effective.

In John 2:1-10, Jesus does His first miracle when He turns water into wine. Mary, mother of Jesus, says to Him, "They have no wine" (vs. 3). Jesus asks, "What does that have to do with me?" And says, "My hour has not yet come" (vs. 4). Despite that, Mary says to the servants, "Whatever He says to you, do it" (vs. 5).

Mary wanted Jesus to rescue the hosts of the wedding from humiliation, but Jesus was not getting any direction from His Father about it at first, but then. . . something changed. Suddenly Jesus began to give the servants direction, "Fill the waterpots with water" (vs.7). Did Mary change His mind? No. Jesus was not trying to please His mother; Jesus only did what He saw His Father doing. One minute, the Father wasn't doing anything about it and the next, He was. Father God began to move and gave Jesus direction and the empowerment necessary to turn ordinary water into wine.

What is interesting to me about this account also is why the waterpots were filled and not the containers the previous wine was in. They had wine up to that point at the wedding; the wine had to be contained in something. Why not fill those containers with water?

The scripture says, "Now there were set there six waterpots of stone, according to the manner of purification of the Jews, containing twenty or thirty gallons apiece" (John 2:6 NKJV). These jars were used by the Jews for ceremonial washing. Interesting. Jesus received a Word from the Holy Spirit to do what He did. In fact, through that miracle, Jesus foreshadowed that the Jews would cease to be cleansed with water but would be cleansed with the wine of the New Covenant, His blood, and it would happen at a covenant sealing moment, such as a wedding, when they and all of us would spiritually betroth ourselves to our Bridegroom King, Jesus. Very cool imagery here! But, unfortunately, I'm off topic.

One last example, from the Bible, of a word of wisdom is found in the healing of the woman who suffered from continuous bleeding, found in Mark 5:25-34. We've already talked about that healing, but I just want to point out here, that it wasn't her good idea that led her to seek Jesus out. She was tired and weak. Her flesh wanted to stay in bed! I'm sure of it. It would have made no good sense to any logical mind for her to get up and go anywhere. No, it was God that gave her the wisdom to get up, seek Jesus out, and touch the hem of His garment. It was also God that gave her the faith to be healed.

I remember a time when I was facilitating a small group discussion at church after a conference and there was a woman who was very discouraged about her small business. She owned and managed a salon/spa and was feeling that maybe what she was doing was not spiritual enough and a waste of time. We had just finished listening to some great speakers on how God was doing amazing things through them—rescuing children from child labour in India etc. and her little business suddenly felt too insignificant to matter. The business wasn't overly successful, and she was thinking that maybe she should close shop.

Two minutes after first speaking with her, the power and anointing of the Holy Spirit rose up in me strongly and I began prophesying to her, encouraging her on how God wanted to touch people through her, and I began to speak to her several words of wisdom on how to level up her business. Included were words on re-ordering staff as well as instruction on creating more of an atmosphere of peace by reducing clutter and organizing things better, creating order out of chaos, praying in her space, and asking the Holy Spirit to fill it. (There was more, but this is what I remember.) Now, many years later, she is still in business, and her shop is lovely. She is one of the higher end salons in town. In fact, I was just in there getting a pedicure and it was very busy.

Word of Knowledge
A word of knowledge is information given to you by the Holy Spirit—something you do not naturally know about a person, or about what God wants to do or heal in the moment. Knowing that

the Holy Spirit might give information about you to someone can be a bit unnerving, however, it is always for a good purpose, and He only tells those whom He knows He can trust with the information.

Jesus moved in words of knowledge when He spoke to the woman at the well and said to her, "for you have had five husbands, and the one whom you now have is not your husband" (John 4:18 NKJV). Jesus did not know this on His own. He knew it by the Spirit.

Jesus also moved in words of knowledge in John 1:47-48 when He recognized Nathanael even before meeting him physically and said, "Behold, an Israelite indeed, in whom is no deceit" (vs.47 NKJV)! Nathanael was confused and wondered how Jesus knew him. Jesus said, "Before Phillip called you, when you were under the fig tree, I saw you" (vs.48 NKJV). This was all it took for Nathanael to recognize Jesus as the Son of God. Love Nathanael!

Ask the Lord, "What do you want to do for this person right now?

Words of knowledge are especially useful in evangelism and the Holy Spirit uses them often with those who are open to it. For instance, if there was a person on the street that Jesus wanted to reach, a Spirit-filled, Spirit-baptized Christian who is open to being used this way could speak to that individual and deliver a message right from the Holy Spirit that pierces their heart. For example, you might be on the street, and you notice something about someone (something stands out to you), and compassion begins to stir in your heart for them. This is how you know the Holy Spirit is at work.

A good question to the Lord would be, "What do You want to do in this moment for that person?" The Holy Spirit may answer you directly or show you an area in their life where they need care, love, or encouragement. The Holy Spirit may show you that they struggle with fear, or that they're having nightmares, or give you a nugget of knowledge about them that will give you a launching pad for witnessing and ministering to them. The beauty of this gift is it communicates clearly that God is real, God cares, and God sees what they're going through.

Another type of word of knowledge is when the Holy Spirit reveals to you what He wants to do, or what He wants to heal in that moment, for a particular person, people group, or in a meeting—wherever you are. I was involved with a church group who purposefully went out into the street, stores, and public places to move in this type of gifting. We would pray ahead of time and ask God to show us the people He wanted us to connect with and we would make notes on the features of the people God showed us through thoughts or pictures on the screen of our imagination. We would also ask the Lord if there was something He wanted us to share with them or something He wanted to heal (based on an evangelism method called Treasure Hunting).[41] Sometimes God would give us details ahead of time but sometimes He would wait until we were speaking to the person we found.

> The Lord sees everyone as a treasure and wants His kids to communicate with others on His behalf, representing Him well.

One time we had been ministering in Meijer and at some point, surrounding that event, God dropped an image in my mind of a tall young man (early twenties perhaps) with friends, standing in front of the dairy section. The Lord then dropped the words, *shin splint* in my mind. Then, in my mind's eye, I saw myself ministering to this young man, and I heard the words, "You have pain in the front of your shin (pointing to the left one), and God wants to heal it. You have been playing soccer, though most people assume you play basketball, and you injured yourself playing the game, with such intensity. You're very good at it! The Lord wants to heal you, but

---

[41] Kevin Dedmon, *The Ultimate Treasure Hunt* (Shippensburg: Destiny Image Publishers, 2007).

He also wants you to come back to Him. When you were a child, you used to kneel at the edge of your bed and pray but as you grew, you stopped doing that. The Lord misses you. The Lord misses hearing your voice. Return to Jesus. He loves you with an everlasting love. If you will once again kneel and pray to your Savior acknowledging Him, He will heal you."

I didn't have the opportunity to deliver that word to anyone that night as I didn't see anyone that fit that description. I'm not sure why. Perhaps I missed him or perhaps I have not yet met him. Regardless, the word I received was full of supernatural words of knowledge and wisdom from the Holy Spirit.

We did speak with a few people in Meijer at the outreach event previously mentioned. I don't usually remember exactly what I say to people as I am in the Spirit when I speak, but I do remember speaking to one young woman and delivering a word of encouragement to her about something she was worried and concerned about—that God was intervening on her behalf etc. I remember she was overcome by emotion as the Holy Spirit ministered to her heart, and she revealed to us that her cat was sick, and no one could figure out what was wrong. She received encouragement and a sense of peace about the situation, and we parted ways. She already knew Jesus and just needed a touch from Him.

Gift of Faith
The gift of faith from the Holy Spirit is a supernatural deposit of massive, fully persuaded faith that suddenly drops in our spirit which supercharges the faith we already carry. It is over and above the faith that is in our spirit every day and shifts us into sudden, aggressive faith for something we may not have been *fully* persuaded of before. It very often will propel us into action.

Gift of Healing
The gift of healing is the supernatural ability to heal others by the power of the Holy Spirit which is above and beyond the normal

supernatural working of the Holy Spirit resident in every Spirit-baptized believer. "Healing" implies that what is already in existence is put into proper order according to God's will. For example: to heal someone who is blind but was born seeing. I believe that when the *gift* of healing is in operation, complete healing happens immediately.

Working of Miracles

The working of miracles is a gift which provides believers the supernatural ability, by the power of the Holy Spirit, to heal an issue that would require the creation of something that is not already in existence. For example, when a person who was born blind without the necessary physical organs in their eyes to see, suddenly sees.

Prophecy

Prophecy is a gift of the Holy Spirit that is in operation when a believer discerns, in various ways, the heart, will, and voice of God regarding people (personal prophecy) and/or geographical regions and releases a "word" or "utterance" to express it. It could include (but not always) the foretelling of possible events. I say "possible" because prophecy is an utterance based on the present and whether the prophecy comes true or not can depend on the response of the hearer.

Paul tells us in 1 Corinthians 14:1-3 to earnestly desire the gifts, especially the gift of prophecy:

> Pursue [this] love [with eagerness, make it your goal], yet earnestly desire and cultivate the spiritual gifts [to be used by believers for the benefit of the church], but especially that you may prophesy [to foretell the future, to speak a new message from God to the people]. For one who speaks in an unknown tongue does not speak to people but to God; for no one understands him or catches his meaning, but by the Spirit he speaks mysteries [secret truths, hidden things]. But [on the other hand] the one who prophesies speaks to people for edification [to promote their spiritual growth]

and [speaks words of] encouragement [to uphold and advise them concerning the matters of God] and [speaks words of] consolation [to compassionately comfort them]. (1 Corinthians 14:1-3 AMP)

Discerning of Spirits

The gift of discerning of spirits is a gift of the Holy Spirit giving believers the ability to know when the Holy Spirit is at work and when a demon is at work. It also gives the believer the ability to know WHAT demon, in particular, is at work around them, in the atmosphere, in people and in geographical regions with the purpose of dealing with it in prayer and/or casting it out.

Different Kinds of Tongues

The gift of tongues is a supernatural ability to speak another earthly language unknown to the speaker or a heavenly language for the purpose of

Knowing the gifts of the Spirit and receiving them is part of honoring the Spirit well.

delivering a message from God in a corporate setting (when in order) or to use in personal prayer to draw closer to God, hit the mark in prayer, stir oneself up in the spiritual realm to activate discernment and/or to war in the spirit realm. There are whole books written on why we should pray in tongues so the benefits I've listed are in NO way the only benefits, just the ones off the top of my head.

Interpretation of Tongues

The gift of interpretation of tongues is a message from the Holy Spirit, given in the language of the corporate setting, which interprets an utterance already given in a heavenly language.

These are the manifestation gifts of the Holy Spirit, and He wants us to move in them as He releases them and empowers us. They are for our benefit and the benefit of everyone around us and can cause a pre-believer to take the leap into relationship with Christ.

Embracing or rejecting the gifts is your choice but rejecting them could have consequences.

Have you ever given a gift only to have it rejected by the person it was given to? No? Me neither. That would be rude, wouldn't it? Well, in this conversation we are talking about God, not people. The last thing I would want to be toward God is rude. It wouldn't help in our relationship and our fellowship together; it would only hinder. This past year I received a teaching from Christian International regarding the prophetic and the instructor said, "Never return to God with an unopened gift." This is profound. Gifts are to be opened and then used; nothing speaks indifference and dishonor more than someone not even bothering to open a gift they are given, so let's discern the gifts that the Spirit has given us and open them, then use them as we are led and trained.

It's okay to be a bit nervous and it's okay to be unsure. Moving in the gifts of the Spirit takes practice so get with some spiritual Christians who are like-minded—who are forgiving and will allow you to make mistakes.

Above all, honor the Holy Spirit. Welcome Him in your presence and give Him the space and opportunity to move in your life. Receive the gifts He has given you and use them. If you haven't honored Him, repent, change your mind, and turn back toward goodness, thankfulness, honor, and righteousness.

Throwing the baby out with the bath water because of fear only produces religion without power and that's no good to anyone. So, embrace the supernatural instead of running from it or rejecting it. It is *only* by the breaking in of supernatural power from the Holy Spirit that we will be healed in this earthly realm.

Chapter 7

PRAISE AND WORSHIP

What breaks the enemy's oppression over us faster than anything else? Praise and worship! Opening our mouths and choosing to celebrate God for Who He is, singing His praises, declaring His goodness and mercy, through every circumstance sends the devil running every time. The devil hates it. The devil wants us to wallow in disappointment and fear, feeling sorry for ourselves sitting under defeat. He wants us to focus on what's not working out for us so that it consumes us and controls us. God on the other hand wants us to focus on Him and His victory, shouting out His praises with a voice of triumph, all the time, even when we don't feel like it. We may have to push our flesh, but when we do, we will win and maintain the victory we already have in Christ.

In 2001, my husband and I went through a very difficult time. We were expecting our third child but days after my eighteen-week ultrasound, we were informed that our baby had no heartbeat. It was heart-wrenching to say the least. During and right after the ultrasound, I sensed something wasn't quite right and agonized about it until we finally got the call from the doctor's office.

We got the bad news on a Friday and were told that my body would likely miscarry over the weekend, so that is where it was left. Two days later, on Sunday morning, I was feeling fine physically but emotionally wasn't and didn't *feel* like going to church. However, because I am *always* connected to the Spirit, I heard His gentle, still small voice inside, *why do you go to church*? I thought, *to worship God*. Then I heard inside, *am I not worthy to be worshipped this morning? Have I changed? Have I somehow lost my holiness*? I think my heart may have stopped for a millisecond right there in the fear of the Lord.

Well, you can probably guess the rest of the story. Of course, God is worthy to be worshipped, at all times, so we went to church and sat near the front as we always did. I couldn't sing much because of the massive lump in my throat, as I tried desperately not to ugly cry in front of everyone, but I worshipped God in my heart with all sincerity. It was the strangest mixture of grief and praise and worship all at once. That morning, I learned we are to worship, love and honor God for *Who* He is, not only for what He does, regardless of our circumstances.

Unfortunately, ten days later I still had not miscarried and I was admitted to the hospital for an induction. Our little one was stillborn, almost outwardly fully formed having survived about twelve weeks gestation. I don't know why this happened to us, but I chose to continue to trust in the goodness of God and I greatly valued my Sunday morning lesson in honoring God well.

God did not allow me to get away with not worshipping Him and I am so very grateful! Human reasoning told me it was okay to stay home and have a pity party, but God knew what I needed to do to stay aligned with Him and *remain in victory*. Praise and worship amidst sorrow and pain opened the way for God to manifest great favor in our lives. Just two months after my "missed miscarriage" I was pregnant again, but this time with twins. Gabriel and Jonathan, identical twins, were both born healthy in August of 2002. Praise God!

Psalm 100 says the following:

> Shout with joy to the LORD, all the earth! Worship the LORD with gladness. Come before him, singing with joy. Acknowledge that the LORD is God! He made us, and we are his. We are his people, the sheep of his pasture. Enter his gates with thanksgiving; go into his courts with praise. Give thanks to him and praise his name. For the LORD is good. His unfailing love continues forever, and his faithfulness continues to each generation. (NLT)

Exuberant praise should come first. Don't even think about holding back! Praise ushers us into His courts and His presence and He is worthy of it all. He is worthy to be praised with every fibre of our being, with prayer, words, and shouts—with instruments, flags, songs, and even dance. Yes! I said dance! Don't hold back.

We praise God for His pleasure and His pleasure alone. It doesn't matter who else likes it or dislikes it.

I will never forget the first time I broke out in exuberant dance while praising the Lord. As I simply just let go of my self-imposed, self-conscious boundaries and limitations, the freedom and joy I felt was extraordinary. It was a Tuesday night meeting at a friend's home. As the live musicians strummed and beat their instruments and the vocalist sang in the Spirit, we moved seamlessly from praise to worship and back to praise as the Spirit led. It was beautiful. There was freedom as everyone did what the Spirit put on their heart to do. Some stood with hands raised, some knelt, some sat quiet with eyes closed and some lay prostrate on the floor. A holy hush had come over us as the music stopped and the presence of God filled the room. Moments of complete silence passed as we simply adored Him.

Suddenly, as the musicians followed the Spirit, an exuberant sound erupted and beckoned me to dance. Before I even knew what I was doing, I began to dance—to war dance. The Spirit propelled me, and I was completely submitted. My brain wanted to stop. My brain was concerned about who was watching me, but I persisted anyway. It was amazing. I know that personally, I overcame the need to impress others and the concern of what others thought of me but I'm sure it accomplished so much more than that in the Spirit as it was an intercessors' dance and a prophetic demonstration all its own.

I am reminded of another person who broke out in dance before the Lord. His name was King David. Second Samuel 6:12-15 tells the story:

> . . .So David went and brought up the ark of God from the house of Obed-edom to the City of David with gladness. And so it was, when those bearing the ark of the Lord had gone six paces, that he sacrificed oxen and fatted sheep. Then David danced before the Lord WITH ALL HIS MIGHT; and David was wearing a linen ephod. So David and all the house of Israel brought up the ark of the Lord with shouting and with the sound of the trumpet. (NKJV, emphasis added)

King David danced with all his might; he held nothing back and he didn't care what others thought. Was he criticized for it? Yes, he was. His wife, Michal, daughter of Saul, saw him and verse sixteen says that she "despised him in her heart." King David responds to her criticism and says in verse 21 and 22:

> It was before the LORD, who chose me rather than your father or anyone from his house when he appointed me ruler over the LORD's people Israel—I will celebrate before the LORD. I will become even more undignified than this, and I will be humiliated in my own eyes. But by these slave girls you spoke of, I will be held in honor. (2 Samuel 6:21-22 NIV)

King David had no problem humiliating himself for the sake of worshipping God and pleasing Him. Impressing others was of no importance but impressing God was. He danced for an audience of One!

Praise recognizes God for *Who* He is. Praise celebrates Him and all His amazing characteristics: His goodness and holiness, His amazing power, authority, greatness, and beauty. Praise is exuberant, loud, and expressive. It stirs up joy from our inner most being, leads us into His presence and elevates us into a spirit of worship.

Praise shifts to worship as we are overtaken by His love. Praise gets us in the door, but the presence of God brings us to our knees. When the beautiful spirit of worship overtakes us, suddenly everyone else in the room disappears and it becomes just us and God together as one. We go from a party in praise with many others to complete seclusion, privacy, and intimacy with the One we love, where we simply behold and adore Him.[42] As we worship, we are overtaken by His love and end up receiving much more than what we've given.

> *If you've not forgotten where you are while in worship, you've not yet come high enough.*

Worship itself *begins* with a reverent heart toward God but many Christians choose to stay there. Sadly, they choose not to press through into adoration. But we can go higher! We can go higher if we will allow ourselves to fall deeply in love with Him, adore Him and become ravished by His love.

Worship is about turning our hearts completely toward God, putting everything else out of our mind and focusing solely on Him. As we do, we offer Him ALL our heart and ALL our adoration. We let go of every *lesser lover* we have entertained in the past. The more we are willing to focus our attention on God and *demonstrate* our love to Him, the higher we can rise. *If you've not forgotten where you are while in worship, you've not yet come high enough.*

Luke 7:36-50 tells us of a sinful woman who knew how to *demonstrate* her worship. A Pharisee by the name of Simon invited

---

[42] Ruth Ward Heflin, *Glory: Experiencing the Atmosphere of Heaven* (Maryland: McDougal Publishing, 1990, 2000) 88-89. Print.

Jesus to his home for a meal and an uninvited woman with a colorful, sinful lifestyle boldly inserted herself there. We see two very different levels of love and worship being expressed to Jesus between the Pharisee and the woman. Let's have a look at the woman's actions:

> Now one of the Pharisees was requesting Him to dine with him, and He entered the Pharisee's house and reclined at the table. And there was a woman in the city who was a sinner; and when she learned that He was reclining at the table in the Pharisee's house, she brought an alabaster vial of perfume, and standing behind Him at His feet, weeping, she began to wet His feet with her tears, and kept wiping them with the hair of her head, and kissing His feet and anointing them with the perfume. Now when the Pharisee who had invited Him saw this, he said to himself, "If this man were a prophet He would know who and what sort of person this woman is who is touching Him, that she is a sinner (Luke 7:36-39 NASB).

This precious woman washed Jesus' feet with her tears, dried them with her hair, kissed his feet and anointed them with costly perfume. The Pharisee, on the other hand, didn't offer Jesus any such admiration—not even the basic foot washing when He arrived. The woman's demonstration of worship indicates the depth of her love for Jesus and the tenacity of her faith. Jesus says in verse 47, "... whoever has been forgiven little loves little" (Luke 7:47 NIV).

We all have a decision to make. How will we worship? Will we worship like the sinful woman, humbling ourselves, offering the Lord all our heart and affection, or will we hold back and worship like the Pharisee? Will we allow the Holy Spirit to give us revelation on how much we have truly been forgiven as well as the holiness of Christ and worship Him accordingly or will we stay in our limited carnal understanding, pride, and deception thinking we're not all that bad, staying in complacency? I pray you are willing to challenge yourself and push your flesh outside of your comfort zone, into a whole new level of praise and worship.

When the unction comes upon you from the Holy Spirit to raise your hands, to kneel, to dance, to lay prostrate on the floor, *don't hold back* my friend! This grieves the Holy Spirit. Break through your fear. Break through whatever is holding you back and GO FOR IT! I promise you—you will be so blessed by it.

Chuck D. Pierce wrote a book called, *God's Now Time for Your Life*. In it, he gives his and his wife's testimony over barrenness. The final step to their healing was for Pam, Pierce's wife, to worship the Lord in a brand-new way. Pierce lists twelve steps they had to take as a couple to see the fulfillment of their promise including attending a conference that they would not have normally attended and then he writes:

> "As a result of following these steps of obedience, culminating at the conference when Pam, against her nature, raised her hands in worship to God, Pam was healed instantly by the power of God invading her body and actually knocking out the clots that were in her uterus."[43]

Wow! Healing manifested in her body the minute she was obedient to the Spirit's lead to raise her hands in worship. What have we missed out on by not raising our hands in worship!? What have we missed out on by not being obedient? By not surrendering? God only knows. I pray the Holy Spirit is opening your eyes to how important this is for your healing and I pray, the next time the Holy Spirit prompts you to express worship in a tangible way, you will do it, without hesitation.

The Lord is worthy of everything we can give. He is worthy of our words, shouts, adoration, and every expression of the physical body. If we want healing in our physical body, we better be willing

---

[43] Chuck D. Pierce and Rebecca Wagner Systema, God's Now Time for Your Life: Enter Your Prophetic Destiny (Ventura: Regal Books from Gospel Light, 2005), 13. Print.

to worship with our physical body on the outside and not just in our heart.

Here's the thing—if we are completely honest, we would admit that we don't raise our hands or dance or whatever because we don't want to look stupid to others. Come on! Let's just get real. It is an invisible social boundary that we have been trained to adhere to. Don't be weird. Fit in. Do what everyone else is doing and nothing more. Right? The spirit of the world causes us to be ashamed of our passion for the Lord. The spirit of the world convinces us that we shouldn't be *religious fanatics*. Well, that belief is killing us, my friend.

The belief that we are crazy or fanatical or whatever when we raise our hands in worship is of the devil and it keeps people in bondage to the world, including sickness and disease. Don't be of the world! We are called to be *in* the world but not *of* it. God has called us out and right now, I speak courage to you in Jesus' name to be a *called out one*, to be separated, and to be a possession of the Lord who is different, holy, righteous, and *on fire* for God. May our hearts burn for Him! May we be more concerned about God's approval than man's.

Are you with me?

Chapter 8

THE LORD'S SUPPER

I n John 6, Jesus speaks a Word in the synagogue at Capernaum which challenges the crowd beginning with this: "I am the bread of life. Whoever comes to me will never be hungry again. Whoever believes in me will never be thirsty" (John 6:35 NLT). Jesus continues in verse 47:

> I tell you the truth, anyone who believes has eternal life. Yes, I am the bread of life! Your ancestors ate manna in the wilderness, but they all died. Anyone who eats the bread from heaven, however, will never die. I am the living bread that came down from heaven. Anyone who eats this bread will live forever; and this bread, which I will offer so the world may live, is my flesh. (John 6:47-51 NLT)

This Word causes arguments among the people and offends the minds of many, "How can this man give us his flesh to eat" (John 6:52 NLT)? They had no clue what He was talking about as they didn't know Jesus was about to willingly give up His life for them and allow the brutal beating and crucifixion of His own body for them and us.

Jesus continues to speak even more blatantly:

> I tell you the truth, unless you eat the flesh of the Son of Man and drink his blood, you cannot have eternal life within you. But anyone who eats my flesh and drinks my blood has eternal life, and I will raise that person at the last day. For my flesh is true food, and my blood is true drink. Anyone who eats my flesh and drinks my blood remains in me, and I in him. I live because of the living Father who sent me; in the same way, anyone who feeds on me will live because of me. I am the true bread that came down from heaven. Anyone who eats this bread will not die as your ancestors did (even though they ate the manna) but will live forever. (John 6:53-58 NLT)

Many of Jesus' disciples left Him because of this Word. They could not understand it. However, *we* can understand it being on this side of the cross. Jesus demonstrates what He means at the Passover meal which He shares with His disciples right before His arrest:

> I have been very eager to eat this Passover meal with you before my suffering begins. For I tell you now that I won't eat this meal again until its meaning is fulfilled in the Kingdom of God." [19]He took some bread and gave thanks to God for it. Then he broke it in pieces and gave it to the disciples, saying, "This is my body, which is given for you. Do this in remembrance of me." After supper he took another cup of wine and said, "This cup is the new covenant between God and his people—an agreement confirmed with my blood, which is poured out as a sacrifice for you. (Luke 22:15-16, 19-20 NLT)

Jesus demonstrates for us how to partake of His blood and broken body *by faith*, by using symbols of bread and wine. The church has implemented this as a corporate act once a month or once a quarter, depending on the church, but there is no reason why we can't do this at home by ourselves as the Spirit leads—especially if we're ill. It does not have to be given by a pastor, priest, or minister.

We can simply take a little cup of wine or grape juice and a piece of bread or cracker, pray over them, and exercise our faith to partake and receive the renewing power of Jesus' life.

How we take the Lord's supper is also important. First Corinthians 11:27-30 tells us to examine ourselves *before* we partake so we don't partake in an unworthy manner as follows:

> So anyone who eats this bread or drinks this cup of the Lord unworthily is guilty of sinning against the body and blood of the Lord. That is why you should examine yourself before eating the bread and drinking the cup. For if you eat the bread or drink the cup without honoring the body of Christ, you are eating and drinking God's judgment upon yourself. That is why many of you are weak and sick and some have even died. (1 Corinthians 11:27-30 NLT)

I remember being at a women's renewal weekend and we were about to take communion on Sunday morning. It had been a great weekend with the Spirit moving powerfully in my heart. As I held the bread between my fingers, the Spirit reminded me of a painful event in my teen years. I had forgiven the other person involved but I knew it wasn't all his fault. I knew I had a part to play in it too. As I contemplated everything, still seeing the regret in my heart, I heard the Lord say *clear as day*, "Don't you dare put that bread in your mouth until you forgive yourself."

A little stunned, I sat there, motionless for a second or two. Frozen in the fear of the Lord, physically unable to put the bread in my mouth. And here was yet another moment when I knew that I knew God was *very* real, alive, and active in my life. I was not going to get away with anything.

Tears quietly leaked from my eyes as I said, "Yes, Lord." With eyes closed, I brought my heart into alignment with His will and once again, just like He had done many times before, He gave me a wonderful picture confirming my surrender and His acceptance. As a young girl dressed in white, I saw myself in the throne room, before my Father, twirling and dancing before Him. He had such a look of delight on His face! And there was so much freedom in my childlike display. As this wonderful scene played out in my mind, I quietly slipped the bread into my mouth and peace overcame my heart and mind.

Before taking communion, be sure to ask the Lord to search your heart and show you anything there that would cause you to partake in an unworthy manner. Perhaps repent for taking the Lord's supper in an unworthy manner before if this discussion has convicted your heart.

My suggestion for you would be to work through the remainder of this book, then begin to take communion as the Spirit leads.

Take your bread or cracker and pray:

"Lord, before I partake of these elements, search my heart O God, and renew a right spirit within me. Is there anything I need to repent for or anyone I need to forgive? [Allow the Holy Spirit to search your heart and then repent for anything the Lord shows you and forgive those who you haven't forgiven. Then continue...] On the night He was betrayed, Jesus took bread, gave thanks to God, and gave it to His disciples saying, 'This is my body which is given for you. Do this in remembrance of me.' Thank You, God, for this bread/cracker which represents the broken body of Your Son, Jesus. Thank You that His body was broken for my healing and as I eat His body, eternal life is made manifest in mine. As I partake, I remember and honor His sacrifice. I live because He lives [break the cracker and partake]."

Take your juice and pray:

"Also on the night He was betrayed, Jesus took a cup and said, 'This cup is the new covenant between God and his people—an agreement confirmed with my blood, which is poured out as a sacrifice for you." Thank You, God, for this wine/juice which represents Your blood poured out for me for the forgiveness of my sins, sealing our covenantal promise together. As I partake, putting my faith behind my action, may Your blood wash me clean. [Partake of the juice/wine.] Thank You, Lord. I bless You and worship You with all that I am. Amen."

· · · · · · · ● · · · · · · · · · · ·

This concludes the first part of *Position Yourself for Healing*. We have laid a foundation for divine healing as well as an expectation for it. We have also talked in generalities about attitudes of the heart and various other things that could block us from receiving our healing so now we're going to get more specific. And we're going to dive into some prayer examples to get you praying in faith, authority and boldness as the Spirit leads and wants you to.

Notes

_____

_____

_____

_____

_____

_____

_____

_____

_____

_____

_____

PART II

ELIMINATING
BLOCKAGES
TO HEALING

Notes

BLOCKAGES

Ever had a blocked drain in your kitchen? Ever had a blockage so bad a professional had to come in with a drain snake? We have. For some reason, our last house seemed to be particularly bad for this. The plumber had to snake the pipes all the way down under ground and we had to become extra vigilant at not allowing food particles to go down the drain. It became quite a nuisance.

Ever had a plugged toilet? If you've had young children growing up in your home, you've probably become an expert with the plunger. Perhaps you've had unexpected things block your toilet. I think the worst blockage we had was after our 4-year-old tried to flush a bottle of Calamine lotion. My husband had to completely remove the toilet to get it out. Toddlers love to put all kinds of random things in the toilet, don't they? Hopefully, you've not had to part with anything valuable due to a toddler's obsession with the flush.

Why do I bring up pipes, toilets, and blockages of all kinds? Because it's possible for our healing and our blessings from the Lord, financial and otherwise, to be held back or blocked from reaching us, because of issues in our soul which have not been dealt with.

In the Old Testament, we see an example of a gate or portal to heaven in Genesis 28:10-17. Jacob had a dream and saw a ladder stretching into heaven, upon which angels ascended and descended. In verse 17, Jacob says, "How awesome is this place! This is none other than the house of God, and this is the gate of heaven" (Genesis 28:17 NKJV)! How awesome for Jacob to have discovered that place and connected with God's presence there; it was rare for those in the Old Testament to experience such a thing. Conversely, under the New Covenant, we are honored and privileged to be blessed with all the benefits of being reconciled to God. One of those benefits is to have the very presence of God living within us and another is being welcomed right into the throne room, should we wish to go.[44]

Those who know Jesus are invited to come into the Lord's presence whenever they wish but in Revelation 4, John of Patmos is given an explicit invitation to receive a message he was to pass on to us. "Come up here," said the Lord. A divine portal or door suddenly became manifest to John's spiritual eyes in a vision. "Then as I looked, I saw a door standing open in heaven..." (Revelation 4:1 NLT).

As Christ's own beloved, the Spirit of God lives within us, and WE have now become God's dwelling place. Although there may be places in the world, like Israel, where the Lord's presence is easier to discern, technically we don't need to travel to any geographical region to find the presence of God. He is as close to us as we are to ourselves. We as believers are temples of the Holy Spirit.[45] The Spirit of Jesus dwells within us and we have become the point of connection where the natural realm meets the spiritual, where angels ascend and descend.

Inside all of us is a gateway, passageway, or portal to heaven. Jesus said, "I am the way..." (John 14:6). Jesus also said, "I am the door..." (John 10:9 NKJV). The Spirit of Jesus in us, provides a point of access for us to reach God and the heavenly realm, and for God to reach us. This door, where the natural and supernatural meet—where divine power passes from one reality to another, is the meeting place, the touching point, where the Holy Spirit meets our spirit. It's a place of supernatural exchange where healing and transformation happens.

---

[44] "So let us come boldly to the throne of our gracious God. There we will receive his mercy, and we will find grace to help us when we need it most" (Hebrews 4:16 NLT).

[45] "Don't you realize that your body is the temple of the Holy Spirit, who lives in you and was given to you by God? You do not belong to yourself, for God bought you with a high price. So you must honor God with your body" (1 Corinthians 6:19-20 NLT).

What if we don't properly honor the Holy Spirit in us, or submit to the Holy Spirit? What if we don't honor our body which has been created by God and now is the temple or abiding place of God? What if we try to take advantage of grace and continue to partner with sin after being saved? What if we don't exercise our freedom over sin by saying "no" to it? What if we live in falsehood by not recognizing or admitting the negative attitudes in our heart? What if we don't repent? Each of these situations causes the doorway between the Spirit and our soul to be blocked and if access to our humanity, by the Spirit, is blocked, we will have great trouble connecting to God, hearing His voice, and experiencing transformation by His power. As a result, the healing we desire which is supernaturally present in His love and power, can't reach us.

The scriptures confirm that we are *both* sanctified[46] *and* in the process of being sanctified[47] as the natural has not yet been perfected. And just like food particles and grease stick to the inside of a pipe and prevent water from flowing through it, the junk in our soul prevents supernatural healing power from flowing to us. If there are things in our soul that prevent us from being able to receive from the Lord, we would want to clear those blockages, wouldn't we? I know I would. I want to experience every benefit of the cross I can, here, now, on this side of eternity.[48] Why live any less triumphantly than what we were intended to?

Many things can block us from receiving, but they all have one thing in common: they all interfere with our ability to receive the love of

---

[46] 2 Corinthians 5:17, Romans 8:30

[47] Philippians 2:12, 2 Corinthians 3:18

[48] "Bless the LORD, O my soul; And all that is within me, *bless* His holy name! Bless the LORD, O my soul, And forget not all His benefits: Who forgives all your iniquities, Who heals all your diseases, Who redeems your life from destruction, Who crowns you with lovingkindness and tender mercies, Who satisfies your mouth with good things, So that your youth is renewed like the eagle's" (Psalm 103:1-5 NKJV).

God for us, to love God in return, to love others, and love ourselves, as we are called to.

How are we called to love? Jesus tells us in Matthew 22:37-39, "Love the Lord your God with *all* your heart and with *all* your soul and with *all* your mind.' This is the first and greatest commandment. And the second is like it: 'Love your neighbor as yourself'" (NIV, emphasis added).

Loving God with *all* our heart looks like guarding our heart and not allowing anything contrary to love, according to 1 Corinthians 13:4-7, to live there, hide there, or even visit there. Loving God with all our soul, is the same principle. We love God with *all* our soul when we do not tolerate, hold, or allow to remain, *anything* that is contrary to love—not an ounce of hurt, offense or ill-will toward *anyone*, including those who have hurt, offended, cheated, and/or not liked us. And it goes even further than that! *Love* not only doesn't curse but has a *desire to bless*. Love goes out of its way to do good to its enemies.[49]

Lastly, loving God with *all* our mind looks like not entertaining any thought or thinking pattern contrary to love and righteousness and not *feeding* our mind anything of the same. It means keeping our mind fixed on the things of God, including whatever things are true, good, pure, just, noble, lovely, and praiseworthy.[50]

It sounds and feels like a lot, doesn't it? If you're beginning to think it's an impossible task, you're right. We are not capable of loving like God loves, all by ourselves. So how do we do it? Well, the Bible says that we love Him because He first loved us (1 John 4:19), so

---

[49] "'You have heard that it was said, 'You shall love your neighbor and hate your enemy.' But I say to you, love your enemies, bless those who curse you, do good to those who hate you, and pray for those who spitefully use you and persecute you, that you may be sons of your Father in heaven" (Matthew 5:43-45a NKJV).

[50] "Finally, brethren, whatever things are true, whatever things are noble, whatever things are just, whatever things are pure, whatever things are lovely, whatever things are of good report, if there is any virtue and if there is anything praiseworthy—meditate on these things" (Philippians 4:8 NKJV).

our ability to love anyone begins with a deep revelation of how much God really loves us *and* receiving it for ourselves.

Receiving God's love for real, deep into our heart *so it changes us*, is facilitated by the revelation that God does not love like the world loves. God does not love like all the others. He does not love like your earthly parents or your siblings or your spouse or your friends; these are all broken versions of love. God loves unconditionally. His love is perfect and set apart from the others. His love is supernatural, supercharged, spiritual, and sacrificial. There are no requirements, no pre-requisites, no hoops to jump through, and no performances necessary. There is nothing you need to do to earn it. There is nothing you can do to increase it and nothing you can do to diminish it. God's love is simply given because He made you and you are His. Ephesians 3:17b-19 says:

> And I pray that you, being rooted and established in love, may have power, together with all the Lord's holy people, to grasp how wide and long and high and deep is the love of Christ, and to know this love that surpasses knowledge— that you may be filled to the measure of all the fullness of God. (NIV)

Wow. Read that again and chew on it for a bit. First, you need to be rooted and grounded, established in the love of God. Then, you will have the *power* to grasp the great dimensions of His love and notice that it takes *power* to grasp this. Whose power? God's. The Holy Spirit's power. Why? Because His love surpasses all human knowledge. Wow. Our intellect cannot handle it. Our brains cannot be wrapped around it. We need the Holy Spirit to give us the understanding and revelation of it. And He will—when you ask for it. Aaaand I hope you're asking for it right now!

The revelation of God's complete, unconditional love for us comes by His Spirit as we let go of all our preconceived ideas of love, renounce the lies we've believed, and open ourselves to the truth. Once this revelation becomes our foundation, once we truly believe that we are *unconditionally* loved by God, loving God, loving ourselves and loving others becomes possible and almost inevitable in our present reality. Praise God! To Him be all the glory.

So, are you beginning to see the blockages? I think if we were honest, we would have to admit that we have *a lot* of work to do. Or perhaps that's just me. You would need to ask the Holy Spirit for yourself. We may have a lot of healing that needs to happen on the inside before it can manifest on the outside.

Indeed, there can be many things blocking our healing, but there is still hope. It is possible for the greatness of God's mercy to bust right through and manifest at any time, as God chooses and enables. Nevertheless, the issues the Holy Spirit *makes us aware of*, are our responsibility to deal with through repentance and renunciation. Never should we just ignore the conviction of the Holy Spirit expecting God to just overlook what He puts His finger on. The Holy Spirit convicts us to help us come into the fullness of resurrection life. We can expect God's mercy to bust through those things we *aren't aware of*, as long as our heart is soft and open to His leading.

There are too many issues to address in one book, but you will get a feel for how to pray through as we cover the following topics:

- the religious spirit or mindset
- anger and unforgiveness
- wrong judgements
- idolatry
- leaning on our own understanding
- iniquity
- words and power
- negative body perspectives
- injustice
- shame and self-hate/rejection
- the orphan spirit or mindset

- soul ties
- repressed emotions
- false burdens and false responsibilities
- false religions and secret societies

Every prayer to gain freedom will follow a rough pattern with multiple steps. One does not always need deliverance from a demon but when you do, the steps are as follows:

1. Confess and repent, forgive yourself.
2. Forgive others.
3. Renounce.
4. Ask for mercy for what you've missed.
5. Bind demons.
6. Cast demons out.
7. Declare every curse broken.
8. Ask Father to send the Holy Spirit to completely fill you.

Confess and Repent

Effective prayer to be free from sin, heart attitudes that don't glorify God, and the influence of demons always begins with confession. How have you partnered, knowingly or unknowingly, with the demon you are attempting to break agreement with and cast out? What bad fruit has come up in your life that is connected to that demon? These are the things you will need to confess. For example, if you have been bound by a spirit of fear, you have likely participated in worry. You may have also participated with a spirit of procrastination and indecisiveness which may have caused grief for your family members.

When we are living in fear, we cannot and do not love well. Fear can also nullify faith and trust in God. In summary, confession will need to include worry, lack of faith, lack of trust in God, procrastination, indecision, lack of love, causing others grief and perhaps not fulfilling your God-given role in your family. You will need to seek the leading of the Holy Spirit, to know exactly what you need to confess and repent for. Let the Spirit convict you. Confession also includes confessing the truth of your emotions— telling God about all your feelings surrounding the sin you have committed, or others have committed against you.

Repentance is simply a decision to turn around and go in the opposite direction, back to God, and to willfully change your mind about a thought, thinking pattern, belief, or behavior. Repentance is making a decision that says, "This is no longer acceptable, and I choose to no longer allow myself to think this way or act this way." Remember in faith, 1 John 1:9, "If we confess our sins, He is faithful and just to forgive us our sins and to cleanse us from all unrighteousness" (NKJV).

To wrap up this step it is always good to voice acceptance of God's forgiveness and thank Him for it. If you find you *feel* like you need to confess a sin repeatedly, you probably have not forgiven yourself, in which case, you have not allowed yourself to fully receive God's forgiveness. Simply say, "I choose to forgive myself and I fully receive Your forgiveness, Lord. Thank You that You have cleansed me from all unrighteousness. I declare that I am forgiven, in Jesus' name."

Renounce and Break Fellowship
To renounce something is to completely reject something and make a formal declaration to give up on, abandon, cut off, and refuse to co-operate with something. For our purposes, we are renouncing the sinful habits or attitudes and possibly demons we have previously agreed or partnered with.

Ask for Mercy
It is only for mercy that we don't get what we really deserve. Considering the truth that we are partakers of a superior covenant with God, based on the mercy and grace of God, pray that God's mercy would touch and cover anything you've missed or aren't aware of.

Bind

To bind is to restrict by binding or wrapping it up, with chains for instance. Matthew 16:19 says that whatever we bind on earth will be bound in heaven. We, therefore, can declare in the earthly realm that harmful spirits are bound, and they will be bound in the spirit realm, restricting them from operating and using their power against us. This will make it easier for us to be free from them and will restrict manifestations. Simply say, "In the authority of Jesus, I bind the spirit of (name the spirit) and all other demons connected to it. I declare their power is broken now by the blood of Jesus, and I forbid any demon to cause me harm or distress, in Jesus' name." And remember to mean what you say! In other words, make sure your heart agrees with your words.

Cast Out

To cast a spirit out, simply say, "I command the spirit of (name it) to come out of me now, in Jesus' name." Speak this command out as many times as you are led by the Spirit. There may not always be a feeling or manifestation associated with a demon leaving but believe in faith that you are being set free and *activate* your faith by breathing deep and blowing out of your mouth. On the other hand, you may find yourself spontaneously doing things like yawning, coughing, burping, crying or even bearing down signifying the exit of that spirit. Simply co-operate with it and allow it to happen.

Every Curse Broken

Everything we co-operate with, which is not of God, gives curses an opportunity to rest on us and operate in our lives. Proverbs 26:2 says, "Like a flitting sparrow, like a flying swallow, So a curse without cause shall not alight" (NKJV). The opposite is also true. A curse *with* a cause WILL alight.

Deuteronomy 28:1-14 outlines all the blessings that will come upon us for our obedience and Deuteronomy 28:16-68 outlines all the curses that will come upon us because of our disobedience and includes multiple physical ailments such as plague, fever, and inflammation. Curses have not been done away with. They are still real just as blessings are real. Deuteronomy 30:19 says:

> I call heaven and earth as witnesses today against you, that I have set before you life and death, blessing and curse; therefore choose life, that both you and your descendants may live; that you may love the Lord your God, that you may obey His voice, and that you may cling to Him, for He is your life and the length of your days; (NKJV).

As you can see from this verse, for our descendants to live, we must choose life and blessings by loving the Lord, obeying His voice, and clinging to Him, but we know that we are not able to do that on our own. We "all have sinned and fall short of the glory of God" (Romans 3:23 NKJV). So how do we do that this side of the cross, under the New Covenant with Christ as our Redeemer? We choose life and blessings through confession and repentance and warfare prayer that boldly confesses our redemption and the breaking of every curse that has come upon us. We can make this confession because according to Galatians 3:13-14, Jesus Christ has redeemed us from the curse of the law, having become a curse for us by dying on the cross.[51] We do this because we have free-will and we must exercise it, and take dominion over our lives appropriating everything Christ accomplished for us. If we don't confess and repent for sin and iniquity, we end up choosing death and curses by default, without even realizing it.

Beloved, curses are evil, and evil is stubborn. Let's not be passive in our praying. We must be bold, strong, and courageous to dis-empower every evil agenda trying to stand against us.

---

[51] "Christ has redeemed us from the curse of the law, having become a curse for us (for it is written, "Cursed is everyone who hangs on a tree"), that the blessing of Abraham might come upon the Gentiles in Christ Jesus, that we might receive the promise of the Spirit through faith" (Galatians 3:13-14 NKJV).

Let's make sure to use our sword—the Word of the Lord. Declare the truth of who you are and Whose you are. Declare Who God is on your behalf. If something is not working, worship the Lord and pray in tongues, then ask God how to proceed.

Lastly, ask Father to send the Holy Spirit to completely fill you. Believe in faith, that Father is giving you what you ask for.[52] He will not give you a snake or a scorpion when you ask for the Spirit. He is a good, good Father Who always gives good gifts.[53]

Let's begin!

---

[52] "So, I say to you, ask, and it will be given to you; seek, and you will find; knock, and it will be opened to you. For everyone who asks receives, and he who seeks finds, and to him who knocks it will be opened. If a son asks for bread from any father among you, will he give him a stone? Or if *he asks* for a fish, will he give him a serpent instead of a fish? Or if he asks for an egg, will he offer him a scorpion? If you then, being evil, know how to give good gifts to your children, how much more will *your* heavenly Father give the Holy Spirit to those who ask Him!" (Luke 11:9-13 NKJV)

[53] Every good gift and every perfect gift is from above, and comes down from the Father of lights, with whom there is no variation or shadow of turning. (James 1:17 NKJV)

THE RELIGIOUS SPIRIT OR MINDSET

I believe the number one block to believers receiving from the Lord, whether it be healing or anything else, is the Pharisee or religious demon and mindset. This demon or mindset makes Christians believe they are saved because they are *doing* all the right Christian things, and it blocks them from having a real relationship with God. It can keep people stuck in the natural realm going through the motions of church but unable or unwilling to be in the Spirit, connected to and communicating with the Holy Spirit.

A religious demon, in partnership with a few others, can keep people attached to the world, immersed in worldly knowledge, worldly understanding, worldly wisdom, and worldly logic structures. Second Timothy 3:5 describes a person affected by this demon or mindset, "They will *act* religious, but they will reject the power that could make them godly" (NLT, emphasis added). Those influenced by a religious demon many times are *actors* pretending to be something they're not. They are preoccupied with outward appearances and avoid inward transformation and sanctification like the plague.

The religious demon is the spirit that was on the Pharisees in the Bible. It kept them blind to many things, including the love and compassion of God, Who Jesus was, the new way God wanted to relate to them through mercy, grace, and compassion, without the sacrifice of animals,[54] and even their own sinfulness. It kept them locked into the old ways and unaccepting of God's new covenant.

Luke 12:1 says, "Beware of the leaven of the Pharisees, which is hypocrisy" (NKJV). Hypocrisy according to Wikipedia is "the

---

[54] To the Pharisees Jesus said, "But go and learn what *this* means: 'I desire mercy and not sacrifice.' For I did not come to call the righteous, but sinners, to repentance" (Matthew 9:13 NKJV).

THE RELIGIOUS SPIRIT OR MINDSET

practice of engaging in the same behavior or activity for which one criticizes another or the practice of claiming to have moral standards or beliefs to which one's own behavior does not conform."[55] Here's a parable Jesus told that illustrates it well:

> Then Jesus told this story to some who had great confidence in their own righteousness and scorned everyone else: "Two men went to the Temple to pray. One was a Pharisee, and the other was a despised tax collector. The Pharisee stood by himself and prayed this prayer: 'I thank You, God, that I am not like other people—cheaters, sinners, adulterers. I'm certainly not like that tax collector! I fast twice a week, and I give you a tenth of my income.' But the tax collector stood at a distance and dared not even lift his eyes to heaven as he prayed. Instead, he beat his chest in sorrow, saying, 'O God, be merciful to me, for I am a sinner.' I tell you, this sinner, not the Pharisee, returned home justified before God. For those who exalt themselves will be humbled, and those who humble themselves will be exalted. (Luke 18:9-14 NLT)

Self-righteousness, pride, haughtiness, fault-finding, and a tendency to be critical, contentious, and argumentative are a few of the key characteristics of this spirit. The religious spirit or mindset puts heavy burdens on people, holds others to a standard that is impossible and does not allow mercy or grace to cut anyone any slack. This spirit does not discriminate against who it influences or connects to, and I believe is very prevalent in many North American churches.

The religious spirit is seen at work in the Bible every time the Pharisees tried to trap Jesus into an argument and *accuse* him of going against the law/rules of the temple. Each time Jesus healed someone on the Sabbath, and the Pharisees were upset about Jesus breaking a rule, the religious spirit was at work. They should

---

[55] https://en.wikipedia.org/wiki/Hypocrisy

have been rejoicing with the one who was set free, not bemoaning the timing of it.

Many of you, reading these words, are not *full-blown* Pharisees. If a Pharisee had picked this book up at all, they likely would have already become offended and thrown it in the trash. No, the ones that have read this far are not completely controlled by a Pharisee spirit, but perhaps may still be influenced, *to some degree*, by a "little Pharisee" inside. If you have grown up in the church at all, you may need to repent and renounce this mindset. I, myself, have had to kick this demon out, so if you need to do it too, you're not alone.

I remember my daughter as a little girl coming home and telling me about what she had been taught in Sunday School that day. To no fault of her own, she informed me that one could tell if someone else was a Christian by how they acted. In other words, she was being taught to. . . first, segregate people into Christians and non-Christians; second, to draw negative *conclusions* about people; third, to base her opinions and conclusions on outward things; and fourth, to look down on those who weren't like her. This was a religious spirit at work. I quickly corrected what she had learned and made sure she understood that being a Christian was about loving Jesus and there was no way any of us could know the state of anyone's heart (unless God showed us). Additionally, in no way are we to look down on or condemn anyone for perhaps not acting perfectly or exactly how we think they should. Lastly, Jesus loves each and every person despite their actions or mistakes and does not hold their sin against them, so neither should we.

Of course, by the Holy Spirit, we are to discern spirits, discern what is happening, whether it's from God or not, and judge the words we hear and receive. When I listen to a sermon, I pay attention to the Holy Spirit and His witness in me. Does what I'm hearing line up with the Word of God? Is the Holy Spirit telling me He's the author of what I'm hearing? Sometimes I hear a word and I pray on it. I ask God to give me confirmation.

It is also wisdom to discern who to spend time with and who's opinion or advise to listen to. Sometimes the Holy Spirit will give you a sense that something is off about someone, but it's not so you can slap a label on them or have a bad opinion about them. Sometimes it's to warn you, to be careful about how much access you give them in your life, and sometimes it's to get you to pray. I find that when it's the Holy Spirit revealing something to me, He stirs compassion in my heart for them at the same time.

One sure sign of the religious spirit is the rejection of any and almost all manifestations of the Holy Spirit. I used to think that if I was uncomfortable in an environment where there were manifestations, it wasn't of God. I have since learned that this is false. A sense of being uncomfortable around manifestations is usually caused by a demon of religion and we need accurate discernment to know the difference. Unfortunately, though, a demon of religion can cloud our discernment.

We visited Catch the Fire in Toronto in the early 90's when revival broke out and many supernatural manifestations were happening around us. I was uncomfortable because it was new for me. I wasn't used to what was happening. I'd never seen such manifestations before—but I did not become offended, and I did not draw negative conclusions. I did not presume to know whether what was happening was of God or not. I was not so arrogant and self-righteous to think I had all the answers. I simply admitted that I didn't know and remained open to the possibility that it was indeed from God. I understood that I was (and still am) a work in progress and God was still teaching me and revealing Himself to me. Now, more than twenty-five years later, such manifestations don't surprise me at all.

Supernatural things happen when a supernatural God manifests His power. Sometimes God is communicating to us through the manifestation and sometimes it is simply our temporal flesh reacting to the presence and power of God. For example, the presence of God can be "weighty" or feel heavy on someone which can cause their flesh to not be able to stand up straight or to have to get on the floor.

Pastor John Arnott from Catch the Fire spoke at a conference, and he gave an example of someone who crowed like a rooster under the anointing of the Holy Spirit. Their first impression was, *That's odd. What could that be?* At first thought, they didn't think it was God, but then they realized God was trying to tell them something. God was saying, in His not-so-obvious way, "Wake up! It's the dawn of a new day."

God does not speak in clear, obvious ways. He usually speaks in ways that require us, the listener, to pay close attention and to seek Him for an interpretation. He speaks in mysteries so only those who are diligently seeking Him will hear. Proverbs 25:2 says, "It is God's privilege to conceal things and the king's privilege to discover them" (NLT). Matthew 13:10-12 says:

> His disciples came and asked him, "Why do you use parables when you talk to the people? He replied, "You are permitted to understand the secrets of the Kingdom of Heaven, but others are not. To those who listen to my teaching, more understanding will be given, and they will have an abundance of knowledge. But for those who are not listening, even what little understanding they have will be taken away from them. (NLT)

There are times, however, when a person in a crowd of worshippers is not pure of heart and they will manifest what is not God, but the entire corporate move can still be holy despite this. If the corporate body is biblical and the leaders are not in gross unrepentant sin, a supernatural manifestation that seems to affect the whole body is going to be of God, regardless of our acceptance of it or comfort through it.

There was a time, over twenty years ago, when I believe a religious demon caused me to manifest. It happened at a time when I felt very insecure and fearful of others judging me. I was part of a small group of women who met every week. The leader of the group had a spiritual burden on her heart for Israel and wanted all of us to join a group of intercessors, interceding and repenting for antisemitism. Unfortunately, I was not in a place where I sensed that burden at all. Not having that burden made me feel guilty. I wondered if there was something wrong with me and didn't know how I would participate in intercession without the Spirit moving me around that issue. I was concerned about appearances and what the others would think of me.

During intercession, I did manifest in a way that was typical of intercession, crouched on the floor in travail, however, I was very aware of thoughts in my head that didn't agree. In my mind, I didn't want the pastor to come near me. My thoughts were contradictory to what was happening in the Spirit, and I knew this wasn't normal. I spoke to the leader of the group afterward and we prayed it through together gaining understanding of how I opened the door to the enemy through my insecurities and concern about appearances. So, as you can see, this spirit of religion is sneaky and it is easy to be taken advantage of by it, especially when one has a wounded soul and/or grown up in a legalistic, religious environment at church or at home.

Perhaps you have discerned this spirit in operation in your life. Perhaps you have not. Since our purpose in this discussion is to be free, let's consider these scenarios and what our reactions might be if we were to experience them:

Scenario:
   You see someone from your church angrily yelling at the grocery store clerk.

Religious Response:
   • Inwardly you decide that they must not really be a Christian because Christians don't act like that. You resolve never to connect with them again.

Godly Response:

- Understand that they probably had a stressful day, and they are in process like everyone else.
- Pray for them.
- If you know them, connect with them at a later time over coffee to check up on them and encourage them.

Scenario:

Your congregation is petitioned for donations to the local crisis pregnancy centre.

Religious Response:

- Annoyance and judgement: "They got themselves into that mess, let them get themselves out."
- Feeling obligated to donate while being annoyed, thinking, *they're always asking for money*.

Godly Response:

- Compassion and prayer.
- Seeking the Holy Spirit for direction on what to give.
- Asking the Lord how much to give, if anything.
- Following the lead of the Holy Spirit in faith and joy.

Scenario:

You learn that a group of praying women are hosting a table at the local psychic fair for prophetic evangelism, pointing people to Jesus.

Religious Response:

- Shock and annoyance, thinking, *don't they know psychics are of the devil?*
- Feeling obligated to join because you don't want to look any less spiritual than the others.

Godly Response:

- Supportive and understand that the church is meant to be light in dark places.

- Pray for them.
- Seek direction from the Holy Spirit on whether this is something He wants you to do.
- Ask God for wisdom, protection, and words of wisdom and knowledge so people are touched by God.
- Know that God's direction for your ministry may look different and that's okay. You don't need to be like them to be spiritual and effective in ministry.

How would you respond in these scenarios? Would you respond in a Godly way or a religious way?

We have a decision to make. Are we going to allow the Holy Spirit to search our heart? Or are we going to just skim over this material and not do the real work it entails? That is up to you, but you will only get out of this process what you put in.

One of the greatest indicators of a religious spirit is the annoyance that rises up as we are confronted with the possibility of sinful attitudes in our heart. Someone who is heavily influenced by a religious spirit, as I said before, is prideful and refuses to submit to inner transformation. A person who has a relationship with the Holy Spirit doesn't mind allowing the Spirit to search their heart and expose what is there. They are in fact eager to do it as they want to be free and glorify God to the best of their ability.

To begin, spend some time in worship and praying in tongues, if you can. Then move forward and apply the steps previously mentioned. Pray something like this:

"Lord, I thank You for Who You are. I honor You and glorify Your name. You are the Alpha and Omega. You are the beginning and the end. You are the everlasting God. The One Who never slumbers nor sleeps and the One Who sees me and loves me just the way I am. (STEP 1: Confess and Repent) Lord, I fully submit myself to You and I confess my sin. I ask You, Holy Spirit, to show me what those are. Lord, I repent for. . . being self-righteous and prideful. For thinking that I'm better than others and righteous on my own. I have been haughty and puffed up, thinking I had it all together, when I don't. I confess that I have looked down on (name the person); I have held their sin against them and thought poorly of them (repeat for every person this applies to). I confess that I have been critical toward (person or organization). I am sorry, Lord. I repent and choose to turn back to You. I recognize that without You, I am nothing and it is only by Your sacrifice that I am made holy. Forgive me, Lord, for my sin. I confess that I have believed lies—lies that have taught me to hold negative opinions about others and to condemn others by what they do. Forgive me, God. I repent. (Continue to confess any other sin related to the spirit of religion. Do not skip over anything. Ask the Holy Spirit to help you.) I repent, Lord God, for preferring to follow a set of rules than be in relationship with You. I repent, Lord God, for lacking compassion and mercy toward others, for being cold and stingy, for being a miser, always concerned about what things cost, for not being a generous giver, for needing to be in control of my money, and not trusting You to lead me in my spending and giving. Holy Spirit, show me anything else I need to confess. Convict me, God." (Sit for a moment and allow the Holy Spirit to speak to you. If the Lord shows you any moment in time when you treated someone else with anything but love, confess it now.) Lord, forgive me. I lay these things before You now. Thank You, God, for Your forgiveness. I choose to forgive myself and I choose to fully receive Your complete forgiveness right now, in Jesus' name. (STEP 2: Renounce) I don't want to ever operate in these ways again, so right now, I renounce the spirit of religion, the spirit of poverty, the spirit of control, and the spirit of infirmity and all association with these spirits. I renounce and sever my agreement with them now. I fully renounce and cut off from my life all pride, haughtiness, wrong judgements, self-righteousness, criticism, coldness, rigidness, stinginess, misery ways, lack, and (list any other attitudes associated with the sins you just confessed). Lord, I ask for Your mercy and grace to cover anything I'm unaware of. (STEP 3: Bind) In the authority of Jesus, I bind the spirits of pride, haughtiness, self-righteousness, judgementalism, criticism, frigidity, infirmity, stinginess, poverty, lack, control, and all demonic spirits related to my sin, including (name any other demon you think may be associated with the sin you have confessed and renounced) AND I bind the spirit of religion. I speak directly to every demon associated with religion—in the authority of Jesus, I bind you and declare your maneuvers against me to be powerless and ineffective now, in Jesus' name. I break your power and put a gag in your mouth NOW. You will not speak, nor will you cause me harm or discomfort, in Jesus' name. (STEP 4: Cast out) I command every spirit of pride, haughtiness, self-righteousness, judgementalism, criticism, frigidity, infirmity, stinginess, poverty, lack, and control to come out of me now, in Jesus' name (include any other spirit you may have bound earlier in the prayer). Finally, I command the spirit of religion to loose me now—come out NOW never to return in Jesus' name. LEAVE ME NOW! Come out in Jesus' name. (Repeat as many times as you are led by the Holy Spirit. If no natural manifestation occurs, such as coughing, crying, or yawning etc., blow out of your mouth as an act of faith, believing you are being set free.) (If you don't sense a release, ask the Holy Spirit if there is anything else you need to repent for and renounce.) Father, thank You for delivering me. Thank You, Jesus, that all things are under Your feet and since I am in You, all things are also under my feet. (STEP 5: Ask Father for more of the Holy Spirit, to fill you afresh) Father, send Your Spirit to fill me completely. Baptize me afresh with Your Spirit and power. Cause every void in me to be saturated with Your presence. May there

NOT be one place untouched nor overtaken by You. Consume me completely, Lord. I am Yours. Fill me up! Come Holy Spirit, come (wait until you sense the Holy Spirit has fully come). Thank You, God. I submit to You. In Jesus' name, Amen."

(Note: I have included the spirit of poverty and infirmity in the above prayer as these spirits very often operate together with the spirit of religion. Simply skip over whatever you feel doesn't apply to you.)

ANGER AND UNFORGIVENESS

Anger

Anger seems to be one thing that gets overlooked. I have not heard much teaching or direction on anger in the church, but I have learned that suppressed and pent-up anger can be very harmful to our heart, soul and even body. Anger is not something we want to store, save or hide away. Knowing how to process it, is vital to our well being. So, let's talk about it.

Is anger wrong? This seems to be an important question to consider. If we looked to Jesus for our answer, which is always a good strategy, we would consider John 2:13-17. In this scripture, we see Jesus overturning the tables of the money changers and driving out, with a whip made of cords, those doing business in the temple. Sounds like Jesus was angry; the Bible describes it as zeal. '"Take these things away! Do not make My Father's house a house of merchandise!" Then His disciples remembered that it was written, "Zeal for Your house has eaten Me up"' (John 2:16b-17 NKJV). Merriam-Webster describes zeal as being "a strong feeling of interest and enthusiasm that makes someone very eager or determined to do something." Synonyms for zeal are "fervor, fire, passion."[56] In this passage, Jesus is taking a stand for righteousness and against injustice. Standing against injustice is the appropriate response for Jesus and for us. Injustice should make us angry but it's what we do with that anger that can cause us problems. Here's another example of Jesus being angry:

> And He entered the synagogue again, and a man was there who had a withered hand. So they watched Him closely, whether He would heal him on the Sabbath, so that they might accuse Him. And He said to the man who had the withered hand, "Step forward." Then He said to them, "Is it

---

[56] https://www.merriam-webster.com/thesaurus/zeal

lawful on the Sabbath to do good or to do evil, to save life or to kill?" But they kept silent. And when He had looked around at them *with anger*, being grieved by the hardness of their hearts, He said to the man, "Stretch out your hand." And he stretched it out, and his hand was restored as whole as the other. (Mark 3:1-5 NKJV, emphasis added)

Jesus was angry at the hardness of the hearts of those around Him in the synagogue. He was angry that their desire to follow a law superseded their compassion and love for others, which in God's Kingdom is unjust. Justice in the heart of God is to see His children healed and made whole, every day of the week. "He has shown you, O man, what is good; And what does the Lord require of you But to do justly, To love mercy, And to walk humbly with your God" (Micah 6:8 NKJV)? Treating others justly is good. Hating injustice is also good. But how do we handle the anger that rises in us toward the injustice when it happens?

Ephesians 4:26 says, "And "don't sin by letting anger control you." Don't let the sun go down while you are still angry, for anger gives a foothold to the devil" (NLT). Be angry, but don't let it control you. Be angry, but don't hold onto it—not even past the sun going down. In other words, don't go to bed angry. Process it, recognize it, express it appropriately, and choose to forgive every day.

I went to see a friend and pastor for a deliverance appointment and the main thing he dealt with was my pent-up anger. When it came out, even I was surprised. It turns out, we can bury it so deep, we don't even realize it's there anymore. Our heart hides it and deceives us.[57] Unfortunately, unbeknownst to us, it can also control us. Everything we do and say can have an underlying tone of anger, and it can color our perspective of everything. Our expectations can become distorted and bent toward negative outcomes because of anger.

---

[57] "The heart is deceitful above all things, And desperately wicked; Who can know it" (Jeremiah 17:9 NKJV)?

I had thought, in error, that it wasn't appropriate for a Christian to express anger or even to be angry. This of course is not true, but it must be expressed in appropriate ways, calmly, and in wisdom. It turns out, if you don't let anger build up, it *can* be expressed calmly—without blowing your top. If we feel that someone is treating us unjustly, we must confront them in love (when safe) and make our heart known. We must be honest and not let it go unchecked. If that person is unwilling to change their ways, then it might be appropriate to put some distance between you and them—to put boundaries in place.

Lastly, always go to God with anger. He is always eager to help us process what we are feeling. And He is not offended, mad or disappointed in us for being angry or even expressing that anger to Him with passion. Thank God, right! He can handle our emotions. Talk to God about your anger and be specific. Tell Him who you're angry at and why. Tell Him all your grievances and He will speak to your heart. One exception, however, is if we are angry at God. I don't think it is wisdom to unleash angry words against God. That's not cool. And you might find out very quickly how uncool it really is. Being angry at God is sin and is the result of misunderstanding His character. We must repent.

God is the God of the universe. He is Almighty God. Let's not lose sight of His supreme power, majesty, and complete awesomeness. If you are blaming God for unjust treatment by other people, you are misunderstanding God and forgetting that each person has free will to make their own choices. God does not control people like puppets. If you are blaming God for something else like a loss or natural disaster, I encourage you to take a step back and ask the Holy Spirit to give you wisdom and understanding.

The Holy Spirit is here on this earth, inside His followers, but unfortunately, the devil is also alive and well on planet earth. First Peter 5:8-9 says, "Stay alert! Watch out for your great enemy, the devil. He prowls around like a roaring lion, looking for someone to devour. Stand firm against him, and be strong in your faith.

Remember that your family of believers all over the world is going through the same kind of suffering you are" (NLT).

We cannot forget about the devil's influence around us. There are still so many unbelievers here, all empowering the devil through their sin. Even entire nations, actively involved in sin, empowering the devil. We see disaster and loss everywhere because of the consequences of their sin. Sometimes, unfortunately, the sin of others and the sin of nations affects us and causes *us* pain. Remember though, it is only because of the presence of God that we are not ALL entirely consumed by the devil. The power and presence of God hold him at bay. He is held back from annihilating us all by the presence of the Holy Spirit in the earth. Let's be thankful for that. Blaming God for something hurtful is very much going to block you from receiving the mercy and grace of God and being healed. It is a deception from the evil one.

Many precious people try to make sense of their suffering and can't. They don't understand why God *seemingly* did not intervene in their circumstances. *Why did I endure such abuse?* People wonder, *why did God not stop it?* Beloved, I believe, if He could have, He would have. But God cannot control the actions of a person who has free will and is likely under the influence of demons. He can, however, heal you of your wounds and restore you. He can and will heal your heart, if you will repent for blaming Him and being angry at Him. (Forgiving your perpetrator is also an essential step, but we will get to that shortly.)

Four years ago, the reality of how many people blame God for the maladies in their lives gripped me and this prophetic word bubbled up:

> "There's a stirring this morning. There's a voice rising that must be heard. There's a message and a word that is calling, beckoning, and longing to release its freedom. Intercession bubbles. Spirits groan.

The Lord would say to you, "Don't give in to deception. Don't believe the lies of the enemy. Beware, he prowls around like a roaring lion seeking whom he may devour. Don't be devoured by his lies. Have I (God) not said, "I am for your good, not for your destruction?" Have I not said, "I am NOT against you?" Have I not said, "You are mine and I am yours?" Have I not given ALL to rescue your barren soul and have I not said, "It is finished?" Have I not waited and longed to be known by you just as I know you? And I say to you, *know Me*! Know *Me*. *Know* Me."

My heart is gripped this morning with a message I must convey. I have seen it repeatedly and the same issue comes up continually before me as I minister to others. It sits in front of me like a flashing neon sign that *can't* be ignored. It *must* be exposed.

I see beloved ones covered in ashes, the remains of a life and heart once lived but no more. I see beloved ones suffering and trudging through their days with nothing but grief and sickness, their lives completely destroyed by another. Lives crushed in the grip of a viscous spiral of sin, hurt, anger, blame, offense, bitterness, un-forgiveness and hate. It ends in death but where does it begin? Know this. KNOW where it begins, and you can avoid it all together.

Misunderstanding God. Not knowing God and blaming God. Well, He is sovereign, right? He is in control of everything, right? If He wanted to, He could stop that person in my life from hurting me, from sinning against me and knocking the wind right out of me, right? But He doesn't. He just sits by and watches. Yes, or no? This is the question that *demands* an answer. Have you had this dialogue in your head? Is this what you believe? If it is, you my friend are spiraling.

This is where it begins. Your nightmare begins with how you respond to what the other is doing. It begins with a distorted belief about Who God is and Who He is FOR you.

It begins with believing the lies the enemy is feeding your mind about God's stamp of approval on your hurtful circumstances.

Here's a news flash for you: you Christian, have an enemy and his name is Satan and Satan's number one goal is to drive a wedge between you and God, to cause you to become offended at Him. As soon as Satan gets you to agree with that, BOOM, you are off the rails! You are out of bounds, out of fellowship and you are free game for the devil. DON'T DO IT! Know your God!

Here in lies the tension: sovereignty and free will. Contrary to popular persuasion from the enemy, sovereignty and free will are not contradictory; they exist simultaneously, and both are true. God IS sovereign. He is God and there is no other. He is the One Who made you and the universe and put all the laws in place. He is the One that created order out of chaos. He is the One Who decided on the rhythm of life and decided that living things would reproduce after their own. He is the One that breathed His breath of life into you. He is also the One that decided at the beginning of time to place man over the earth—to appoint us to steward the earth and rule over it and He is the One Who is eternal and just and doesn't, in fact can't, go back on His Word, even when we mess up. He is the One that despite His power and authority, chose to give us authority on His earth and to work through man. He is the One Who sovereignly chose to limit Himself also by giving us free will, free choice to serve Him or not serve Him, free choice in all of life, free will to choose our spouse and free will to love or not to love.

God did not want puppets or robots that He could control. He wanted family, one that chose Him and chose to love Him. He wants relationship with us, authentic relationship with a heart connection. Does God attempt to intervene?

Yes! Does God attempt to sway our hearts toward the right choice? Yes! Does He move by His Spirit and put love beyond our own ability in our heart? Yes, of course He does. He can because He's God but ultimately, we do have the final choice. By His sovereign will He gives us extra grace and the ability to say "no" to sinful things (1 Cor. 10:13). He does not allow us to be tempted beyond what we can bear, and He provides a way out for us, but we must choose that way out. We must resist the devil and choose what is right. Unfortunately, some of us fail at that. Sometimes the people in our lives choose the wrong way, even after God has pulled out all the stops, and they end up sinning against us. Sometimes the people in our lives hurt us beyond imagination and GOD'S HEART GRIEVES. He sees and His heart aches. He sees our tears, broken hearts and broken lives and HE WEEPS for us.

Beloved, stop shaking your fists at God. It is only providing the devil with more ground to encroach upon. It is only serving to defeat you further. Realize that none of it is God's fault. Resist being offended at God and praise Him for Who He is. Thank Him for being faithful to you in all seasons. Know that God is good and His mercies for you are new every morning. Know that God's heart for you is for the restoration of ALL things and that He is walking with you, even carrying you through it all, to the other side.

If you will do this and continue, despite what is happening around you, forgiving all who have hurt you, THEN, you will see restoration of joy, peace, hope and love and you will be victorious in Christ. God is your answer and your Defender, NOT your enemy. YOU ARE extravagantly loved by the Creator of all. This is truth that we must bind ourselves to even amid pain and trying circumstances, even amid evil coming against us in its fullest form. Stand with God in truth. Submit to His Lordship, stay rooted and firmly planted in the truth of God's Word and resist the devil. Resist his evil manipulations of your mind. Resist being offended. Resist hate and he must flee. Simply put, God is love. If what's happening to you is not love, it's not God. God is love and God is good. . . ALL the time."

· · · · · · ·•••••●•••••••· · ·

To know God, let's again consider what love is. Love is best described in the well-known passage, 1 Corinthians 13:4-7. Here's The Passion Translation:

Love is large and incredibly patient. Love is gentle and consistently kind to all. It refuses to be jealous when blessing comes to someone else. Love does not brag about one's achievements nor inflate its own importance. Love does not traffic in shame and disrespect, nor selfishly seek its own honor. Love is not easily irritated or quick to take offense. Love joyfully celebrates honesty and finds no delight in what is wrong. Love is a safe place of shelter, for it never stops believing the best for others. Love never takes failure as defeat, for it never gives up. (TPT)

God is perfect love. We can expect God to relate to us with all patience, gentleness, kindness, never putting shame on us, truth, and joy—all while celebrating who we are. We can expect Him to relate to us with perfect love. We, as humans, fail at loving well every day. We are prone to impatience, jealousy and pride, but God is not. He never has an off day or a bad day where He struggles to control His emotions. He is even-keeled, steady. . . rock-solid.

Amidst all God's love however, there *is* something that God *will* do that doesn't always *feel* good, but just because it doesn't feel good doesn't mean it's not love. Since we are God's children, and God relates to us as a Father, God will discipline us. Here's Hebrews 12:5b-6, "My son, do not make light of the Lord's discipline, and do not lose heart when he rebukes you, because the Lord disciplines the one he loves, and he chastens everyone he accepts as his son."

From time to time, a good parent will need to show *tough love* to their children, so they mature and head in the right direction. God does the same thing. To discipline a child is to love them well. Discipline has the best interest of the child at heart. Consider Hebrews 12:10-11:

> For our earthly fathers disciplined us for a few years, doing the best they knew how. But God's discipline is always good for us, so that we might share in his holiness. No discipline is enjoyable while it is happening—it's painful! But afterward there will be a peaceful harvest of right living for those who are trained in this way. (NLT)

God does not discipline His children for sin that they have confessed, turned away from and covered in the blood of Jesus, but He will discipline His children if they refuse to repent. God will also discipline His children to re-direct them and protect them.

Several years ago, I began a new job as a Compassion Caregiver to a senior. There were a few things about the arrangement that I quietly questioned in my heart. I was not a trained Personal Support Worker, and I wondered if my employer was honest with the senior's family about that. Also, my employer did not offer liability insurance. However, the job paid well so I chose to ignore my concerns and went ahead with it. When I applied for the job, I was recovering from a cold. I assured my potential employer that I was not one to be sick like that often, which was true. I had a cold lasting more than 2 days, maybe once a year.

I began work and within a few days, I was sick with a cold again. And do you know, I continued in a cycle of illness for almost 3 months—the whole time I was employed by this employer! It cycled between a head cold to a chest cold with only a few days in between where I felt normal. This was very strange! Some days I wore a mask, others I used a lot of medication, kept my distance, and disinfected the kitchen where I worked. It was not good. I felt guilty the whole time because I didn't want to make my senior sick.

Finally, I gave in to the conviction in my heart. I quit the job. I couldn't do it. As soon as I quit, my health was restored completely, and the cold didn't return. I had no special medical treatment or antibiotics to make it go away. God was trying to tell me something. He was trying to protect me from a bad situation, and I was out of His will. Working that job wasn't necessarily sinful, it just wasn't wisdom and not where God wanted me.

If a Christian continues in their own way (sometimes sinful but not always), ignoring the conviction and discipline of God, I believe He would allow more serious illness in their lives. He would do whatever was necessary to get through to them. He does this to re-direct and make us holy. Other ways He disciplines could involve losing something like a job, position, favor, ministry, or whatever perhaps has become too important to us.

Now is the best opportunity to respond to the conviction of the Lord, to admit all our anger to Him, repent for hanging on to anger and for blaming God for our suffering.

Unforgiveness

In the Spring of 1990, my husband and I took a lovely vacation to Western Canada. We stayed at the amazing Chateau Lake Louise, visited Banff, Alberta, and took many scenic hikes through the Rocky Mountains. We decided to begin to try to start a family with this marker trip. I expected to be expecting very soon after, but my expectations were dashed when over a year later, I still was not pregnant.

I had experienced much trauma as a young girl regarding pregnancy—watching my mother go through two painful miscarriages, receiving evil reports from my mom regarding her doctor, way too much information for my age and experiencing maternal neglect due to my mother's mental illness. All these emotionally traumatic events left marks on my soul that were still affecting me as I tried to conceive.

After some prayer counselling (more on that later), I conceived for the first time but quickly found myself in tears, grieving a miscarriage at eight weeks gestation. I held the phone to my ear as I solemnly explained to my parents that I had miscarried. Dad's words of compassion were comforting but my mother's comments were far from it. "Well, you weren't really pregnant anyway." Jaw dropped, breath. . . stopped. I don't remember my response. All I remember is the blade cutting my heart, creating yet another wound.

After hanging up the phone, I sat with my prayer counselor friend, while I talked to her about all the ways my mother had hurt me. (We happened to be living with our friends at the time as our new house was being built.) She calmly but very directly asked me, "Do you hate your mother?" Her question shook me. It felt like time stood still as the conviction of the Holy Spirit overtook me. The Lord pulled back the curtain of my heart and I was mortified by what was there. Hot tears streamed down my face as I whispered my confession, "Yeah, I guess I do. Jesus! Forgive me!" *What kind of person was I?* I thought. The answer of course was, "A person with wounds of the soul who had been purchased by Jesus and invited to be renewed by grace," but for a moment I felt the shame of my sin. It was not my finest moment, but the Holy Spirit did His work. The Lord forgave me, I forgave myself, and I forgave my mom for many things.

As it turned out, forgiving my mom and releasing the hate that was in my heart, was the final doorway to my healing of childlessness. (For my full story, see my book "Barren No More.") My husband and I went on after that first miscarriage to have four children, including a set of twins. Perhaps I will have an opportunity to share more on that later.

Of course, your story won't be the same but there may be similar elements. It's not uncommon to have been hurt by a parent either due to neglect, abuse or hurtful words spoken. Family life can be horribly demanding and challenging—especially when one is still carrying emotional burdens from the past. My mother had been through so much as a child and did not have any opportunity for healing. People who are hurting on the inside can't love others well as they are still trying to cope with their own pain. They can't help but focus on themselves, trying to survive and they end up hurting others in the process. It is inevitable.

Forgiving others is a very important key to unlock healing. Many, many people, if not all of us, have multiple opportunities to forgive others. We have all been hurt by someone. Romans 3:23 says, "For everyone has sinned; we all fall short of God's glorious standard." Sometimes, the infraction against us is so horrific, forgiveness feels impossible, and we have absolutely no desire to extend it. However, forgiving others is not an option according to God if we ourselves want to be forgiven. Mark 11:25 says, "But when you are praying, first forgive anyone you are holding a grudge against, so that your Father in heaven will forgive your sins, too" (NLT). This truth is further reiterated in the parable of the unmerciful servant found in Matthew 18:23-35.

You probably know it, but the parable of the unmerciful servant begins with a king forgiving a servant of a debt too large for him to ever repay. Of course, he was grateful, happy and relieved, however, that servant then went out and demanded payment of a much smaller debt from a fellow servant. When that servant couldn't pay, the forgiven servant threw him in prison. Other servants reported the incident to the king and the king confronted the forgiven servant saying, "You wicked servant! I forgave you all that debt because you begged me. Should you not also have had compassion on your fellow servant, just as I had pity on you" (Matthew 18:32-33 NKJV)? That servant, who refused to have mercy on others, was delivered to "the torturers" until he paid the original debt back. Matthew 18:35 says, "So My heavenly Father also will do to you if each of you, from his heart, does not forgive his brother his trespasses" (NKJV). This parable says it all. Forgiving others is required if we want to be forgiven. Refusing to forgive others will lead to us experiencing torture or torment somehow, either through mental or physical anguish.

How do we forgive others? Forgiving others is a choice and an act of the will. We do not wait to "feel" like forgiving someone. We just do it because we are required to. As we continue to make that choice, eventually, our feelings will soften and change, and we will find ourselves feeling compassion for our perpetrators. That may seem impossible now but trust me, it will happen when you lean into Christ to be empowered through grace. Remember what you have been forgiven of and then ask the Holy Spirit for the compassion you need to move forward in His will.

Remember also in the parable above, one servant owed a HUGE debt and the other owed a small debt. The King expected both to be treated equally. Very often this is true in life. We may have *seemingly* been forgiven a small debt, but we may be required to forgive, in many cases, a debt that SEEMS so much larger than our own. It's non-negotiable friend. If you want to enjoy relationship and eternity with the King as well as a healthy body this side of heaven—forgive.

Prayer

First, we're going to sit down with a pen and paper and ask the Holy Spirit to reveal to us every person we are angry with and need to forgive. Write their names down. Secondly, we are going to ask the Holy Spirit to show us why we are angry and how that person made us feel. Then in prayer, first, sanctify your imagination and then tell the Holy Spirit about the experiences you listed above.

> "Lord Jesus, thank You for being with me. Thank You, for showing me my heart and being patient with me. I confess to You, God, that at times I have not honored You with my imagination; I have used it for ungodly purposes, and I am sorry. Please forgive me. Thank You, Jesus, I receive Your forgiveness and I declare Your blood over my imagination, purifying it and setting it apart for Godly purposes. I ask You,

Holy Spirit, to help me guard my imagination, so I don't slip into ungodly imaginings in the future. Right now, I sanctify my imagination for You, Lord, and I bind all deception right now, in Jesus' name. Lord, I ask You now to give me the desire to confess my anger and to forgive every person who has hurt me."

Now go through the list, one person and event at a time:

"Lord, I confess that I am and have been angry at (say the person's name). I am sorry that I have held on to that anger for so long. Please forgive me. (Say the person's name) hurt me deeply when she/he (say what the person did). She/he made me feel (list every feeling you had due to the injustice)."

As you confess how they made you feel, imagine, with your eyes closed, putting those feelings into a bowl. When you are done confessing your feelings, imagine giving that bowl to Jesus. See Jesus in your mind's eye standing before you, taking the bowl from you, making sure to take notice what Jesus does with the bowl. I learned this exercise from Dr. Douglas E. Carr and I pray that you are able to engage with it. Each time I have done it, it has brought great healing to my heart. Repeat this exercise with each person and injustice on your list.

Now, pray to forgive each person for each event:

"I know Lord, that since You have forgiven me, I now need to forgive others. So right now, in the name of Jesus, I choose to forgive (name the person) for (name what they did). I choose to release them and their sin against me into Your capable hands God and trust You to be their righteous judge and redeemer. I pray, Lord, that she/he would come to know You and be healed of the pain in her/his heart that caused her/him to hurt me. Thank You, God, for Your empowering to live by Your Spirit in the realm of health and healing and to truly desire good things for myself, my family

and (name the person) and their family. Fill me with Your
Spirit, Lord, in Jesus' mighty name. Amen."

After praying this prayer, you may find the memory of what you
have just voiced forgiveness for continues to come back to your
mind. Each time it does, refuse to re-hash hurt emotions and
negative thoughts about that person, but voice again, forgiveness
toward them and pray for them. Pray for them more and more,
allowing the Holy Spirit to elaborate your prayer according to His
heart and the compassion for them in your heart will grow.
Rehearse forgiveness toward them often until it becomes part of
your heart and emotions.

WRONG JUDGEMENTS

As we continue our discussion on possible issues that block us from receiving from the Lord, let's dive right in to understanding judgements—what to judge and what not to judge, as well as how to judge righteously. And if you just chimed in and said, "Wait a minute! The Bible says, 'Do not judge.' What do you mean, *judge righteously*?" Well, let's look at it and see.

A Christian is called to live in the power of the Holy Spirit, a life worthy of the blood of Jesus—a life of consecration. We are called to first cooperate with the Lord in the process of sanctification through responding in repentance to the conviction of the Holy Spirit as He identifies the planks and the splinters in our own eyes. Only then, after we have been filled with the Spirit and submitted every area of our life to the Lord, will we ever be called to come alongside a brother or a sister *in love* to remove a speck from their eye. Only then are we prepared to encourage and exhort others for the purpose of restoring, building, and calling others to a higher place in Christ. Please note, I am not suggesting we must be perfect, but fully submitted. Galatians 6:1 encourages us to do this:

> Brothers, if anyone is caught in any sin, you who are spiritual [that is, you who are responsive to the guidance of the Spirit] are to restore such a person in a spirit of gentleness [not with a sense of superiority or self-righteousness], keeping a watchful eye on yourself, so that you are not tempted as well. (AMP)

Notice the phrase, "in a spirit of gentleness [not with a sense of superiority or self-righteousness]." This is key!

Matthew 18:15-17 gives us further instruction if the person we have come along side, in humility, refuses to listen to us. We are told by Jesus Himself to go as far as exposing their sin to church leaders:

> If your brother or sister sins, go and point out their fault, just between the two of you. If they listen to you, you have won them over. But if they will not listen, take one or two others along, so that 'every matter may be established by the testimony of two or three witnesses.' If they still refuse to listen, tell it to the church; and if they refuse to listen even to the church, treat them as you would a pagan or a tax collector. (Matthew 18:15-17 NIV)

This is serious stuff. Those in the church *who are followers of Christ*, are not supposed to still be entangled in a *pattern* of sin. And if it's obvious that they are, they need to be encouraged *in gentleness* to repent.

Some versions of Matthew 18:15-17 specifically speak about those who sin *against us*, however, some versions like the NIV quoted above, do not. I would say that if a brother or sister in Christ is part of our church family and they are involved in a *pattern* of *blatant* sin, they *are* sinning against us; they are pretending to be something they are not. Their sin affects the whole church family whether it is done in private or against us in particular. Having said that, I think it's also important to mention here, the following: the local church isn't the same now as it was in the New Testament (at least in North America). Most churches in North America *do not* follow the New Testament blueprint. In the NT, the apostles went out into the community, preached in the streets, and brought *converts* into their church gatherings. They did not invite pre-believers into "church." Their gatherings were private.

In the popular North American church with open doors, some purposefully made palatable to pre-believers, not everyone who attends has surrendered their lives to Christ; not everyone in the church has been regenerated by the Holy Spirit nor have they been empowered to live free of sin. Today, believe it or not, some people only come to church for its social benefits. So, greater discernment is needed! Let's be sure that if we're confronting someone in kindness regarding something we see in their lives, that they have *indeed* made a decision for Christ, been born-again and possess the empowerment of the Spirit. We can't expect someone who still lives in darkness to behave like they're in the light.

It's always good to have sisters (and brothers) in the Lord who are willing to be sharpened and who will sharpen us in a loving and respectful relationship. What's not good is when someone leaves a conversation feeling less than, shamed, unheard, unloved, and even humiliated by an exchange. If this happens, it's *possible* that we have not communicated well and *possibly* have operated in a spirit of haughtiness or self-righteousness. However, realize too that there could be situations where a person doesn't want to be sharpened and would rather stay in their sin. This person may be defensive and come away offended regardless of how much compassion and love you attempt to communicate.

The point here is that there are times we are called to judge *righteously* or perhaps better said, *spiritually discern*, when a brother or sister needs help. Other scriptures that support this are 1 Corinthians 2:14-16:

> But the natural man does not receive the things of the Spirit of God, for they are foolishness to him; nor can he know *them*, because they are spiritually discerned. *But he who is spiritual judges all things*, yet he himself is rightly judged by no one. For "who has known the mind of the LORD that he may instruct Him?" But we have the mind of Christ. (NKJV)

As well as 1 Corinthians 5:11-13:

> But now I am writing to you that you must not associate with anyone who *claims to be a brother or sister* but is sexually immoral or greedy, an idolater or slanderer, a drunkard or swindler. Do not even eat with such people. What business is it of mine to judge those outside the church? *Are you not to judge those inside?* God will judge

those outside. "Expel the wicked person from among you."
(NIV, emphasis added)

We are absolutely to discern and make righteous judgements about the behaviors, attitudes and opinions *of our brothers and sisters without looking down on them* for the purpose of praying for them, as well as knowing how much time we want to spend with them or if we want them speaking into our lives. Sometimes it's our place to address things that we see and sometimes it's not. Sometimes we are called simply to pray for them.

A brother or sister *who has been trained by righteousness* may be *called* by God to lead those they are close to and even the Body of Christ at large, through exhortation; this may include calling believers back to the fear of the Lord and to holiness. To some it can sound critical or like they are judging others, but they are not; they are fulfilling their mandate from God. Think Jonah and Elijah, John the Baptist, and the Apostles.

I wonder how the people felt initially when Peter stood up among them in Acts 2 and boldly confronted them about their sin? Peter stated to them plainly when talking about Jesus, "...you, with the help of wicked men, put him to death by nailing him to the cross" (Acts 2:23b NIV) and called them to repent. Was Peter being judgmental? Was he being critical? No. He was preaching boldly and doing what he was called to do. Peter was called to confront people in their sin so they would turn away from it. Three thousand people were added to the church of Acts in one day because of Peter's bold confrontation.

In John 7:24, Jesus addressed a crowd in the temple court where He had been teaching, regarding judgments made against Him for healing on the Sabbath. Jesus says to them, "Do not judge by appearance [superficially and arrogantly], but judge fairly and righteously" (John 7:24 AMP). Jesus had come into the temple teaching something different—something fresh—and moving in a way that seemed wrong on the outside (healing on the Sabbath) because it challenged the way they had always done things (according to the law), so they had to make a judgment. Was what they were hearing and seeing, God, or was it not? They had to decide whether they were going to believe what He taught.

We are faced with the same thing every day. We see "Christian" memes on Facebook, and we need to make a judgment whether it lines up with our belief system—the Word of God. We listen to a preacher online and we must qualify everything they say with the Bible and decide, *are they biblical in their teaching and are they led by the Spirit? Is it beneficial to listen to this person? Will it build me up in my faith or lead me into deception?*

Other questions to consider are, "Do they have pure motives?" "Do they have integrity?" and "Can they be trusted?" The answers to these questions we can't possibly know by outside appearance because many people are very good actors. They say all the right things. They are funny, charming, knowledgeable, and likeable. Yet, some are influenced by demons of pride, people pleasing, flattery, greed, and/or lying. The only way we will know is by asking the Holy Spirit to lead us and show us the truth of who a person is. *This* is making a *righteous judgement*—by and with the wisdom of God through the Holy Spirit. *However*, making a righteous judgement still does not include forming a negative opinion of someone from a place of hate, offense, or bitterness.

Let's look at the scriptures in the Bible that tell us not to judge. The first one we'll consider is Matthew 7:1-5 which says:

> "Do not judge, or you too will be judged. For in the same way you judge others, you will be judged, and with the measure you use, it will be measured to you. "Why do you look at the speck of sawdust in your brother's eye and pay no attention to the plank in your own eye? How can you say to your brother, 'Let me take the speck out of your eye,' when all the time there is a plank in your own eye? You hypocrite, *first take the plank out of your own eye, and then you will see clearly to remove the speck from your brother's eye.* (NIV, emphasis added)

Next, let's consider Romans 2:1. Romans 2:1 begins with the word, "Therefore," and anytime we see *that* word, we should look back in the scriptures to establish context. Let's begin with Romans 1:28-32 which is talking about those who have chosen to reject God. Here's the New International Reader's Version for simplification:

> They didn't think it was important to know God. So God let them continue to have evil thoughts. They did things they shouldn't do. They are full of every kind of sin, evil and ungodliness. They want more than they need. They commit murder. They want what belongs to other people. They fight and cheat. They hate others. They say mean things about other people. They tell lies about them. They hate God. They are rude and proud. They brag. They think of new ways to do evil. They don't obey their parents. They do not understand. They can't be trusted. They are not loving and kind. They know that God's commands are right. They know that those who do evil things should die. But they continue to do those very things. They also approve of others who do them. (NIRV)

> Romans 2:1 now follows:
> *Therefore* you have no excuse or justification, everyone of you who [hypocritically] judges and condemns others; for in passing judgment on another person, you condemn yourself, because you who judge [from a position of arrogance or self-righteousness] are habitually practicing the very same things [which you denounce]. (AMP, emphasis added)

It's obvious from Romans that those who are in gross sin certainly have no business judging anyone. However, those who are spiritual and led by the Spirit also need to be extra careful what they think about people and what they do with what they see in the natural and in the Spirit (or what they discern by the Spirit).

Google's dictionary defines the verb, *to judge* as: "to form an *opinion* or *conclusion* about."[58] The word "conclusion" indicates something that is *final*, which means *we've made up our mind*.

We naturally form opinions and draw conclusions about words, messages, and behaviors all the time and this is good. We need to discern what is godly and what is not, without becoming offended. What we're not supposed to do is draw *definitive negative conclusions* about *people* and their character; this is the danger zone.

I may see or observe that a person is not behaving in a godly way, but the *only opinion* or *conclusion* I should come to is that *they're struggling*, or *they need Jesus (or more of Jesus)*, and I should pray for them. *Never should I decide that they must be a bad person without hope or redemption—without the capacity to grow or change.* We do not know anyone's heart outside of the revelation of the Holy Spirit and we are all in a process of sanctification. Just as we see that another person is not perfect, we are also not perfect.

There may be times when we may wonder, *has that person really experienced new birth by the Spirit?* Maybe we haven't seen the fruit of repentance or transformation in their lives. But let's pray for them and give them grace—just as we would want to receive grace from others.

So, when is judging a problem? What does it look like when it causes us to be ill? Some examples can be found throughout this book (page 197-198 for example). Bitter judgements can play a part in anger, unforgiveness, ungodly vows, and words that we have spoken against others. Bitterly judging someone (looking down on

---

[58] Google dictionary:
https://www.google.com/search?q=judge+meaning&oq=judge+mea&gs_lcrp=EgZjaHJvb
WUqCQgAEEUYOxiABDIJCAAQRRg7GIAEMgYIARBFGDkyBwgCEAAYgAQyBwgDEAAYgAQy
BwgEEAAYgAQyBwgFEAAYgAQyBggGEEUYPDIGCAcQRRg8qAIIsAIB&sourceid=chrome&i
e=UTF-8

a person in bitterness) will cause you to become like that person or cause you to experience the same misfortune they have.

In my late twenties, I personally had to work through anger, hate, and unforgiveness toward my mother. She had mental health issues which caused her to be very self-focused and emotionally fragile. She did not look after me well. Because of this I had made *bitter judgements* against her. I had *decided* that she was emotionally weak; she could be heard crying in her bedroom behind a closed door often. I remember it well. I could not depend on her for much and I felt to some degree, abandoned by her. Additionally, the fear my mom lived in was obvious. She and my dad tried to instill faith in us from a young age, but my mom seemed unable to live it out. Because of all these things, as a teenager and young adult, I looked down on her and *concluded* that she was not a good mother.

In God's perfect time, the Holy Spirit led me to repent for holding judgements *against* my mom and helped me to see her heart from His perspective—from a heart of love, compassion and understanding. Had I not repented, I could have given the enemy a legal right to afflict me in the same way my mom was afflicted with physical illnesses. But in God's kindness, He alerted me to the condition of my heart so I could be whole and in divine health. I love the goodness of God and His faithfulness to correct us when we need it.

What *conclusions* have you made about others? Have you made decisions that define anyone's character negatively which in turn have caused you to look down on them in your heart? Perhaps you've witnessed them being unfaithful or disloyal. Perhaps you've heard them exaggerate or tell half-truths. Or perhaps they've not protected you or defended you as they should have. Perhaps you've been hurt by them, repeatedly. If you've looked down on anyone because of their weaknesses and held bitter judgements against them, I invite you now to dig deep—to invite the Holy Spirit to help you and have a conversation with God. I invite you to repent so you too can be released from the bondage of bitter judgements. Doing so will bring immense freedom to your mind, heart and possibly even your body.

If you're willing, I invite you to pray something like this:

> "Lord, I confess to You now that I have held bitter judgements against (name the person). I have thought her/him to be (state your opinions) and I repent now in Jesus' name, and I ask You to forgive me for looking down on them and thinking less of them than You do. I'm sorry. God give me Your heart and perspective of who they are. Help me to see them through Your eyes. Thank You for Your forgiveness, Lord. I choose to forgive myself and receive Your forgiveness fully. I also choose to forgive them for their sin and/or weakness (be specific). I know that You died for them too, Lord, and as soon as they repent, they are forgiven also. I now release myself from them and them from me, in Jesus' name. Thank You for Your blood, Jesus, that cleanses us and makes us whole. Lord, heal every wound in me that has caused me to have a negative opinion of them. I renounce every negative word I've spoken about them now, in Jesus' name and I command every negative word to fall to the ground, unfruitful. Thank You, Lord. In Jesus' mighty name, amen."

If you prayed through, way to go! God is smiling down on you, strengthening you and cheering you on.

IDOLATRY

Idolatry clogs up our spiritual gateways like nothing else and prevents us from receiving healing. Why? Because it doesn't reflect whole-hearted love for God nor complete trust in Him—in fact, it demonstrates the complete opposite. For Christians, idolatry is covert, disguised in deception and can be falsely clothed in good intentions. No genuine Christian knowingly engages in it, it's not obvious, we live in denial, and we don't actually understand what idolatry is.

First, any time we recognize, attribute spiritual power to, call on, worship or sacrifice to any other god or deity, other than the One true God of the Bible, Jehovah, we are guilty of idolatry. Idolatry many times, involves the worship of idols or graven images that have been crafted to represent a so-called "god." If you've ever been to Prague, Czech Republic, you may have seen an example of this. Found at the center of Prague's Zoo is a statue of Radegast, the (false) god of hospitality, fertility and crops;[59] you may even have seen "gifts" people have left there at the base of the statue as they have attempted to gain its favor.

Idolatry though is not just active in these obvious ways. It is more prevalent in a passive sense when we have EXTREME admiration, love, or reverence for something or someone to the point that they or it is more important to us than God. This is the type of idolatry that trips up many Christians without realizing it.

Idolatry happens to be the subject of the very first commandment God gives Moses in Exodus 20:

> You shall have no other gods before Me. You shall not make
> for yourself a carved image—any likeness of anything that

---

[59]https://www.waymarking.com/waymarks/WMMX16_Radegast_statue_Prague_Czech _Republic

is in heaven above, or that is in the earth beneath, or that is in the water under the earth; you shall not bow down to them nor serve them. For I, the LORD your God, am a jealous God. (Exodus 20:3-5a)

What does it mean for God to be jealous? In short, it means He wants ALL of us and not just part. The longer answer involves recognizing that God has loved and continues to love us with everything. He has given us ALL He has. He loves us with an everlasting love, a love that never fails and a love without condition. He loves us so much He gave us His only Son for our redemption. God expects us to reciprocate that same love to Him, by loving Him first, with all our heart, mind, soul, and strength and by loving Him the most out of everything and everyone in our lives, including our children and family. God is not interested in sharing the throne of our heart with anyone or anything else.[60] We are in a love relationship with God (even to the point that we are called "The Bride of Christ") and when we give our attention, affection and adoration to things or people to the extent that it surpasses that for God, we are being unfaithful to Him. To God, it feels as though we are having an affair and it is dishonoring to Him.

We can identify obvious examples of idolatry in the Old Testament. For example, when the Israelites got tired of waiting for Moses to come down from the mountain and told Aaron they wanted to make a gold calf out of their jewelry. Moses had been gone for forty days and forty nights and they did not know what had happened to him, so they were anxious. They desperately needed God to lead them and help them but the only way they heard from God was through Moses. Since Moses didn't seem to be coming back any time soon, they felt they needed to create their own god. (It was that very common trap we all seem to fall in from time to time—

---

[60] Kyle Idleman, *gods at War: The Battle for Your Heart that Will Define Your Life* (Louisville: City on a Hill Productions, 2012) DVD.

God is silent, or we can't hear God, or God takes too long to answer/act, so we take matters into our own hands.)

The Israelites fashioned a gold calf and they said, "This is your god, O Israel, that brought you out of the land of Egypt" (Ex.32:4b NKJV)! (Yikes!) When Aaron saw the calf, he built an altar before it and the following day, they had a festival. They offered burnt offerings to the calf, brought it peace offerings, and ate and drank in merriness. In verse seven of Exodus 32, God saw what they had done and urgently told Moses, "Go, get down! For your people whom you brought out of the land of Egypt have corrupted themselves" (NKJV). Reading further in Exodus 32, God becomes so angry at the Israelites for their rebellion and disloyalty, Moses had to plead with God not to destroy them.

We also see idolatry alive and well in the New Testament, especially at Caesarea Philippi where there were seven sites and/or temples for the worship of pagan gods and where people sacrificed their children to the god of Pan.

In our world, currently, there is *still* the worship of other deities and even Satan (Satanists) but among Christians, idolatry looks different. However, is still very much alive and well. There are well-meaning Christians who think they can worship nature and the stars in the practice of wicca, astrology and horoscopes. They think they can practice yoga (originating from Hinduism),[61] look to crystals for healing and certain charms on a charm bracelet for increased fertility, and other health benefits.

The truth is, there are only two spiritual powers that exist—God and Satan, good and bad, and there are only two spiritual kingdoms, the Kingdom of Light and the Kingdom of Darkness. That means, if the God of Abraham, Isaac and Jacob, Jesus or the Holy Spirit is not the spiritual One you are addressing, inviting, or

[61] This article explains the spiritual significance of each yoga pose and its connection to the false god of Hinduism, Shiva: https://www.livestrong.com/article/395082-spiritual-meanings-of-yoga-postures/

POSITION YOURSELF FOR HEALING BY BARBARA DE SIMON

interacting with, the spirit you are interacting with is very likely from Satan's kingdom—there is no other option. (One exception may be when you are interacting with an angel from the Lord, but this event would be part of the worship of Jesus/God, not be independent of it.) There are NO good spirits that are part of a neutral kingdom or spiritual space. Don't be deceived! Satan and his entourage can transform themselves into angels of light for the purpose of tricking you into playing their games.[62] And just because you're speaking or casting a positive "vibe" onto someone does not make it pure or good. Anytime we are attempting to control someone else's life, for good or bad, we are dabbling in witchcraft, and witchcraft is of the devil.

I know that there will be some who don't want to give up their pagan practices, like expecting crystals to heal or a fertility charm to bless fertility because at times, they seem to work. Here's the problem though: as soon as you ascribe spiritual power to a physical object of any kind, you dishonor God and give demons an opportunity to attach to that object. Now the object *does* have spiritual power but it's of the bad kind. The demon attached to that object will appease you for a time and perhaps cause something good to happen in your life for the sole purpose of drawing you in to enslave you further. Over time, that demon will begin to wreak havoc in your life as you get deeper and deeper into bondage. Eventually you will experience great torment and strife. If I've just described you, you can be free from its grip through the steps already described in this book, confession, repentance, renunciation etc., but also it is necessary to destroy any physical object you've turned into an idol. (If you are experiencing deep bondage, you may need help getting free.) Please see Appendix B,

---

[62] "And no wonder, since Satan himself masquerades as an angel of light. So it is no great surprise if his servants also masquerade as servants of righteousness, but their end will correspond with their deeds" (2 Corinthians 11:14-15 AMP).

188

at the back of the book, for a list of Pagan, occult, idolatrous practices for which you may need to repent.

Perhaps this previous discussion doesn't apply to you. Perhaps you have been able to identify this type of idolatry already and you have stayed clear of it. That's great! But it doesn't mean you're not involved in idolatry some other way. As previously mentioned, idolatry can show up in our lives covertly when we admire, adore, love, regard, honor or pursue someone or something more than God.

I ministered to a woman once who struggled with deep depression and suicidal ideation. She had been through deliverance and received freedom from a spirit of heaviness, but she was not able to maintain her freedom. (This is a dangerous situation as the oppression that comes back can be way worse than the first.) I watched this precious woman go into a phone call free of depression, but end the phone call bound again, so I asked her about it. She desperately wanted her daughter's forgiveness but was denied it. Through the Holy Spirit, it was revealed to me that she was becoming bound by depression again because she held her daughter's forgiveness in a high place; it was higher and even more important to her than God's forgiveness. This is idolatry. We dealt with her sin before the Lord, in prayer, and her bondage was broken once and for all. A few years later, her daughter also finally found it in her heart to forgive and re-establish a relationship with her.

We are forgiven when God forgives us and if our loved ones don't forgive us, frankly that is between them and God. Yes, it can be very sad when our loved ones refuse to forgive us and re-connect but it does not determine our standing before God. Have faith that the Lord is working on your behalf to soften your loved one's heart toward you. Give them the space and time they need to recover and heal with the Lord.

Kyle Idleman and City on a Hill Productions has produced an excellent small group Bible Study DVD curriculum addressing this very issue called, "gods at War: The Battle for Your Heart that Will Define Your Life." The DVDs include powerful personal testimonies from people just like you and me. In the study, Kyle identifies gods of our culture that many of us worship without even realizing it, like pleasure, money, sex, power, and even love.

How do we identify idols in our heart—the gods that are warring within us for pre-eminence demanding our adoration and affections? It's not an easy task as Jeremiah 17:9 says, "The human heart is the most deceitful of all things, and desperately wicked. Who really knows how bad it is" (NLT)? We tend to live in denial, and you may have already assumed that nothing about this conversation applies to you either, but I would encourage you to dig a little deeper. Look beyond your initial assumptions and the surface of your heart. Be willing to allow the Holy Spirit to draw the curtain back and reveal to you what's really there.

Kyle Idleman suggests some probing questions to help us identify idols. They are as follows:

1. What has left you feeling the most disappointed?
2. What do you complain about?
3. What do you sacrifice your time and money for?
4. What do you worry about?
5. Where do you go when you are hurt and need comfort?
6. What makes you unreasonably mad?
7. What do you dream of?
8. Whose encouragement or approval means the most to you?[63]

In addition, consider these questions as follows:

---

[63] Idleman, *gods at War: The Battle for Your Heart that Will Define Your Life*. DVD.

1. What do you allow to affect your self-worth? What makes you feel bad about yourself? What do you turn to, to help you feel good about yourself?

2. Is there a circumstance in your life that needs to be present for you to *feel* successful?

Also, fill in the blank:

"My life and happiness ride on this one thing:_____."

"I will never be completely happy until _____."

What if you don't get that promotion at work, that pay increase, or that four-bedroom house with the double garage? What if you never get the recognition you've worked hard for? What if you don't achieve the goals you've set out for yourself? Will you still be able to find joy in life or will your life be ruined?

After reflecting on these questions, can you now see if anything has become too dear to you? There could be various things you've identified. I would encourage you to make a mental note of them or write them down for reference later. In the upcoming paragraphs, we're going to dig a bit deeper and focus on a few things which are particularly prevalent as idols with women: romantic love and family relationships.

It is well known, we as humans, have an emotional need that is universal across races and cultures—that is the need for love. God created us that way. He is a relational God and He created us in His image. God created us for love and to be loved, but that love is supposed to come primarily from God Himself—through relationship with Him. A problem occurs when we don't have enough intimacy in our relationship with Him or enough spiritual discernment to experience it. We end up desperately searching for love in all the wrong places trying to fill the void. We look to other people, a spouse, children, pets and sometimes even material things. The elusiveness of perfect love in our lives drives us to do whatever it takes to get it and to latch onto things and people with all our might—turning those things and people into idols. Love is such a deep need in us that not experiencing it can make us utterly desperate.

When I was young, I longed to find that one man who I would marry—that one man who would love me and cherish me properly. I know now *that* One Man is Jesus, but when I was young, I didn't know Him. When I was young, I wrongly believed that once I found the right romantic relationship, all would be right with the world. I believed that once I married, I would finally have true love and happiness. Now I know, I was wrong. It turned out that expecting one man to meet all my needs, including my deepest emotional needs, was too high an expectation for a human being. It turned out that my husband was not and is not and never will be, God. Shocking, I know. It turns out some types of love, the unconditional kind that meets our deepest need, that loves through our worst mood and worst sin, comes only from God.

Now, there may be some women reading this who have trouble fully relating to this. There may be some women who might say, "Actually, I think my husband is pretty good at loving me unconditionally. He's quick to forgive and gives me grace when I need it," and that's awesome. I'm very happy for you. Some men have had an excellent role model in this area and have been taught well. Be careful though. Don't allow your relationship with your husband to become more important than your relationship with God. Be diligent to nurture your connection and intimacy with Jesus and be careful not to look to your husband for what only God can and should provide. Your husband is human, and he will make mistakes. Expecting your husband to be like God puts unreasonable pressure on him to be what he is not. There should not be ANY relationship that is more important to you than God's—not your marriage, not your relationship with your mother, nor your relationship with your children, future or existing. God should always be first.

A friend of mine had an experience while visiting a church for a special meeting. The offering plate was being passed but she had no cash. Surprisingly she heard the Spirit tell her to put her "promise ring" in the plate. Yes! God told her to give up the very first ring her now husband had given her while dating. That one! She explained to me her shock and said to the Lord, "But Lord, he's my love!" Jesus was calling her to release that which she held dear and to come back to Him as her "first love." She did comply and do what God called her to do, and I know she will be blessed for it. Perhaps there is a prophetic act God is calling you to do, to demonstrate to Him your enduring love and faithfulness?

One final area that needs to be considered is our children. We must release them back to the Lord so He can protect them. It is imperative that we realize that we cannot control everything in their lives, and it is beyond us to keep our children safe, 100% of the time. We must partner with God in this. We must have faith and peace in our heart that God is protecting them and working on their behalf. God cannot work with anything we insist on keeping in clenched fists. Let them go. They must be in the Great Potter's hands for Him to fashion and protect. "And yet, O LORD, you are our Father. We are the clay, and you are the potter. We all are formed by your hand" (Isaiah 64:8 NLT).

Prayer

"Lord, I thank You for Who You are. I honor You and glorify Your name. You are the Alpha and Omega. You are the beginning and the end. You are the everlasting God. The One Who never slumbers nor sleeps and the One Who sees me and loves me just the way I am. Lord, I confess that I have not put You first in my life.

I confess that… (confess all occult activity, looking to find out information about your future from psychics, tarot cards or tarot card readers, and horoscopes, spirit guides, attempting to converse with the dead, etc. Please see Appendix B.)

I am sorry, Lord, that I have knowingly or unknowingly looked to demonic powers for help and wisdom. I repent and I choose to forgive every person who introduced me to occult activity or encouraged me to connect with demons. I choose to forgive (name each person specifically) for (name how they led you into idolatry). (An example may be: "I choose to forgive Aunt May for taking me to that psychic or I choose to forgive Liz for sending me that video that introduced me to Tarot cards.") Lord, please forgive me and cut off from my life all influence demons have acquired through my participation with them. I renounce all demonic spirit guides, demon influences, psychic abilities, and divination in Jesus' name. I renounce idolatry and false idols. (If you have been worshipping specific false gods, or deities, renounce them by name.) I renounce every prayer I have uttered to false gods, and I renounce every false covenant I have made with them. I renounce putting my faith in them. Deliver me and wash me clean from their influence, Lord.

I also confess that I have made things and/or people into idols; I have loved them too much and have held onto them too tightly. Specifically, Lord, I have loved... (name all the things you have loved more than God) more than You and I am sorry. I confess that (example: the approval of man, my family, job, bank account etc.) has become too important to me and I have turned them into idols. I am sorry, God, for finding my worth in these things. I am sorry, God, for finding my success in these things. All I need is found in You, so help me, God, to connect with that reality and experience Your approval, acceptance, and love, for real. Open my spiritual senses to sense You and Your presence with me. I let go of worldly things now and accept that You, God, are the most important person in my life, and You provide for me the most important things. I understand that Your approval is the only approval that matters, so I let go of the need to be approved by man right now, in Jesus' name. Please forgive me, God, for idolatry and spiritual adultery. I repent and turn back to You completely. Cleanse me, Lord. Thank You that You are merciful and full of grace. Thank You that when we confess our sins to You, You are faithful and just to forgive us and cleanse us from all unrighteousness. I choose to forgive myself and I receive Your forgiveness Lord in its fullness. I declare that I am forgiven of my sin.

I completely renounce idolatry and I turn away from it now, in Jesus' name. I bind all demons that have gained access to me through idolatry. I bind all deception, lying, trickery, and false voices and I bind idolatry now, in Jesus' name. I declare that my sin is now under the blood of Jesus' so every curse that has touched my life because of my sin is broken now and no longer has any right to operate. I cancel every curse coming from idolatry and I command the spirit of idolatry and all its cohorts to leave me now, in Jesus' name. Every legal right they have had over me is now gone and cancelled. Idolatry no longer has a hold on me. GO NOW, in Jesus' name! (If no physical manifestation occurs, blow out of your mouth in faith.)

I declare the blessing and favor of the Lord over my life. Goodness and mercy shall follow me all the days of life and I shall dwell in the house of the Lord, in freedom, forever. I will love the Lord my God with all my heart, mind, soul, and strength with His help and I will see the goodness of the Lord in the land of the living. The land of my life will be called blessed and fruitful in Jesus' name. Fill me up, God, with Your Spirit. Possess every place in me that has been vacated and saturate me with Your love and power. In Jesus' name, amen."

LEANING ON OUR OWN UNDERSTANDING

> Trust in the LORD with all your heart and lean not on your
> own understanding; in all your ways submit to him, and he
> will make your paths straight. Do not be wise in your own
> eyes; fear the Lord and shun evil. *This will bring health to
> your body and nourishment to your bones.* (Proverbs 3:5-8
> NIV, emphasis added)

These verses say two things I'd like to highlight. First, "lean not on
your own understanding" and secondly, "do not be wise in your
own eyes."

"Lean not on your own understanding" is key for us as we pursue
healing. This means, *don't think you know it all* and don't rely on
your own way of understanding something or explaining
something. Does this mean we aren't to seek understanding at all?
No. It is good to seek understanding *from the Lord*—to seek the
Spirit of understanding which is a facet of the Holy Spirit.[64] *Any*
understanding we are leaning on or trusting in, needs to come from
the Spirit and not the world, Satan, or our own flesh. If we are not
discerning *divine* understanding, we must be careful not to *default*
to our own and *most* importantly, not put the *need* to understand
in a high place. Psalm 32:8-9 says:

> I will instruct you and teach you in the way you should go; I
> will counsel you with my loving eye on you. Do not be like
> the horse or the mule, which have no understanding but
> must be controlled by bit and bridle or they will not come
> to you. (NIV)

---

[64] Isaiah 11:2, "The Spirit of the Lord will rest on him—the Spirit of wisdom and of
understanding, the Spirit of counsel and of might, the Spirit of the knowledge and fear of
the LORD" (NIV).

Seek the Spirit of understanding. The Lord wants you to understand, but we may need to be patient with ourselves as we seek Him for answers.

There was a lady the Lord brought to me who had multiple types of cancer in her body—who had been fighting *different* cancers for many years. Some cancers she had victory over, but others she didn't. When I met her, she had lost all hope of surviving. The doctors had exhausted all protocols and had advised her to begin to plan a move to hospice. We'll call her Lois (not her real name). Lois felt *she knew and understood* why she had so much cancer in her body.

Lois had worked in agriculture beginning at a young age, in the greenhouses, tending to tomatoes and vegetables grown in our local area. Back in the day, no one knew that pesticides were harmful to one's health, so they didn't think anything about handling it with their bare hands and breathing it in as it wafted in a cloud above their heads. Knowing what we know now in the world about pesticides, it made perfect logical sense to Lois that she had cancer. And it probably makes perfect *natural* sense to you too *if* we just think in terms of the natural, worldly realm. But as I prayed for her, God gave me His divine, supernatural wisdom and understanding of the situation, which is not of this world, as follows:

> These miraculous signs will accompany those who believe: They will cast out demons in my name, and they will speak in new languages. They will be able to handle snakes with safety, and *if they drink anything poisonous, it won't hurt them*. They will be able to place their hands on the sick, and they will be healed. (Mark 16:17-18 NLT, emphasis added)

This verse does *not* mean that we can *intentionally* do unwise things like pick up venomous snakes, drink poison, inhale poison or handle poison with our bare hands and survive, but it does mean we can do these things *accidently*, or *unknowingly* and expect God to protect us from harm. This is God's Word and promise to us. I

197

shared this truth with my friend, Lois, but because of her immaturity as a Christian, she struggled to believe what I was telling her. She defaulted to her *own* understanding rather than the Lord's. My heart grieves that she possibly missed out on her miracle because of unbelief.

Even though the Word of God flies in the face of what we think we know on this earth, the Word of God is TRUTH. The world does NOT get to define truth! Now, what we *experience* in the world seems like truth also, but the facts of our experience are just facts—facts that are not eternal and can change on a dime. Facts are not truth. So, the question is, *what will we believe? What belief or understanding will we decide is higher and more important to us? God's understanding/perspective or the world's?* So, if you think you know *why* you are ill, if you have your *own* understanding of the cause of your illness, I implore you to be willing to let it go and let God give you His understanding and perspective instead.

Why do you think we, as God's people, can escape threats in the world like venomous snake bites or harm caused by poisonous substances? Because we are *set-apart* ones. We are Glory carriers. We carry the very presence of God within us. When we repent and turn to God, we are spiritually translated from the kingdom of darkness into the Kingdom of Light *immediately* and we become *citizens of heaven as soon as we believe* and surrender. Philippians 3:20 says, "But we are citizens of heaven, where the Lord Jesus Christ lives. And we are eagerly waiting for him to return as our Savior" (NLT). We are *in* the world but are no longer *of* the world. John 15:19 says, "If you belonged to the world, it would love you as its own. As it is, *you do not belong to the world*, but I have chosen you *out of the world*. That is why the world hates you" (NIV, emphasis added).

I was born in Canada. Naturally in the world, this means I am a citizen of Canada. I abide by the laws of Canada, and the laws of Canada govern my life here. I enjoy the privileges of being a Canadian citizen and my citizenship dictates my obligations and my freedoms (or lack thereof) in the world. However, now that I'm a disciple of Christ, the Bible tells me that I have become a *citizen of heaven* and with it comes a whole *different* set of obligations and *true* freedoms that supersede any others. I am no longer of the world. I have been re-born as a *supernatural* spiritual being who carries the very presence of God within her, which gives me access to heaven's realities now. My citizenship in heaven supersedes my citizenship in Canada. As a result, *heaven now governs my life* instead of Canada or the earthly realm. If you're a disciple of Christ, the same is true of you. We can expect, as a citizen of heaven, to see the realities of heaven, such as righteousness and supernatural protection, to manifest in our lives here and now.

As believers and Glory carriers, we can expect to have a very different experience of the world than other people, who are both in and of the world—who are pre-believers. We can expect to flourish financially, even though the world around us is going through a financial crisis. We can expect to experience great light in our lives, even though the rest of the world is experiencing gross darkness.[65] All we need to do is read Psalm 91 to see the benefits of living as a citizen of heaven, in the shelter of the Most-High God:

> Those who live in the shelter of the Most High will find rest in the shadow of the Almighty. This I declare about the LORD: He alone is my refuge, my place of safety; he is my God, and I trust him. For he will rescue you from every trap and protect you from deadly disease. He will cover you with his feathers. He will shelter you with his wings. His faithful promises are your armor and protection. Do not be afraid of the terrors of the night, nor the arrow that flies in the day. Do not dread the disease that stalks in darkness, nor the disaster that strikes at midday. Though a thousand fall

---

[65] Isaiah 60:1-2, "Arise, shine; for your light has come, And the glory of the LORD has risen upon you. For behold, darkness will cover the earth And deep darkness the peoples; But the LORD will rise upon you And His glory will appear upon you" (NASB).

at your side, though ten thousand are dying around you, these evils will not touch you. (Psalm 91:1-7 NLT)

This, of course, does not mean that life will be perfect, as we are still *in* the world. Jesus Himself said, "In this world you will have trouble...,"[66] We will experience rejection, injustice, and persecution. The enemy will also resist us, cause us confusion, and try to put sickness and disease on us.

Romans 12:2 says, "Don't copy the behavior and customs of this world, but let God transform you into a new person by changing the way you think. Then you will learn to know God's will for you, which is good and pleasing and perfect" (NLT). Let's allow God to change our thinking from a worldly perspective and understanding to His perspective and understanding—in all things. For example, someone with type 2 diabetes may think, "I have type 2 diabetes because I didn't watch my diet." What they're really saying is, "I got what I deserved." But the Bible says, God's mercies are new every morning and what is mercy? Mercy is *not* getting what you deserve! Jesus died so God could show us mercy, grace, and favor! So, let's elevate our thinking and realize God is so good, He doesn't give us what we deserve. Let's allow ourselves to receive His extravagant mercy by coming out of agreement with our natural worldly understanding of why we might be sick. Let's not lean on our own understanding but allow God to give us His! (At the same time, let's also understand that we may need to make some lifestyle changes to come out of some sinful habits.)

The second tidbit of direction we get from Proverbs 3:5-8 that will bring health to our body and nourishment to our bones is, "do not be wise in your own eyes."

There was a guy in the Old Testament by the name of Job who struggled with being wise in his own eyes and suffered dearly for it. This may surprise you as it surprised me, but the New King James

---

[66] John 16:33, "I have told you these things, so that in me you may have peace. In this world you will have trouble. But take heart! I have overcome the world" (NIV).

Version says in Job 32:1, "So these three men ceased answering Job, because *he was righteous in his own eyes*" (emphasis added). The New Living Translation says, "Job's three friends refused to reply further to him because he kept insisting on his innocence" (Job 32:1). But Job was not innocent! In fact, Job 34:7-9 says, "Tell me, has there ever been a man like Job, with his thirst for irreverent talk? He chooses evil people as companions. He spends his time with wicked men. He has even said, 'Why waste time trying to please God'" (NLT)? However, we can't have this discussion without also addressing Job 1:1, can we? I know there is someone out there quoting it verbatim, right now.

Job 1:1 says, "There once was a man named Job who lived in the land of Uz. He was blameless—a man of complete integrity. He feared God and stayed away from evil" (NLT). This *appears* to be a contradiction to Job 34:7-9, but let me ask you this, "Have you ever been in a conversation with someone who was dead wrong, but vehemently insisted they were right and despite what you said, you couldn't convince them otherwise?" Yes? And I would bet that since you couldn't convince them, the only option was to agree that they were right with a condition for them to prove themselves. Some people simply can't be convinced of their fault. The only way to get through to them is to allow Satan to sift them. This is how God had to deal with Job. God in effect said, "Okay Job. Yup, you're sinless. You're innocent. But now let's prove it." Job 1:1 narrates how Job was seen in the world and how Job saw himself, but not what was actually true of his heart. God saw deeper, so He put Job to the test, and exposed what was *really* there.

I say all this about Job to simply say, "Don't be like Job!" Don't be wise in your own eyes. Don't be puffed up in pride as "pride goes before destruction, and haughtiness before a fall" (Proverbs 16:18 NLT).

In summary, be humble. Seek God's understanding and don't nullify the miracle of mercy and healing by thinking you know better than God. Let go of all your reasonings, arguments,[67] and understandings that are worldly, rational, intellectual, logical, and carnal. *Sometimes, we know too much, and our knowledge gets in the way of our miracle.* Command your carnal mind to submit to the Lord and the ways of the Kingdom of God.

Allow me to suggest praying something like this:

"Father God, thank You that I am Your son/daughter. I repent for leaning on my own understanding, Lord, and I repent for regarding my understanding superior to Yours. I also repent, God, for pride and a haughty spirit. Please forgive me. Thank You that when I confess my sin to You, You are faithful to forgive and cleanse me from all unrighteousness. Thank You that my citizenship is first and foremost in Heaven and I can enjoy the benefits of that citizenship right here, right now. I surrender to You, God, every thought and argument in my carnal mind that explains my illness and convinces me that this is "normal" and "acceptable." I renounce the lie that I am ill because... (I am old, I ate too much, I didn't exercise, I was irresponsible/foolish etc.) and I choose to forgive myself for the foolish things I have done, for not using wisdom, not living holy, and for any and all mistakes, bad decisions, and misguided steps. Right now, God, I receive Your mercy and the benefits of heaven, like undeserved favor, forgiveness, and redemption by the blood of Jesus, which allow me to bypass the negative outcomes of the world and the negative consequences of sin and bad decisions in my life. I thank You, Lord, that Your rescue plan for my life is complete and a done deal and I can expect it to manifest now, this side of eternity. I renounce pride and I surrender my understanding to You, God. I surrender my intellect, my

---

[67] 2 Corinthians 10:5, "We are destroying arguments and all arrogance raised against the knowledge of God, and we are taking every thought captive to the obedience of Christ," (NASB).

logic, and all my reasonings to You, God, and I receive my healing from You, right now, in Jesus' name. I take, with gratitude, my healing from Your banqueting table, right now! In Jesus' name, amen."

We can escape the consequences of our dumb decisions and unwise actions! Consider the parable of the *Prodigal Son* beginning at Luke 15:11. The prodigal son made some of the dumbest decisions ever and when he came back home to his father, there were no more consequences for him to bear. (Yes, he did suffer consequences, like eating with the pigs, but only until he decided to return to his father.) The prodigal was received back into his father's house with all the benefits of sonship. There was no probation period. Nothing was withheld from him. There was not even any disciplinary action when he returned. . . only a celebration of epic proportions. This parable was told to illustrate to us, those in the Kingdom of God, that even after we mess up, the Father receives us back to His home and into His arms, with mercy, grace, full restoration, and extravagant blessing, when we repent. Turn back to God and receive it today!

INIQUITY

Iniquity. This word tends to be misunderstood. Many think it's just another word for sin, but it's not. Sin is something we do, think, say, or feel that is NOT aligned with righteousness and faith.[68] Iniquity is a pattern or bent of *character* that is passed down through the generations in your bloodline that threatens to cause or causes you to sin in a certain way. From Dr. Carr's book, *Breaking Patterns of Perversity*, he says iniquity can be defined as, "A bent, twisting, perversity, distortion of character, or pattern of ungodly behavior/perversity passing down ancestral lines."[69] He later goes on to say, "The English word "iniquity" comes from the Hebrew word "avon." Iniquity describes character flaws behind the action of sin."[70] Iniquity is a propensity to sin a certain way or a weakness. We may not have actively sinned according to that iniquity, but when considering Isaiah 64: 6-7, the distortion of character separates us from God nonetheless:

> But we are all like an unclean thing, And all our righteousnesses are like filthy rags; We all fade as a leaf, And our INIQUITIES, like the wind, Have taken us away. And there is no one who calls on Your name, Who stirs himself up to take hold of You; For You have hidden Your face from us, And have consumed us because of our iniquities. (NKJV, emphasis added)

Why is it important to consider iniquity when contending for healing? Because iniquity that has not been confessed and cleansed by the blood of Jesus, blocks us from receiving

---

[68] "But he who doubts is condemned if he eats, because he does not eat from faith; for whatever is not from faith is sin" (Romans 14:23 NKJV).

[69] Dr. Douglas E. Carr, *Patterns of Perversity: Freedom from Iniquity* (Sturgis: Doug Carr Freedom Ministry, 2022), xi. Print.

[70] Carr, *Patterns of Perversity*, 18. Print.

resurrection life and is passed down through the generations—three to four generations deep. Here are two passages from the Bible supporting this truth:

> You shall not make for yourself a carved image—any likeness of anything that is in heaven above, or that is in the earth beneath, or that is in the water under the earth; you shall not bow down to them nor serve them. For I, the LORD your God, am a jealous God, visiting the iniquity of the fathers upon the children to the third and fourth generations of those who hate Me, but showing mercy to thousands, to those who love Me and keep My commandments. (Exodus 20:4-6 NKJV)

> The LORD is longsuffering and abundant in mercy, forgiving iniquity and transgression; but He by no means clears the guilty, visiting the iniquity of the fathers on the children to the third and fourth generation. (Numbers 14:18 NKJV)

It is important to actively confess and repent for iniquity. The Israelites in Nehemiah 9 are an example to us:

> Now on the twenty-fourth day of this month the children of Israel were assembled with fasting, in sackcloth, and with dust on their heads. Then those of Israelite lineage separated themselves from all foreigners; and they stood and confessed their sins and the INIQUITIES OF THEIR FATHERS. (Nehemiah 9:1-2 NKJV, emphasis added)

Just in case there are a few well-meaning readers who are thinking, *we're under grace now so it's not necessary*, consider the following: Jesus died for the sins of every person in the whole world, so does that mean that every single person in the world is just *automatically* saved, without repentance, without acknowledging their sin or their need for salvation? Without submission to God? Without *knowing* Jesus? No, it doesn't. Each person must accept the gift of salvation through repentance (which includes confession) and believing that Jesus died and rose again—by being born of the Spirit and by confessing with their mouth, "Jesus is Lord." Each person is required to enter salvation by taking these steps. It is this submission to God that *activates* the miracle of re-birth. Just as we submit to the principle of repenting for our own sin, so we also must submit to the principle of repenting for iniquity, to be free.

Do you remember we talked about the first Passover earlier? The Israelites were told to slaughter a spotless lamb and then to apply the blood of that lamb to their door frame, the gateway to their home, so that the spirit of death would pass them over. It wasn't enough that the blood was shed. It wasn't enough that the blood sat in a bucket at their door. No, they had to dip the hyssop branch into the blood and smear that blood over their door frame, at the top and on both sides.

Jesus' blood was shed for us. But, in the same way, it isn't enough that it was just shed. It isn't enough that His blood spilt and dripped down His body. To activate its power in OUR lives, Jesus' blood also needs to be applied by faith to our doorframes symbolically, to our spiritual and inner gateways, so the spirit of death passes over us too (our inner "gateways" are the places of entrance into our body and soul). Confessing our sins and the iniquity of our fathers and mothers and speaking the blood of Jesus over our spirit, soul and body is just like taking that hyssop branch and smearing the blood where we need it most.

To understand iniquity better, let's have a look at an example in the lineage of Abraham. In Genesis 20:2 we see Abraham being fearful, deceitful, disrespectful, and selfish when he lies to King Abimelech about who Sarah is, in an effort to protect himself. (He told the king that Sarah was his sister because he was afraid the king would kill him to take Sarah as his wife.) As a result, King Abimelech believed it lawful to take Sarah as his concubine and did so. Not only did this cause great grief and embarrassment for Sarah, but it also almost cost King Abimelech his life and the lives of his whole household. Abraham was caught in his lie as God revealed the truth to

Abimelech in a dream. King Abimelech confronted Abraham and returned Sarah to him. Later, in Genesis 26, Isaac, Abraham's son does *exactly* the same thing to his wife, Rebekah. Then in the next generation, deception, lies, disrespect, and selfishness continue as Jacob steals Esau's blessing (Genesis 27). The propensity to deceive to get what one wants or because of fear, continues down the line, entangling them all in sin.

I'll never forget the day I lay face down, on the carpet in my living room, repeating the phrase, "I submit to You, God." I had found myself parenting badly and I *saw* my father in my actions. When I was young, he had trouble controlling his temper and now, so was I. I didn't like what I felt. And I didn't like how I was acting. I had already repented for acting out in anger, but I didn't seem to be able to stop. I felt caught in a vicious pattern, unable to break free. I had had enough, so I passionately pursued God, confessing the iniquity in my family line including fits of rage, poor anger management, yelling, violence, and even murder, and ended up lying prostrate on the floor. As I confronted the demons that wanted to hold me, the Holy Spirit put me on my face in submission to Him, to protect me and set me free. He knows what He's doing! Thank God. It was a real-life James 4:7 moment, "Therefore submit to God. Resist the devil and he will flee from you." Sometimes, submitting to God by specifically confessing iniquity is the key to deliverance and sometimes you've got to get on your face—quite literally.

Another moment came, as I homeschooled our daughter, for the first time, when she was only 6. This time however, I reminded myself of my mother. I had lost patience with Jessica as I tried to explain the lesson and again, I had come to a place of deep conviction by the Holy Spirit. I was no longer able or wanted to make excuses for myself, so I prayed. As I prayed, asking the Lord to help me have more patience, a very sinister voice in my head told me, "But you don't know how to do anything else!" I knew that thought was not from God nor from myself. No, I knew this was directly from the devil and I wasn't going to agree with his lies. I called out the "father of lies," told him to shut his mouth, and confessed the truth the Holy Spirit showed me. I confessed that God, my Father, was shifting everything and taking me on a wonderful journey where He would teach me everything I needed to know about being a good, patient mother and teacher. I saw with eyes of faith my heavenly Father filling my need for a righteous role model in the parenting department. Again, I had to confess the iniquity in my bloodline and forgive my mother to be released from the iniquitous pattern of yelling and speaking harsh words out of frustration. Praise God for His mercy and grace that sets us free from every bondage.

· · · · · · · · · · ● · · · · · · · · · · ·

Iniquity is directly related to many diseases. You know how when you enrol as a patient with a new doctor, you are required to complete a questionnaire about your family's medical history? This is because some diseases run in families. They are genetic and carried along through the DNA. These diseases are held in place by iniquitous patterns that have not been dealt with through the following steps:

- confession
- repentance
- renouncing
- asking for forgiveness and accepting forgiveness
- applying the blood of Jesus
- adjusting behaviors

Notice the last step—adjusting behaviors. And remember, we are not talking about sin here; we are talking about iniquity. There are some iniquitous patterns that are *reinforced* through our behavior. This means, we could pray and repent for the iniquity in our family but then continue to give it legal right to continue through what we do. For example, deep rooted fear in the bloodline can influence behavior. So, ask the Holy Spirit to show you anything you are doing that is rooted in, or *began* in fear. This is not necessarily your fear but fear from previous generations so don't just use your carnal mind to decide what's from fear and what's not. Ask the Holy Spirit! Keep in mind, your answer from the Holy Spirit may not come right away but may come as you are going about your day, doing the things you normally do. He may just quietly whisper to you, "This is fear."

To illustrate, consider a woman who doesn't wear any makeup. There's nothing wrong with not wearing makeup—unless the reason why is linked to fear or some other lie regarding her identity. Perhaps a young woman from a *previous* generation was severely chastised and called a "whore" by her father when she tried makeup for the first time and as a result, never wore makeup again because of the hurt in her heart and the fear of not being loved by her father. This woman then raised her daughter not to wear makeup as well, teaching her skewed beliefs and attaching shame to the use of makeup. This then was passed on through the generations, keeping the pattern of emotional abuse, shame, and self-loathing alive and well. A woman who does not wear makeup might do well to ask the Holy Spirit, "Why don't I wear makeup? What is at the root of that decision in my life?" You might think, *I don't like makeup.* But why? Is it fear? Is it shame? Is it because you believe you won't be loved or accepted if you do? Is it because you're afraid of rejection or do you think that women who wear makeup look cheap or sleezy? Perhaps there's nothing more to it but be brave and ask the tough questions of yourself. Allow the Holy Spirit to show you anything that may be lying beyond the surface.

Another example is connected to superstition. There could be behaviors, habits, items, or traditions that have been modeled to you and passed on that are rooted in suspicion or superstition. I still remember as a youngster having a rabbit's foot key chain for luck, walking along the sidewalk being careful not to step on the cracks saying, "Step on a crack, break your mother's back," and seeing

POSITION YOURSELF FOR HEALING BY BARBARA DE SIMON

adults throw salt over their shoulder at the dinner table. Wanting or needing *good luck* is a sin as it doesn't reflect faith in God. Make sure to get rid of any item said to be a *good luck* charm, whether it was passed on through the generations or not.

I see in my mind's eye someone turning the deadbolt on their front door twice in a row, just to make sure it's locked properly. I don't understand why someone would do that, but I'm seeing it so it must be important to mention. I believe this kind of behavior could be considered *obsessive compulsive disorder* which of course includes other behaviors too, like washing hands compulsively because of the fear of germs, hoarding because of a fear of not having what is needed later or shame about being wasteful, compulsively cleaning household surfaces, and others. These behaviors will keep the iniquity of fear rooted in your blood despite what you pray.

What about the family tradition of opening Christmas presents on Christmas Eve? Why do some families do that? Is it just for fun? Or was there another reason for which that tradition was started in the first place? I remember hearing of a family whose ancestors had their home broken into overnight on Christmas Eve and all their gifts stolen. They woke up on Christmas morning to devastation. From that time on, they opened their gifts Christmas Eve instead of Christmas morning and that tradition was continued through the generations. In summary, the family *began* opening their presents on Christmas Eve because they were fearful of their gifts being stolen again and continuing in that behavior kept the entire family partnering with fear and trauma.

What about the tradition of eating fish every Friday as some Catholics do? Why do that? What happens if you don't? Is it motivated by fear? Is it biblical and rooted in faith? These are important questions for us as we untangle ourselves from ungodly generational behaviors, traditions, and iniquity.

· · · · · · · · · ●· · · · · · · · · ·

Iniquity has a very broad scope. It could be any bent, perversion or weakness of character that causes or attracts sinful behavior. Some common weaknesses resulting in negative patterns seen in families are fear, shame, lust, sexual perversion, abuse, rage, pride, addiction, greed, deceit, frustration, rejection, victimization, and idolatry.

Patterns in most of these areas are easy to detect. A pattern of lust and sexual perversion will manifest in obvious ways like addiction to pornography and/or sex, fornication, adultery, habitual masturbation, homosexuality, voyeurism, sexual abuse, molestation, rape, sodomy, sadomasochism, bestiality, pedophilia, and any other sexually deviant behavior. Also keep in mind that lust is not just about sex. Sometimes people lust after power, influence, money, and material things.

Rage obviously manifests as yelling, throwing things perhaps and the like. Addiction can manifest in many ways as well. Addiction to pornography/sex was already mentioned but people can be addicted to *many* things including food, sugar, caffeine, prescription drugs, legal and illegal drugs, smoking, alcohol, shopping, attention, social media, games etc.

Pride can manifest as arrogance, arguments, condescension, not accepting advice or help, unwilling to submit, unwilling to be taught or to be wrong, unwilling to see one's own faults, boasting, bragging, anger, frustration, competitiveness, contentiousness, criticism, control, deception (hiding the truth), egocentrism, narcissism, entitlement, greed, and others.[71] Greed, deceit and frustration can easily be seen in people's behaviors when they lie, tell half-truths, keep secrets, steal, hoard, withhold from others, pinch pennies, freeload off of others, get angry, yell, throw things and perhaps verbally abuse others. Victimization and rejection

---

[71] Douglas Carr, *Free Indeed from Root Spirits* (Sturgis: Doug Carr Freedom Ministry, 2014), 142-143. Print.

perhaps are not so easy to identify, so let me explain these a bit further.

Victimization

Victimization manifests in our lives when we are victimized *repeatedly*. Sometimes we accept it as normal, and at times don't even realize we're being victimized. It operates in those who have been abused, by convincing them of lies associated with the original abuse. These lies could include, *it's my fault, I deserved it, I'm not worth anything more, I'm unlovable*, or *I'm trash and will always be abused*. It can be identified when a PATTERN of abuse arises in one's life. For example, a child is abused, perhaps repeatedly, and when they grow up, they are abused by boyfriends/girlfriends, then they marry someone who is covertly abusive, they are treated badly by friends and bosses, and they may even abuse themselves at times with negative self-talk or worse. A *spirit* of victimization acts like a magnet, attracting abusers to further victimize people and LABELS a person as a victim. Ever felt like you had a "kick me" sign on your back,[72] or an "open for abuse" sign? Well, it's not a sign, but a spirit that has labeled you as a victim.

A spirit of victimization could be attached to us if we are experiencing repeated abuse or victimization. Mentally we can be convinced that we are above it, but if the manifestation of it is still happening, our spiritual health is not lined up to what we believe in our head. The good news is deliverance is available to every child of God, and it will give us a new level of freedom.

To be free from victimization, if as an adult, we've been abused and have not recognized it as such, we first need to call it what it is and forgive our perpetrators. We then need to ask ourselves where it first began. Where, when and under what circumstances did we first accept abuse as normal?

---

[72] Carr, *Patterns of Perversity*, 43. Print.

A child who has been raised in abuse ends up confused about what love should look like and can very often not even identify abuse in their life as an adult. Abuse feels like "home" to them, so that's what they gravitate toward. The good news is, God understands and He is full of healing power and compassion. As adults, let's recognize our broken perceptions and pour our heart out to God in prayer.

Ask the Holy Spirit to remind you when the very FIRST instance of abuse occurred in your life, what happened and who was involved. Also ask the Holy Spirit what lies you have believed about the abuse. Make notes for reference in prayer. Then, focussing on the event the Holy Spirit revealed, tell Him about it, what happened, what it did to your heart and how it made you feel. This is a necessary step in acknowledging the event and releasing it all to Jesus, including every hurt emotion and feeling. Ask the Holy Spirit to heal you and show you where He was in the room at the time of the abuse. According to the Word, the presence of God is with us ALL the time. He never leaves us nor forsakes us, so He was there! You just weren't aware of it at the time. Ask the Holy Spirit to make you aware of His presence in that event, now.

You may ask, "Well if He was there, why didn't He stop it?" Beloved, sometimes people will ignore God and follow the evil inclinations of their heart instead. God is sovereign but He sovereignly chose to limit Himself when He gave us free will. We all have the capacity to make a decision apart from God and His influence. Believe and understand that God did not endorse or author your abuser's actions.

Next, *forgive the abuser*. I know this is difficult. Remember though, forgiving your abuser is not letting him/her off the hook; it is getting the devil's hook out of you. Your abuser is still responsible and accountable to God for what he/she has done.

Next, *renounce* the lies, if any, that you believed about the abuse (example: It was your fault, you asked for it, it was normal, you had to allow someone to abuse you to keep them happy or to be loved etc.), *renounce* the spirit of abuse and the spirit of victimization, *bind them* in Jesus' name, and forcefully command the spirits to get out.

Lastly, ask Father God to send the Holy Spirit to fill you afresh and as a follow through, ask God to help you identify any abuse that is currently happening in your life. If there is anything, you will need to confront it, call it out and refuse to continue to allow it or co-operate with it anymore. This may require you to make a plan first though! Don't put yourself in a vulnerable situation where you don't have a roof over your head. Use wisdom and ask God to show you your next steps.

Rejection

Rejection operates similarly. A hurtful rejection happens, and the one being rejected believes lies about it and themselves that sound like, *I deserved it; it's my fault; I'm ugly; I'm unlovable; I'm unlikeable; I'm a reject; I never fit in; something's wrong with me,* etc. A pattern of rejection then shows up in the person's life as the demon of rejection labels them "a reject" attracting even more rejection. The demon of rejection will even cause us to reject others as a self-preservation coping mechanism. We will reject others before they have a chance to reject us.

The process to be free is the same. Ask the Holy Spirit to show you where the *pattern* of rejection began and pray it through. Forgive all those who have rejected you. Renounce rejection and renounce all the lies connected to it. Cast that demon out and be filled with the Holy Spirit.

It is imperative that we understand and believe the truth about ourselves. We are not rejects and we are not rejected! God the Father sent His One and Only Son to die for us, just so we could be back in relationship with Him—so we could be adopted as His. We are the beloved of God! We are CHOSEN, pre-destined, and highly favored in His sight and that is ALL that matters. If another person has not valued us, it is not because there is anything wrong with us but because they did not see our worth. It's also possible that their own internal wounds caused them to want to tear us down. If we get hung up on people rejecting us, then we are putting a greater value on the opinions of people than on the opinion of God. Don't do that! It's a trap. It will get us entangled with idolatry which will just be another thing that will make us sick.

Idolatry

As we've discussed already, idolatry is the worship of other gods, looking to other (false) deities for healing or spiritual power or it can simply be placing a higher value on something else above God.

It can manifest in many ways. On the more obvious side of things, our ancestors may have done the following:

- looked to the stars for guidance (astrology).
- worshipped nature.
- looked to crystals for healing.
- participated in rituals or witchcraft.
- been superstitious.
- believed in horoscopes.
- were psychic or went to psychics.
- read Tarot cards.
- believed in the power of other gods (examples might be, the goddess of fertility (isis), the god of weather (zeus) or the goddess of volcanos, fire and lightening (Hawaiian goddess of pele)).
- used dreamcatchers or other things to try and ward off evil spirits.
- made sacrifices to other gods.

On a tamer note, idolatry can be loving or valuing others or things more than God and pursuing those things more passionately than pursuing God. Some common things that people tend to hold too dear are money, power, career, sex, romantic love, opinions of people, acceptance by others, material possessions, spouses, children, and sometimes other family members. Take an inventory and ask the Holy Spirit to help you identify ways your ancestors may have been involved in idolatry.

Before praying to be free from iniquity, spend time in praise and worship. Begin by praying in tongues, then ask the Holy Spirit to help you take a *complete* inventory of ALL iniquity your ancestors and family have been entangled with. Think back about your parents, siblings, and grandparents. Make a list of things you think may apply to your family. Look for patterns in multiple people and generations. Ask the Holy Spirit to help you. Then begin praying something like this:

> "Lord, I thank You for Who You are. I honor You and glorify Your name. You are the Alpha and Omega. You are the beginning and the end. You are the everlasting God. The One Who never slumbers nor sleeps and the One Who sees me and loves me just the way I am.
>
> Lord, I confess to You that my family has not obeyed Your commands; we have not kept Your laws nor honoured You with our lives. *As a family*, we have been involved in things that have broken Your heart. We have worshipped other gods—worldly things, worldly success, (name other things that your ancestors may have valued higher than God, like money, status, power, false religion, creation). I confess to You, on behalf of my family, the iniquity of (name all iniquity the Holy Spirit revealed to you earlier such as anger, violence, abuse, murder, hatred, bitterness, unforgiveness, lying, cheating, adultery, fornication, perversion, lust, whoredom, gluttony, rejection, abandonment, covenant breaking (divorce), complacency, abdication of responsibility/authority/leadership, and so on) and I repent. Lord God, I am sorry, and I ask for Your forgiveness. God, I thank You that You are a merciful God and a God Who is patient and longsuffering. I turn from the iniquity of my ancestors now and I receive Your forgiveness in my life and the lives of my family and all future generations. I now

choose to forgive my ancestors for their sin, iniquity, and weaknesses and for the negative effects that have come upon my life and the lives of my children. In the name of Jesus, because we are forgiven, I renounce and cut off from my life and the lives of my children, even since the womb, the sins and iniquity of my ancestors including... (name as many as you can). I renounce and cut off from my life and my children's lives since the womb, every consequence of these sins and iniquity and every demonic spirit empowered by them, and every curse associated with them. I bind every hereditary, familiar, and generational demon of (name them individually if you can) in my bloodline, and I command each and every one to leave me and my bloodline now, in Jesus' Mighty Name. I declare that every curse is broken by the sacrifice and blood of Jesus and that my bloodline is now cleansed and set free from every evil intent and assignment. Thank You, Jesus that You became a curse for us and have nullified every curse in our lives. We receive Your family, Lord, as our new family heritage and bloodline and declare that Your blood flows through our veins. Holy Spirit, come and fill us afresh and fill us completely. Don't leave any spot untouched by Your presence. I welcome You, Holy Spirit, and give You control. In Jesus' Name. Amen.

Finish with praise and worship and thank Him for setting you free. "Raise a Hallelujah" and "Rattle" are awesome songs that will lead you into victory, if you will declare it out of your own mouth. Allow yourself to come out of complacency and come into overcoming, victorious faith.

WORDS AND POWER

There are many scriptures that talk about the power of the tongue and words. Proverbs 18:21 says, "The tongue can bring death or life; those who love to talk will reap the consequences" (NLT). Proverbs 13:3 says, "Those who control their tongue will have a long life; opening your mouth can ruin everything" (NLT). Proverbs 15:4 says, "Gentle words are a tree of life; a deceitful tongue crushes the spirit" (NLT). Psalm 34:12-13, "Does anyone want to live a life that is long and prosperous? Then keep your tongue from speaking evil and your lips from telling lies (NLT)! And then we have James 3 which teaches us that the tongue can do incredible damage, completely direct our lives like a rudder on a ship and even set a whole forest ablaze with one little word. Yikes! We best be careful how we speak!

King David confirms in the following scriptures that the tongue is very often used by evil to cause much damage:

> Hide me from the plots of this evil mob, from this gang of wrongdoers. They sharpen their tongues like swords and aim their bitter words like arrows. (Psalm 64:2-3 NLT)

> O Lord, rescue me from evil people. Protect me from those who are violent, those who plot evil in their hearts and stir up trouble all day long. Their tongues sting like a snake; the venom of a viper drips from their lips. (Psalm 140:1-3 NLT)

Have you ever been hurt by words? That old childish saying, "Sticks and stones may break my bones, but words will never hurt me," is one big fat lie. Words can hurt *more* than breaking bones and the damage can last a lifetime. Words have power!

The New King James Version of Proverbs 18:21 says, "Death and life are in the *power* of the tongue," (emphasis added). Very often words and phrases spoken to us, over us or about us, from long ago still haunt us today. But God can set us free from those words and set our life back on track according to His will!

There was a time when I was young. I had been disobedient somehow, or too much to handle, so my mother sent me to my room. Unbeknownst to her, I had snuck down the hallway and planted myself just outside the kitchen as she spoke to my grandmother on the telephone. She complained to her mom about her life and said words about me she shouldn't have. Those words stuck with me deep on the inside, but I blocked the memory from my mind. It wasn't until I had given birth to Jessica, my first-born, that the memory began to stir and press for attention.

I began to feel emotionally upset and triggered but I wasn't sure about what or why, so I contacted a good friend who was a prayer counsellor. I asked her to meet with me for ministry and she agreed. We met and as soon as we sat down to pray, the memory surfaced. I shared it with my friend, and she began to minister healing prayer. Within minutes, the grace, power, and compassion of God washed over me and a vision from the Holy Spirit began playing on the screen of my imagination.

> I was a little girl amidst a crowd of other children, waiting for the arrival of a special guest who was coming to greet us and bless us. There was a barricade that kept us back, but there wasn't enough room for everyone along the front where we were sure to be greeted.

> It was crowded—six, seven children deep, all pushing and vying for a position where they could be greeted and received. Not surprisingly, I was at the back, not able to make my way forward, feeling rejected and unseen. We all waited as the excitement grew and voices got louder. *He won't greet me; He probably won't even notice me*, I thought, as I allowed the others to push and jostle me back.

> Suddenly. There He was! He had arrived. He began coming down the line greeting and smiling at the children in the

front. I watched Him, longing to be included. Again, *He won't greet me*, I thought, *I'll just be left out again*, but suddenly, everything changed.

In the blink of an eye, supernaturally, my position changed, and I found myself propelled right to the front—right before our guest, Jesus. Clothed in bright white, He took my hands in His and fixed His eyes on mine. I became lost in His gaze and everyone else disappeared. His fiery blue eyes pierced right into mine—right into my soul, cutting away lies and eradicating everything warring against the truth.

"Barbara, I love you," He said. Time slowed and His Words hung in the air with fresh breath and new life. Once again, slower this time, "B-a-r-b-a-r-a, I. love. you." A few moments passed as I tried to take it all in; His eyes locked on mine, communicating past human limitations. As love overtook me, eyes wet with salty tears, I thought astonished, *He said my name! He just said my name. How does He know my name? I never told Him my name.*

Over the next few moments, the truth of my value in His eyes, enlightened my heart. He greeted me. He knows me. He sees me. He loves me. I am His. It was all I needed. One encounter with Jesus and the Word transformed me from the inside out. Forgiveness flowed and healing came.

Words. They can hurt or they can heal. They can build up or they can tear down. But Words spoken by God Himself right into our heart, are in a league all their own; they are sure to mend the most broken places and heal the worst pain.

If you have been hurt by words spoken by others, I would encourage you to forgive that person and pray something like this:

"Lord, thank You for Who You are. Thank You that You are for me and not against me. Thank You that You see all and hear all and You redeem all. Lord, there have been words that have been spoken to me and over me that have literally haunted my mind and life. You know. You saw it when it happened, but I confess it to You now. [Name of person] told me that, [repeat what the person said], and I believed them. Their words pierced my heart, God, and I need Your healing. I renounce the words, [repeat what the person said], and I come out of agreement with them now. I know they were not of You, God, so I repent for believing them and receiving them, and in the authority of Jesus, I break their power over me, now. I say, those words are now powerless, and I command them to fall to the ground, in Jesus' name. Forgive me, God, for believing lies. Thank You, Lord. I now choose to forgive [say the person's name] for speaking lies to me and over me and making me feel [confess how those words made you feel]. I choose to release her/him into Your hands as their judge, God, and I ask You, Lord, not to hold it against them. Have mercy on their soul. Thank You, God, for Your faithfulness to me and them. In Jesus' mighty name, amen."

Have you ever spoken words about yourself that tear you down — perhaps words that sound like, "I can't believe I did that. I'm so stupid," or "I'm such a loser. I can't ever seem to get ahead." If you find yourself saying things like this, renounce them as soon as you realize what you've done. Say, "I renounce that in Jesus' name. And I repent for tearing myself down with my words." We have enough enemies to contend with, without having to contend with ourselves!

There are two further scenarios I'd like to address when it comes to words that hurt. One scenario happens when a prophetic person gives us a "word" they think is prophetic, but it's a negative word and the other is when we respond to negative circumstances by wanting to control and we end up saying things like, "I'm *never* going to do that," or "be that" or "I'm always going to..." This last scenario leads us into making vows to ourselves, which leads us into bondage.

Negative Prophetic Words

Back in chapter 4, we talked about how God created everything through words. God said, "Let there be light'; and there was light" (Genesis 1:3). All He did was say it and it was. God's Word is powerful! His Words create and will always accomplish what they were sent for. Modern-day Prophets or people operating in the prophetic gifting also may utter powerful words that are legitimately from God's heart and mind, blessing us greatly. However, occasionally a prophetic person may miss it and speak something prophetically of a negative nature that ends up empowering negative outcomes. It's very unfortunate, but it does happen. To guard against being blindsided or becoming sick because of it, let's talk about it.

All words spoken over us for personal prophesy are supposed to be for the purpose of encouragement, edification, and comfort.[73] The word should therefore be of a positive nature and should never include the foretelling of negative things like accidents, calamity, misfortune, or disasters. A prophetic person is to seek the Lord for His will and heart for the person they are speaking with. In light of this, everything they perceive should come from a place of peace, love, and healing.

If a prophetic person perceives that there is a challenging circumstance coming our way or discerns the enemy is trying to mess with us somehow, they should seek the Lord for His *redemptive* word that cancels the enemy's plans and deliver *God's* Word to us and only that word. The last thing we need is for a prophetic person to prophesy the devil's plans into existence.

If we are given a prophetic word that foretells an accident, illness, or bad event, don't receive it, no matter who the person is. Even if that person is seen as reputable and even if they follow it up with something positive, don't receive it. If it happens in a corporate

---

[73] "But the one who prophesies speaks to people for their strengthening, encouraging and comfort" (1 Corinthians 14:3 NIV).

setting, don't make a scene, and embarrass them, simply renounce, and cancel their words on your own in prayer later. Simply say, "I renounce the lie that... [repeat the negative word]" An example may be if someone prophesies that you're about to go bankrupt, but God will restore you later. In this case, I would pray, "I renounce the lie that I'm about to go bankrupt." You could also pray, "I know Lord that it is not Your will for me to go bankrupt nor to be stolen from; I know that Your mercies are new every morning and it is Your heart for me to prosper in all things. If there is anything I am doing that would give the enemy a legal right to cause me to go bankrupt, show me God and I will repent immediately." *In a private setting*, if someone says to you, "You're about to go bankrupt, but God will restore you after," you could say, "I'm sorry, I don't receive that. I don't believe it is God's plan or will for me to go bankrupt; based on Jeremiah 29:11, His plans for me are good and for my benefit and prosperity."

Always test the word that you are given from a person who claims to speak anointed words from God. Ask yourself, "Does it line up with God's Word? Does it reflect God's heart and character?" If it doesn't, renounce it, and always forgive the person who spoke the misguided word(s). No one is perfect and growing in prophecy is a journey that can begin with more blunders than we want. So, let's be gracious.

Also, realize that a personal prophetic word can be a *mixture* of true prophetic words and the soul of the person speaking and/or their own flawed interpretation. For example, someone may speak a true word from the Lord but interpret it wrong. They may assume it means something literal when it doesn't.

I once had a friend tell me prophetically that I would have a daughter and name her Sarah. I happened to be pregnant at the time. My friend had assumed this was a literal word, but when I lost the baby, I was carrying, she was disillusioned with the prophetic and was, unfortunately, chastised by church leadership because they didn't understand it either. I knew she was not speaking about the baby I was pregnant with because Sarah was not the name we had already chosen. I later understood *that* prophetic word to be speaking about ministry, and *not* a literal child at all. It was an accurate word from the Lord, but it was interpreted wrong. I am a prophetic person, so I understand the learning curve it entails. We all need so much grace, don't we?

Personal Vows and Promises to Self

Sometimes when we go through abuse, trauma, or injustice when we are young, we make vows (spoken or inner) to ourselves to try and control our lives and avoid pain. A vow is simply a promise made to oneself with deep conviction to "never" or "always" do or be something and may involve a bitter judgement against another person who has caused us pain. It is an attempt to protect ourselves from being hurt, either because we've been hurt already, or we've witnessed others being hurt.

When my husband and I were trying to start a family and couldn't, I realized that I had made three vows regarding having children and they were holding me hostage. Firstly, because of trauma in childhood, including watching my own mother go through two miscarriages, being told very graphic information I didn't need to hear, and accumulating ridiculous amounts of fear around doctors and hospitals, I made a vow when I was an adolescent to *never* have children. Secondly, shortly after moving into our first home after getting married, I didn't like the neighborhood we lived in, so I made a vow not to have children while living there. I did not want to raise my children in that neighborhood. Thirdly, I made a vow not to have children while driving the car we drove as it was very unreliable; it had left us stranded on the highway a few times and I certainly didn't want to have a baby on board in that situation. I was not successful at conceiving and birthing our first-born until all three of these vows were either met or broken in prayer.

I became pregnant for the first time just *one* month after renouncing my vow never to have kids. Unfortunately, I miscarried but became pregnant again with our first-born, Jessica, *four* months after moving into a new house and *one* month after buying a *new-to-us* car. All three vows were sin because they were all an attempt to control, but in addition, the first vow was made because of fear, the second was made because of judgements against our neighbors and the third was made because I knew it wasn't wisdom to drive an unreliable car with an infant. Instead of making that third vow, we should have just listened to wisdom and bought the newer car when we needed it!

Once we make commitments to ourselves, we step out of God's plan and into our own. We decide God is not trustworthy and we take things into our own hands. When we do this, we lock the Holy Spirit out of those aspects of our lives and because of our obstinate independence, end up giving the devil an opportunity instead. Unfortunately, the devil is not going to waste an opportunity.

In my situation, the devil was preventing me from conceiving, and he also caused me to miscarry, but the devil can also cause sickness because of vows. I would encourage you to ask the Holy Spirit to remind you of any time you may have stubbornly and emphatically said, "I'm never going to [blankety blank]!"

Were you abused in any way as a child? Abuse can cause us to decide to never be like our parents or to never treat our own children the same way. This sounds reasonable as it would be good not to parent the same way, however, every *vow to self* always comes from an independent spirit that does not trust God and this vow usually includes a *bitter judgement* against our parents. Now we have two sin issues operating in us giving the devil a foothold.

Scripture is clear that we are to honor our father and mother, even when they don't do the best job. Understanding that our parents did the best they could with what they had and knew, is key to having our heart in the right place. Exodus 20:12 says, "Honor your father and your mother, that your days may be long upon the land which the LORD your God is giving you" (NKJV).

In his book, *Shadow Boxing*, Dr. Henry Malone gives a real-life example of someone who was held hostage by her inner vow and bitter judgement against her father, as follows:

> "A grandmother once came to me seeking help. With tears in her eyes, she confessed that she was abused as a child and that she abused her three children. She was troubled by watching her adult children physically abuse her grandchildren. Often, she found herself abusing them, too. "I can't take it any longer. You must help me," she begged.
>
> I asked her to share about her childhood abuse. She was the third of six children. Whenever one child did something wrong, her father punished all six of them."[74]

Dr. Malone goes on to describe the horrific abuse the children suffered but I will spare you the details. He continues as follows:

> "When she was ten years old, she made an inner vow. She promised herself that "if I ever have any children, I will never do to them what Daddy does to us." While she didn't punish them in the exact same way, she beat her children with whatever was at hand... Quickly I saw that the vow she had made had imprisoned her and set her on a track that she could not get off simply because she had judged her father. When she repented of her inner vow and asked God to forgive her for judging her father, freedom came. We broke the vow and its results ceased."[75]

Recognizing our mistakes, repenting, asking the Lord for forgiveness, and breaking our vows will also lead us into freedom and we can do that now. Pray something like this:

> "Lord, I confess that I have tried to control my life, that I have attempted to protect myself in my own strength by making a vow and I have also looked down on and judged

[74] Dr. Henry Malone, *Shadow Boxing* (Lewisville: Vision Life Publications, 1999), 78. Print.
[75] Malone, *Shadow Boxing*, 78. Print.

(the person's name) for his/her behavior toward me. I choose to forgive (person's name) for hurting me and/or mistreating me. Father God, I now repent for being bitter, for making bitter judgements against (name the person), for wanting to be in control of everything, for pushing You out of my life, for not trusting You and not submitting to You and Your authority. I repent for thinking that I could do a better job than You of keeping myself safe. I repent for relying on my own strength instead of You. Lord, I ask for Your forgiveness. I now renounce the vow that I will (repeat the vow). I cancel those words in Jesus' name, and I now break my agreement with them. I command them to fall to the ground, and I decree them powerless over my life. Father, I bring every part of myself and my life back under Your authority, care, and protection and I choose to trust You with my life. I ask You again, God, to be Lord over EVERY part of my life. I choose to forgive myself for making this vow and I now break and cut off every curse that has come from my disobedience and self-protection. I break the power of every evil force that was released to carry out these curses over me, my family, my destiny, and my future. I thank You, Lord, that my family and I are covered in the blood of Your Son, Jesus, and that He has redeemed us from every curse by becoming a curse for us. Thank You, Lord, that when we confess our sin to You, You are faithful and just to forgive and cleanse us from all unrighteousness. I receive Your forgiveness and cleansing, and I give You praise. Fill me afresh, Lord, with Your Holy Spirit to overflowing and baptize me again in Your power. In Jesus' most powerful name, Amen."

BODY PERSPECTIVE

When I was young, I hated my hair, my teeth, overbite, and prominent chin; unfortunately, orthodontics was never an option for me, and I could never figure out how to manage my curly, frizzy hair (hair straighteners didn't exist when I was young). I now have long hair for the first time in my life and am grateful for its fullness in middle age, but my teeth, overbite, and chin remain the same. None the less, I have learned to see myself through my Father's eyes and love myself the way I am.

I am sure most every person reading this has had similar thoughts about themselves. Maybe it wasn't your hair, but your nose or perhaps your high forehead. We have all had critical things to think and say about our looks and body, haven't we? Unfortunately, this does not honor God nor His creation (us).

Additionally, as we are aging, our body may fail us somehow—perhaps getting weaker, softer, and not as flexible. Being diligent to continue to move and stretch becomes vital to everyday life. This can be annoying and difficult to cope with at times. Inside we're still young, but we can't act young anymore. We may not feel we have the energy to keep up with the grandkids, exercise, or maintain our homes and yards as we want. I used to do a "WOG" in the morning—an intermittent walk/jog route that I really enjoyed, but I haven't been able to do that for several years now as my joints cannot tolerate it.

Is there something your body refuses to do now that you're older? Perhaps you used to enjoy roller coasters, but now you can't handle them. Perhaps you used to enjoy water skiing but now it's a thing of the past. We're not sick really, just aged. How does this make you feel? Are you angry about it? Are you angry at your body for getting old? Releasing and repenting for these attitudes, plus gaining a new perspective of our body so we can celebrate and bless it, will help us come into healing.

God created us. He created our inner parts and our outer parts. Psalm 139 says He formed us in our mother's womb, knitting us together and there are so many amazing things about our body that only a Creator could think of and design. He is a master builder, intricately wiring us and connecting all our systems together.

Genesis chapter one gives us the account of God creating everything, including us. In an overview, Genesis, chapter one, tells us that God created man in His own image and likeness. Genesis chapter two gives us a closer look at the creation of man, specifically the creation of our body. I don't know about you, but because of my upbringing, I've always thought of the body as an inferior creation to the spirit, but this is wrong thinking. We need to elevate our thinking and understanding with regard to the human body; God did not create our body as they are now. God created our body before the fall, in Glory with perfect intentions.

Genesis 2:7 says, "Then the LORD God formed the man from the dust of the ground. He breathed the breath of life into the man's nostrils, and the man became a living person" (NLT). As Patricia King so perfectly points out in her "Women of Influence" online course, the *dust* of the earth which God used to form man, was not dust as we know it today. Dust is not a desirable thing now; we continually try to eliminate it from our homes but before the forbidden fruit was eaten, the earth was full of Glory. In fact, the *dust* of the earth was Glory particles infused with the very presence of God. The human body was a thing of beauty, shimmering and shining with Glory, perfectly made, and expertly functioning.

I mentioned before, but see fit to reiterate now, that we are primarily spiritual beings, we have a soul, and we live in a body of which all have been magnificently created by God. All three parts of who we are, are integrated and connected. No one part functions on its own. We were created in the image of God, Who also is three parts in one. Just like God, our three parts are in agreement, in unity and harmony, one with the other. Proverbs 17:22 says, "A cheerful heart is good medicine, but a crushed spirit dries up the bones" (NIV). The condition of the heart (inner man) and the spirit affect the body and the bones.

I used to think of the spirit as a light living in a person's belly, kind of like an orb. I'm not sure where that came from, but it's not an accurate picture. The truth is, the spirit gives life to the body. It's impossible for a human body to live without the spirit inside.[76] A more accurate picture of how the spirit and soul are integrated into a body is to see each physical cell infused with both. Indeed, the field of epigenetics is beginning to discover that human DNA carry emotional and soulish data like "tags" turning genes on or off which in turn affects a person's physical well being. Hence, each and every cell has a soul and a spiritual component, not just physical.

Patricia King explains in her "Women of Influence" online course, if our soul and spirit were able to step out of our body and appear separately, they would look the same as our body in appearance. Our soul and our spirit are not blobs in the center of our bellies; they are expressions and exact replicas of who we are. They function differently but they appear the same.

Why is this important? Well, at the moment of salvation, the Holy Spirit comes to make His dwelling—His abiding place—inside of us. He actually comes and makes His home in us, but not in some obscure, unknown place in our belly, but in EVERY CELL of our body! The Holy Spirit is not confined! His presence is alive in every cell and His power can be invited to operate throughout our entire being, even *possessing* our organs, muscles, tendons, and any body part not behaving as it should. Praise God! Renewing our mind— hearing the revelation of the Holy Spirit is the gateway to faith and healing.

---

[76] "For just as the body without the spirit is dead, so also faith without works is dead" (James 2:26 NASB).

Once again, in Luke 13:10-16, a *daughter of Abraham* was bent over for eighteen years because of a demon in her body. If a demon, which is a spirit, can cause this kind of physical problem, how much more can the *Holy* Spirit, Who is God the Creator of all, possess your body and cause it to function according to God's perfect will?

Let's consider 1 Corinthians 6:19-20:

> Don't you realize that your BODY is the temple of the Holy Spirit, who lives in you and was given to you by God? You do not belong to yourself, for God bought you with a high price. *So you must honor God with your body.* (NLT, emphasis added)

The original Greek word in the text translated here as *body* is *sōma* which means the body as a sound *whole*, an organized whole made up of parts and members, a *living* body. This word *sōma* is different from another Greek word translated as *body* in other passages which is *sárx*. *Sárx* in contrast, refers only to the flesh, denoting only the natural, physical material of the body.[77] So, in other words, *sōma* in 1 Corinthians 6:19 is talking about the whole person—spirit, soul, and flesh.

Even more truth can be pulled out of this scripture. It says, we were bought at a high price, but which part of us? All of us! Each part of who we are, spirit, soul, and body, was purchased and now belongs to Jesus. Our body has become His body. Considering this, how much more should we love, appreciate, and bless our body with our words and actions, taking care of it properly? How much more should we guard against sin—especially sexual sin which defiles the body? How much more do you think Jesus wants it functioning properly, being free of sickness and disease?

---

[77] The Hebrew-Greek Key Word Study Bible: New American Standard Bible Revised Edition, ©1984, 1990, 2008 by AMG International, Inc. (Chattanooga: AMG Publishers, 2008) 2287. Print.

Allowing all this good revelation to sink deep into our heart and mind, let's also make sure we are aligning ourselves with righteousness. You may want to:

1. Confess and repent for hating or disliking your body.

2. Repent for not celebrating your body.

3. Confess, repent, and renounce any curses (negative words) *spoken* over your body (eg. "I hate my…," "I'm sick and tired of…," "I'm fat," "I'm ugly," etc.).

4. Confess, repent, and renounce any negative *thoughts* and *beliefs* about your body.

5. Confess and repent for all sexual sin.

6. Confess and repent for any other sin you've committed against your body (e.g., overeating, alcohol abuse, drug abuse, eating too much junk food, treating your body like a trash can, whatever HS convicts you of, *perhaps* even unnecessary surgeries or surgeries you've had without first asking God for His opinion and direction).

7. Confess and repent for all anger you've held against your body.

8. Confess and repent for any judgements you've made against your body.

9. Forgive your body for aging and not functioning as it should.

10. Repent for dishonoring your body.

11. Repent for overworking your body and not knowing when to allow yourself to rest.

12. Repent for not keeping the sabbath—one day every week to rest and focus on the Lord.

13. Forgive yourself for all the above.

14. Release to God, by speaking it out loud, any sin that was committed against your body by someone else. Tell God about it and confess to Him your feelings (not because they are bad or sinful but to get them out of your body). Forgive anyone who has committed sin against your body.

15. Ask God to give you a new love for your body.

16. See your body from God's perspective.

17. Break curses over your body.

18. Cast out a spirit of infirmity.

19. Remove trauma from your cells by praying, "I pull out trauma from every cell of my body right now, in Jesus' name."

20. Speak love and blessing over your body—even specific body parts. For example I may pray, "I speak blessing over my body. I speak over my teeth in Jesus' name, and I thank God for them and how they function, allowing me to eat good food. I declare health over them and proper alignment in Jesus' name. I say they are blessed of the Lord and in their rightful place, in Jesus' name."

21. Anoint your body with oil.

22. In prayer, give your body to God. Romans 12:1 says, "And so, dear brothers and sisters, I plead with you to give your bodies to God because of all he has done for you. Let them be a living and holy sacrifice—the kind he will find acceptable. This is truly the way to worship him" (NLT).

23. Treat your body with respect and honor going forward by taking proper care of it. Eat properly, allow yourself to rest appropriately, get enough sleep, perhaps work less, exercise, move, don't stay sedentary, shower, groom yourself appropriately, and even wear nice clothing. If you don't care about what your clothes look like, have you ever really thought about why? Perhaps you've convinced yourself that it's about not being vain, but I would challenge you to think again. Wearing baggy, ratty clothing could be an outward sign of how you *really* feel about yourself. Allow the Holy Spirit to examine your heart friend and get on the same page with Him. Honor yourself by wearing descent clothing.

Following through with the previous suggestions will help you come into alignment with God and bring about divine health. Remember to believe what you pray to activate faith.

Facts Verses Truth

As a believer, your job when praying regarding the healing of your body is to *declare the truth* of what already is, *not* ask God to heal you and *not* moan and complain about the facts. Your job is to stand in faith. Jesus has already provided for your healing. In the Spirit realm, you are already healed. Your healing simply needs to be pulled into the earth realm through faith. We can, however, still admit the facts. We must be truthful about everything. Let me explain.

The fact may be that you have pain somewhere in your body. I am not suggesting you deny the facts. Let's look at Abraham. Abraham had a promise from God that an heir would come from his own flesh, but he was way past the years of physically being able to biologically father children, as was Sarah. The only way he was going to have a biological child was through a miracle. Listen to Romans 4:19-21:

> Without weakening in his faith, he (Abraham) *faced the fact* that his body was as good as dead—since he was about a hundred years old—and that Sarah's womb was also dead. Yet he did not waver through unbelief regarding the promise of God, but was strengthened in his faith and gave glory to God, being *fully persuaded* that God had power to do what he had promised. (NIV, brackets and emphasis added)

Abraham was able to face the facts but still be strengthened in his faith and be *fully persuaded* of what God was *able and willing* to do. We also can be strengthened in our faith and be fully persuaded of what God has already provided for, regardless of what we see and feel in the natural realm.

Assuredly, a fact and the truth according to God are two very different things. The facts about our circumstances are volatile, temporary, earthly, always changing and can totally turn around in an instant according to our faith. The facts come from a worldly, natural perspective of our situation. The truth, on the other hand, is eternal and comes from a heavenly perspective. The truth is constant and does not change. The truth is God's view of a situation and comes straight from His Word. Potentially, our confession of the facts and truth could sound something like this:

"The fact is I'm in pain, but the truth is, Jesus bore all my pains when He was beaten and crucified and has carried them all away, far from me never to return. Jesus has already paid for my healing and has purchased me as His very own possession. I belong to Christ and nothing apart from Christ can reside or stay in my body. I am His. Jesus Christ bore upon Himself all pain, infirmity, sickness, disease, and adverse conditions that may want to attach themselves to me, but I do not give them permission. I renounce all permission I may have unknowingly given them in the past. Complete healing and wholeness is available to me right now and in Jesus' name, I receive it now. I take it from the heavenlies, and I apply it to my earthly body right now. I take it because it belongs to me and I thank God for it. I praise God and give Him the glory that the natural facts must submit to the supernatural truth of God right now, in Jesus' name. I speak to my (name the body part or organ causing trouble) and I say, "Be healed in Jesus' name." The Lord rebukes every malady. The Lord rebuke (name problems specifically). The Lord rebukes sickness and disease and I cut my agreement with them now in Jesus' name. Thank You, Lord! Every argument in my mind that has set itself up against the knowledge of God, I now pull down with force, in Jesus' name. Every lie of the devil, I renounce and rebuke in Jesus' name. If I have somehow agreed that *I deserve this illness*, I repent for believing it and I renounce that lie, in Jesus' name. (If there are other lies that the Holy Spirit brings to mind, renounce them.) Thank You for cleansing me of all lies and all unrighteousness, Lord. I know that I will see Your goodness and Your complete faithfulness in my life, despite my shortcomings because that is just Who You are. Your mercies are new every morning and I receive them now. In Jesus' name, amen."

INJUSTICE

We've talked a bit about injustice and the righteous anger that can come up in us when we witness it. However, right now, I want to quickly mention injustice in a slightly different context. Injustice can be a blockage to our healing when we are the ones who are perpetrating it. If that doesn't sound like it applies to you, please don't skip over this section. Injustice can be *very* subtle and sneaky, so please read through and allow the Holy Spirit to speak to you.

When we are ill and seeking the Lord diligently for answers, it is common and helpful to fast. We can fast food completely (so long as we are physically able to do this), or fast certain foods, but either way it is a great way to pull on God to satisfy every appetite, craving, and hunger with His love, His Word, and His voice. Deuteronomy 8:3 says, "...man shall not live by bread alone; but man lives by every *word* that proceeds from the mouth of the LORD" (NKJV).

Food in general, particularly sweets and "comfort" foods tend to dull our spiritual senses—they put cotton in our spiritual ears so to speak. Restricting access to these comfort measures forces us to find our comfort in God and helps us to hear the Spirit's voice distinctly and receive the revelation we need. *Hunger* helps us to hear God. Satisfying that hunger with earthly things causes us to no longer be hungry, thus we don't seek to be filled with His Word. When we fast, however, we should take Isaiah 58 into consideration to make sure it is as effective as it could possibly be.

Isaiah 58 is an amazing passage of scripture calling us to "fast" the right way—the way that God has chosen. It's not just about restricting food but re-aligning ourselves to God's ways. Isaiah 58 speaks for itself so here it is:

> "Cry aloud, spare not; Lift up your voice like a trumpet; Tell
> My people their transgression, And the house of Jacob their

sins. Yet they seek Me daily, And delight to know My ways, As a nation that did righteousness, And did not forsake the ordinance of their God. They ask of Me the ordinances of justice; They take delight in approaching God. 'Why have we fasted,' *they* say, 'and You have not seen? *Why* have we afflicted our souls, and You take no notice?' "In fact, in the day of your fast you find pleasure, And exploit all your laborers. Indeed you fast for strife and debate, And to strike with the fist of wickedness. You will not fast as *you do* this day, To make your voice heard on high. Is it a fast that I have chosen, A day for a man to afflict his soul? *Is it* to bow down his head like a bulrush, And to spread out sackcloth and ashes? Would you call this a fast, And an acceptable day to the LORD? *Is* this not the fast that I have chosen: To loose the bonds of wickedness, To undo the heavy burdens, To let the oppressed go free, And that you break every yoke? *Is it* not to share your bread with the hungry, And that you bring to your house the poor who are cast out; When you see the naked, that you cover him, And not hide yourself from your own flesh? Then your light shall break forth like the morning, YOUR HEALING SHALL SPRING FORTH SPEEDILY, And your righteousness shall go before you; The glory of the LORD shall be your rear guard. Then you shall call, and the LORD will answer; You shall cry, and He will say, 'Here I *am*.' "If you take away the yoke from your midst, The pointing of the finger, and speaking wickedness, *If* you extend your soul to the hungry And satisfy the afflicted soul, Then your light shall dawn in the darkness, And your darkness shall be as noonday. The LORD will guide you continually, And satisfy your soul in drought, AND STRENGTHEN YOUR BONES; You shall be like a watered garden, And like a spring of water, whose waters do not fail. Those from among you Shall build the old waste places; You shall raise up the foundations of many generations; And you shall be called the Repairer of the Breach, The Restorer of Streets to Dwell In. "If you turn away your foot from the Sabbath, *From* doing your pleasure on My holy day, And call the Sabbath a delight, The holy *day* of the LORD honorable, And shall honor Him, not doing your own ways, Nor finding your own pleasure, Nor speaking your own words, Then you shall delight yourself in the LORD; And I will cause you to ride on the high hills of the earth, And feed you with the heritage of Jacob your father. The mouth of the LORD has spoken." (NKJV, emphasis added)

Fasting is a powerful key for healing. However, fasting is not just about limiting foods or limiting comfort measures, but as Isaiah says, letting the oppressed go free, undoing heavy burdens we may have put on others and giving to the poor and needy. When you're fasting, ask the Holy Spirit if there is an act of kindness toward others you should engage in or if there is any way you are acting unjustly toward someone else. If He reveals something, make it right. Do what you need to do to come out from under that injustice.

What does injustice look like? Well... it might not be obvious as many ways that are acceptable in this world are unjust according to God. The ways of the world are opposite of the ways of the Kingdom of God. For instance, an employer must follow the labour laws of the country they do business in, but many of those labour laws only enforce a bare minimum of fairness to the employee. God does not call us to treat people in a way that is barely fair, but He calls us to be generous and loving toward them. As an employer, are you taking advantage of anyone in any way? Are you paying them what they deserve? Are you over-working anyone? Are you looking for loopholes in the system so you can legally dismiss employees (who have not done anything wrong), simply because you don't like them or they're of an older demographic? Are you really treating people—everyone—with respect, fairness, and dignity? If not, mend your ways and begin to treat others according to the heart of God, with generosity, compassion, and kindness.

Isaiah 58 says that if you are willing to do this, "your healing shall spring forth speedily!" Thank You, Jesus! Lord, let it be so!

SHAME AND SELF-HATE/REJECTION

We've already touched on body image, but now we're going to touch on the rejection of self and self-hate partnered with shame. Perhaps it's not your body you're unhappy with, but your soul. Perhaps you're disappointed in yourself for some reason or a past injustice has left you feeling unlovable, dirty, or tainted. I'm sorry friend if you find yourself in this situation.

Healing follows cleansing. When a wound is cleansed, then it can heal. Cleansing equates with applying the blood of Jesus over your wound and pursuing holiness, through prayer, spending time in the secret place with God, and reading the Word. Pursuing holiness is a process where we allow God to lead us and make the necessary adjustments in our heart, sometimes, one step at a time, empowered by the Holy Spirit. Perhaps you have felt overwhelmed by this book. It would not be surprising—it's a lot to cover and confront all at once. Perhaps it would be best for some to digest one chapter at a time and take it slower. It is completely acceptable if you do. Perhaps this is a book that you need to re-visit time and time again.

Many believers, I think, when pursuing holiness, will focus on what they do and don't do—how they behave, but good behavior is the *fruit* of holiness, not holiness itself. Holiness is more about loving God, believing God, agreeing with God about everything, believing who we are in Christ, and aligning our heart with truth.

Perhaps one of the main areas people struggle with is seeing themselves through the eyes of Christ and loving themselves as Christ loves them. To the extreme, some people are stuck in life or are sick because they have agreed with self-rejection and even self-hate. Somewhere amid that, shame lives and operates kind of like glue, keeping them there, unable to get free. Only you can determine where you are on the scale of shame and rejection of self.

Here's the thing—Christ saw enough worth in you to die for you. Christ values you even above His own life. So, when we reject or hate ourselves, we're not agreeing with God. When we have believed and allowed shame to take hold of us, believed and accepted rejection and received the negative report from others, we are NOT believing God—we have not aligned ourselves with God's Word, but we have aligned ourselves with the enemy of our souls.

Yes, we needed redemption. We needed to be saved from our sin and decrepit state, so we accepted God's forgiveness AND we also let ourselves off the hook at the same time. In order to live forgiven, we must allow ourselves to receive the fullness of God's grace and mercy. Let God be God and call the shots. Let God determine our worth and our status as forgiven and cleansed, no matter what.

Shame may have come on us from:

- things we've done and regret.
- experiences of being *caught in the act*, perhaps by a parent (possibly embarrassing situations).
- words spoken over us like: "Shame on you!" or "You should be ashamed of yourself!"
- sin that others have committed against us.

To illustrate my point of how God can heal us of shame, I'm going to be completely vulnerable with you. I wasn't saved until I was twenty-two years old, so my teen years were lived as a sinner. Thank God, He has forgiven it all. Anyhow, when I was sixteen, my father saw my boyfriend and I touching each other's bodies as we were watching television in the basement TV room. I didn't know or hear him come down the stairs. It wasn't until my father confronted me later when he advised me to "use discretion" that I realized what had happened. At the time, I was so embarrassed and ashamed by what he saw. I was devastated, but time went on and it soon faded away and I forgot about it (or so I thought).

Fast forward about thirty-six years. One night, out of nowhere, I had a dream. An unnamed man and I were in the act sexually. In the dream I was hesitant to be in the situation, but didn't resist necessarily, when suddenly, Father God came around the corner and entered the scene. Suddenly, everything and everyone else on the scene disappeared and I went to Father God. We embraced. He brought me close, drawing me right into Him until I *melted* into Him and became one with Him. I felt with such intensity the absolute perfect love He had for me. There was absolutely no shame in His demeanor, countenance, or heart for what He walked in on, only complete and perfect love.

When I awoke, it still felt so real. I asked the Lord what it was about, and He gently reminded me of the experience I had with my earthly father that was filled with shame. I had forgotten about it, but it was still buried in my soul. God showed me that He graciously allowed the dream to *re-form* my experience with a father walking in on or witnessing me in a sinful act and as a result, transformed my past memory and *expectation* for the future. I hadn't thought about that experience in a long time, but God knew it was an open door for the enemy, so He sovereignly took care of it. Father God completely undid and removed the shame over that situation. My mind has now been renewed as to what I can expect when Father God knows and sees me not being perfect. I can rest and be assured that there is no shame in it at all. I can expect only love, mercy, and compassion at its best. Praise God!

I pray this has ministered to you and helped you to see that you too can be relieved of shame. Shame is not of God. Shame is from the devil and meant to keep you in torment, outside of the love of God. If you let Him, Father God will communicate to you in similar ways to set you free. Ask God to heal you as you give to Him all shame and regret. Enter the fullness of forgiveness and mercy as you boldly and courageously choose to trust Father, God, with your deepest secrets.

Go into the secret place with Him and imagine yourself before Him. In your hands is a bowl into which you can place every shameful experience and every regret. Imagine yourself giving Father the bowl and "see" in your mind's eye what He does with it. If you will focus and allow your Godly imagination to be controlled by the Spirit, God will communicate to you through images on the screen of your imagination. I can tell you what God thinks of you, but it is so much more powerful when it comes directly from Him.

Trust Him beloved. He will meet you where you are and He knows exactly what you need.

THE ORPHAN SPIRIT OR MINDSET

On August 8, 1975, Prophet Bob Jones died temporarily and had a significant spiritual encounter with the Lord where the Lord asked the saints an important question. Jesus asked, "Did you learn to love?" In this death experience, the answer to this question determined the rewards that each saint received as they were embraced by Jesus and entered heaven.[78] Bob Jones was sent back to us that day with a new mandate, but He has since gone again to Glory, for good. Bob Jones' testimony gives us great clarity on where we fall short and reminds us of Jesus' mandate: love others and do it well. Are you surprised by the suggestion that we may need to learn, all over again, how to do that?

Before the fall, love was not a problem; it came naturally. We were made from love, out of love, and to love. Unfortunately, one bite of the forbidden fruit changed everything. Love became elusive and loving others well became impossible as we focused on ourselves. Consequences of the fall rippled on down the generations touching our lives right from conception, causing strife in families and marriages. Perhaps you know exactly what I'm talking about. Perhaps images and memories are bubbling up as you relate to love gone wrong or love never expressed in any form or fashion. While it's true, most parents do the best they know how, for many, it has not been enough, and they have grown up feeling more like an orphan than a son or daughter.

I'll never forget my mother coming out of the funeral home after her mother's memorial service. I quickly exited through the back door to escape the stuffy, depressing atmosphere, and my mom followed soon after. I turned to look at her, and she said with a childlike voice, "My mother never loved me." My heart sank as I

---

[78] https://www.youtube.com/watch?v=FrDtDTAD184&t=1213s

realized that apart from any intervention from the Lord, we learn to love by how we were loved. I had never felt tremendously loved by my own mother and now she was confessing the same about hers. This was a moment of clarity for me. Lack of love is a cycle—a cycle with no end until someone rises up in relationship with the Breaker Himself, Jesus Christ, and intentionally refuses to cooperate with it. The cycle is broken when someone sees it, forges a life-transforming relationship with Jesus, embraces their identity as a son or daughter of God, is empowered and taught by the Holy Spirit to love like Jesus and then lives that love out in their world.

Forging a relationship with Jesus, the Holy Spirit, and the Father, puts us in a spiritual position to be loved perfectly as a son or daughter of God. Galatians 3:26 says, "For you are all children of God through faith in Christ Jesus" (NLT). But how much of your new spiritual condition gets passed on through to your soul and physical experience? Are you able to walk with the Lord, in the cool of the day through the garden, as Adam and Eve did, in the Spirit? Are you able to communicate with the Lord? Do you hear His voice? Do you trust Him to meet all your needs according to His riches in Glory? Have you stopped striving and toiling to meet your own needs?

Restoring our relationship and experiencing it is a process. The time we have spent living apart from Father God and sometimes the experiences we've had with our earthly fathers have trained us to continue living independently, like an orphan, looking after ourselves. It takes healing, a paradigm shift in our thinking, a de-programming and renewing of the mind to really be able to believe and trust God to be a good and perfect Father. We don't even know what that is or what it looks like, as none of us has ever had one. All our earthly fathers (even the good ones) and all of us too, have fallen short of the glory of God, somehow.

So how do we know if we're still behaving and living as an orphan despite our new identity in Christ? Well, asking the Holy Spirit is a good start, however, considering how an orphan lives, also helps. An orphan lives independently and relies on oneself. They struggle for what they need, and they earn everything by the sweat of their brow. They work like dogs and strive to be accepted. They hoard and save things because they don't know when they will need that thing they never use. They eat fast fearing they won't get enough, and they stash food in their pockets for later, just in case. They are jealous of others, lack peace, lack a sense of security and belonging and they don't feel loved. Orphans don't feel protected, they don't trust, fears plague their mind, and they desperately search for safety in things and human relationships, going from one person to the next.

Does any of the above sound familiar to you? Do you have a witness in your spirit? If so, don't worry. We are going to be free of the orphan spirit today.

In order to understand Father God's acceptance, let's consider the parable of the prodigal son, in Luke 15:11-32. The story paraphrased goes something like this:

The youngest son severely insults his father and severs ties with him and his family by asking for his inheritance early. He basically says to his father, "You're dead to me." He then leaves to go out on his own and squanders all his money on wild living. Eventually, he runs out of money, lives in a pigsty for a time and finally when he has nothing to eat, decides that he will swallow his pride and go home. He plans on asking his father for forgiveness so that perhaps he can work as a hired hand on the family farm—at least then he would be able to eat. The son begins his journey home and even while he is still a long way off, his father who has been watching for him, sees him in the distance. His dignified Jewish father, ditches his dignity, pulls his robe up above his knees, and RUNS to meet him—no hesitation, despite what the son has done.

The son says to his father, "Father, I have sinned against heaven and against you. I am no longer worthy to be called your son" (Luke 15:21 NIV). But here's the part I want to highlight: His father's reaction is not one of anger, rejection, or disappointment, but excitement, love, forgiveness, and total acceptance.

> But the father said to his servants, 'Quick! Bring the best robe and put it on him. Put a ring on his finger and sandals on his feet. Bring the fattened calf and kill it. Let's have a feast and celebrate. For this son of mine was dead and is alive again; he was lost and is found. (Luke 15:22-24 NIV)

Wow! What a reception! It didn't go at all like the son expected. He expected to be a servant, but instead he was totally restored as a son, with all the benefits, including a new portion of inheritance. The son received everything the father gave him with no resistance or false pride or insistence on earning anything back. There was no probation period and no consequences to endure.

This is how our heavenly Father treats us when we come back to Him, and this is what true sonship looks like. Every time someone returns home, Father runs to meet them, throws open His arms, has a big party, rejoices, and celebrates, while restoring everything that was *given up by them voluntarily through their disobedience*, all without question or explanation. What an amazing, gracious Father we have!

The Holy Spirit is ready and willing to take you on a healing adventure, to change your experience and heal your emotions. Many people don't want to rehash the past, but if you don't allow the Holy Spirit to take you there, the wounds will remain and fester, possibly infecting your whole life. It begins by simply opening your heart to Daddy God, admitting to Him what has hurt you and asking Him to heal your heart. Healthy emotions and healthy expectations will be restored when you continue in prayer and forgive your earthly dad and mom. We must forgive, to break any curses resulting from a lack of love and orphan mentality. Hopefully you're well on your way there by now after covering the previous chapters.

Some of you have been told and trained to *suck it up*, *shake it off*, *get over it*, and *don't be a cry baby*. You've gone to dad or mom in need of compassion and consolation and all you received was chastisement. You needed a hug, and you got a rebuke. Is that you?

Are you afraid to be rejected by Father when you admit that your heart is hurting? Do you need to be strong? Push it down? Does that voice play on repeat in your head? Does it stir something in your heart? If so, I'm sorry you were treated that way. It was wrong and it was not a healthy way to handle your pain and brokenness. You will need to forgive those who treated you that way.

There is a place that we need to be that is totally secure in the love of the Father. There is a place of total acceptance, where we can walk with Him and talk with Him every moment of every day if we choose, to trust Him to be everything He has promised. Most importantly, we must remain in that place even when things around us tell us something different; when our physical circumstances don't line up, we must be unwavering in who we are to Him and in Him. We must know that we know, He fights for us, and He is good all the time—without question and without doubt.

Let's throw off the reasoning of our natural mind and the lies that get our emotions all stirred up and stand solid on a foundation of truth. Let's take every thought captive and make it obedient to Christ—arrest the fear and throw it out. Rest, my friend, in His unfailing love for you. Rest in His arms of grace and mercy. Hear Him sing over you with joy and rejoice over you with gladness. You belong to Him, and He only has your very best interest at heart. He longs to release to you His very best gifts.

Before we get to a final prayer to break the orphan mindset, there are two specific issues I want to target. They are as follows:

1. Not being wanted by our earthly parents.
2. Being mistreated or neglected by our earthly fathers.

Not Being Wanted
You could be carrying a stigma of not being wanted if:

1. Your conception was not planned, expected, or wanted.
2. Your parents or a relative clearly favored a sibling over you.
3. You were told you were an "accident" or even a "mistake."

4. Your parents complained about the financial burden of meeting your needs.
5. Your father was not present at your birth.
6. Your parents did not celebrate your arrival/birth.
7. You were conceived out of wedlock.
8. You were adopted.
9. You were conceived in rape.
10. Your mother tried to abort you.
11. Your mother thought about aborting you.
12. Your mother tried to intentionally cause her body to miscarry.
13. Your mother was abused physically with the intent of causing her to miscarry.

If any of these previous scenarios describes you, you may have felt like you have a "looser" sign on your back. You may struggle with a sense of feeling inferior or not good enough. These are false identities we must confront and renounce.

It is important to come out from under the false identity of not being wanted. You may say, "But I wasn't wanted! I was given up for adoption." Indeed, it may be true—it may be a fact that you were adopted, but not being wanted is not true of who you *really* are. Your *earthly* parents may not have planned you, but it really doesn't matter. Your *earthly* parents are not the Creators—God is! God is the One Who creates. He simply uses our bodies to get the job done. Psalm 139:13-18 says:

> You formed my innermost being, shaping my delicate inside and my intricate outside, and wove them all together in my mother's womb. I thank You, God, for making me so mysteriously complex! Everything you do is marvellously breathtaking. It simply amazes me to think about it! How thoroughly you know me, Lord! You even formed every bone in my body when you created me in the secret place, carefully, skillfully shaping me from nothing to something. You saw who you created me to be before I became me!

Before I'd ever seen the light of day, the number of days you planned for me were already recorded in your book. Every single moment you are thinking of me! How precious and wonderful to consider that you cherish me constantly in your every thought! O God, your desires toward me are more than the grains of sand on every shore! When I awake each morning, you're still with me. (TPT)

You were VERY much wanted by your *heavenly* Father! In fact, according to Ephesians 1:4-6, you were chosen by God before the creation of the world to be holy and blameless in his sight and you were predestined to be adopted as His child through Jesus. So why are we putting more importance on being wanted by earthly parents than being wanted and even chosen by God? Isn't that what we're doing if we choose to stay in a mindset of not being wanted? I encourage you today, right now, to come out of that mindset and reject the lie the enemy wants to hold you in.

Please forgive your earthly parents for not affirming you and loving you appropriately by communicating to you your intrinsic value. Pray something like this:

"I choose to forgive my earthly father and mother for not loving me well and not communicating to me my worth and value. Right now, I come out of agreement with the lie that I was not wanted. I renounce that lie and I confess that I was wanted and planned by my Heavenly Father Who knit me together in my mother's womb and chose me to be His before the foundation of the world. I choose to value God's acceptance of me over the acceptance of the world and my earthly parents, and I choose to value God's love for me over the love that is in the world. I confess that God has wonderful plans for my life—plans to prosper me and not to harm me—plans to give me a hope and a future. In Jesus' name, amen."

Mistreatment or Neglect from Earthly Fathers

Our experiences with our earthly father can skew our beliefs about and trust in God, our heavenly Father, as we project our hurt feelings and experiences on *all* fathers. Our expectations for the future are very often set according to our experiences in the past.

I remember a time when I was young. My father was angry about my mom spending more money on me for something I needed. In his eyes, I didn't need it, but in reality. . . I did. I was hurt by his reluctance to provide for me, and I was fearful when he was mad. I'm sure he was overwhelmed by the expenses of a family of five, but as a ten-year-old, that went right over my head. I projected that experience onto God, and it caused me to see God as stingy, angry about providing for me, and reluctant to do so, though the truth about God is the complete opposite. Philippians 4:19 says, "And this same God who takes care of me will supply all your needs from his glorious riches, which have been given to us in Christ Jesus" (NLT). Second Corinthians 9:8 says, "And God will generously provide all you need. Then you will always have everything you need and plenty left over to share with others" (NLT).

There's a beautiful song on YouTube by Misty Edwards called, "All Men Are Broken" that will soak your soul in love and truth as you listen. She is an incredibly anointed minister of prophetic song. Go find it and receive truth and healing into your heart. Let yourself feel what you need to feel and tell God about it. Then forgive your father, release him to God and receive Father God deeper than you ever have before. Father God wants to re-father you and redeem the time you spent in despair, depression, and grief over the lack of love in your father connection or the lack of having any father figure at all. You are deeply loved, and Papa God is turning it all around for you. You'll see. He'll touch every place that needs to be healed.

And in the name of Jesus, I cancel the curse of fatherlessness over you NOW! I decree that you have the greatest and best Father in the whole world, and you have never been without Him by your side. Every moment and every memory you have where you missed your father, Father God is now stepping into and filling that gap, rearranging, and redeeming it all, causing love to replace fear, attachment to replace detachment and belonging to replace estrangement.

Finally, pray this to renounce the orphan spirit and mindset:

"I thank You, God, for being my perfect loving Father. Open my eyes to see Who You really are on my behalf. Help me to understand that I am not alone, and I never have been without You. I choose to forgive my father for being (absent, unloving, angry, unavailable, disinterested, disconnected, stingy, abusive etc.) I choose to release him to You, God, to be his judge and I ask, God, that You would have mercy on him, just as You have had mercy on me. I repent for being super independent, detached emotionally from You, God, distant, not seeing You as my help and not relying on You as my Father. I now renounce and reject the orphan mentality, thinking that I don't belong, or that I must look after myself because no one else will. I bind the orphan mentality and spirit, and I command it to go from my life now, in Jesus' name. I accept You, God, as my heavenly Father and I look to You for my help, my confidence, my sense of belonging, my provision, and my worth. Fill me up, Lord, with Your Holy Spirit that I may pour out to others around me. In Jesus' name, amen."

SOUL TIES

A soul tie is a deep emotional connection with another person or even with animals or things. This connection can be godly in certain situations but is very often ungodly. A soul connection can be made a few different ways. It can be made through sexual intercourse (husband and wife become one flesh), or it could be made through relying too heavily on someone else (a mother for instance) or even some*thing* to meet our emotional needs.

As I began writing this chapter, a curiosity rose in me as to what the internet would say about a soul tie. I thought, *is it something that is recognized in the world?* Sure enough, it is. I am not suggesting we accept the world's opinion regarding this, but this one definition might help us understand what a soul tie is, and the dangers associated with them.

A simple Google search brought this definition up: "A soul tie is an intense *spiritual* connection between two people that results in a *mutual learning experience.*"[79] Notice the last part: "that results in a *mutual learning experience.*" This means that both parties end up experiencing and learning the same thing, going through, *or* very often *suffering* the same thing. Interesting. And true. But is this a good thing or a bad thing? I would suggest most of the time, this is bad because the devil uses these ungodly connections as opportunities to bring harm to people, especially in families. Have you ever known someone who was just like one of their parents, parroting their bad habits and behaviors? Have you ever known someone who transitioned to heaven exactly or *almost* exactly like their parent, suffering with the same illness?

In some instances, soul ties can be godly, such as in marriage between a husband and wife, and in *healthy* parent-child

---

[79] https://www.brides.com/soul-tie-explained-5498605

relationships, however, in each instance, soul ties can very easily develop ungodly portions that don't serve us, don't glorify God, and give the enemy a foothold in our lives. This is due to the wounds we accumulate as children and the sin that so easily entangles us and distorts God's design.

As mentioned, the main way a soul tie is formed is through sexual intercourse. This is why God's design was for us to have sex in the confines of marriage—and *only* in the confines of marriage. When we have sex outside of this boundary, we form soul ties with multiple people, and we are in sin which makes the soul tie ungodly. The connections with previous partners hang on and cause all sorts of problems in our lives—especially in our marriage.

God's design was for each person to connect with Him and rely on Him as their *source* of love, acceptance, and self-worth (think of the original garden, the Garden of Eden, and how Adam and Eve were secure in their identity because of their relationship with God the Father). So, if we look to and *depend* on someone else to love us, validate us, make us worthy, comfort us, and keep us safe, we end up trying to derive our value and security from another person. We then create a connection of emotional dependence on a person, which was never God's design. This creates in the spiritual realm an ungodly soul tie. It causes a person's identity to become overly intertwined with and dependent on someone else in a toxic way. In fact, it's as if that other person has taken on the role of God in their life.

How do we know if we have depended too heavily on another person to help us feel secure and loved? Well, have you ever said anything like the following: "I don't know what I would have done without her/him." "I don't think I would have survived if she/he hadn't been there (or been who she/he was to) for me." "She/He rescued me." "She/He is (was) everything to me." "I don't know what I would do if I lost her/him."

We must have the proper and godly perception of Who is the *most* important person in our lives. As a Christian, that person should always be God (Father, Son and Holy Ghost). God is our Rescuer. God is our Sustainer. He is our Deliverer. In Him is everything we need. Had that person (mother, father, sibling, spouse, whoever) NOT been in your life or not been as awesome as she/he was, GOD would have provided love and care for you some other way— whether it was through another person or directly to you through your relationship with Him.[80] Our confession should therefore be: "I don't know what I would have done without *God* providing such an amazing mother/father/spouse/sibling for me. She/He wasn't perfect, but she/he was amazing." "I don't think I would have survived had *God* not been there for me and made my mom/dad/spouse/sibling who she/he was." "*God* rescued me." "*God* is everything to me." The first set of confessions above put someone else on a pedestal, elevating them to a place they don't belong. The latter confessions conversely and rightly give *God* all the glory and put Him in His proper place. . . on the throne of our heart. Don't think this is just semantics. It's not. It's a heart attitude and a righteous perception that gives all the glory to God.

Lastly, a soul tie can actually be formed with just about anyone or anything if we become *dependent* on that person or thing for love, comfort, and security. I'm not talking about an infant being dependent on its parents. This is normal. But take note, the infant gradually grows up and out of that dependence. This is the healthy progression of life. The problem comes when a child doesn't grow up and out of that dependence on mom/dad for love and safety, or as they grow, they begin to look for other people and things to attach to and draw love from, creating other toxic relationships of dependence.

I once heard a story of a child who became overly attached to the kittens that the family's cat bore. When it came time for the kittens to go to their new homes, the child had an absolute emotional melt

---

[80] Psalm 68:5-6, "A father to the fatherless, a defender of widows, is God in his holy dwelling. God sets the lonely in families, he leads out the prisoners with singing;" (NIV).

down each time one left. Her mother realized what had happened and prayed to break the soul tie her daughter had developed with the kittens. The success of her prayer became evident very soon after when the next kitten left their home. This time, the child had very little emotional response, in fact, didn't even notice as she continued to play in her bedroom. The young girl had apparently been cured of her temper tantrums and melt downs around the kittens she had grown attached to.

Every ungodly soul tie is an opportunity for the devil to oppress us. It is also an opportunity for demons that may be attached to the souls of others to also attach to us for the purpose of oppressing us, making us sick, or just plain making our lives miserable. It is therefore imperative that we break ungodly soul ties through repentance and prayer.

Prayer to Break Soul Ties with Sexual Partners:

"Lord, I confess that I have not kept Your commands or followed Your ways in regard to sex. I confess, God, that I have had sexual relations with others outside of marriage. (Also confess any other sexually deviant behavior.) I confess that through my fornication I have placed my partner(s), the need for their love and affection, and my fleshly desires above and before You in my heart. I have replaced You as my first love, broken my covenant with You and formed ungodly covenants with others. I am sorry, God, and I repent. I ask for Your forgiveness. Thank You, Lord, that when I confess my sins to You, You are faithful to forgive me and cleanse me from all unrighteousness. Thank You for Your forgiveness. I choose to forgive myself and receive Your forgiveness in its fullness. I now break and renounce all ungodly soul ties, unions, influences, and covenants, in body, soul, and spirit that I have formed with (identify partners by name). I release (say each name again) back to You, God, and I ask You to heal the wounds in her/him/them that caused her/him/them to seek out our union, and I ask You, God, to cause her/him/them to become all You created her/him/them to be. I pray that she/he/they would come to know You and experience Your love. I also ask, Lord, that every part of myself that has been tied to the others would be washed in Your blood and brought back to me. I call back to myself every piece of my heart that I gave away in sin and I ask You, Lord, to heal every wound in me that made me seek out an ungodly union. Heal me and make me whole in You. Thank You, God. In Jesus' name, I now break every ungodly union and transference from their bloodline to mine and every curse empowered through our sin I now cut off from my blood, my life, my soul, my body, my marriage (if applicable), my family/children (if applicable), my destiny, and my future. I break and dis-empower every evil force sent to carry these curses out. In Jesus' name, I renounce every unclean spirit, every spirit of lust and perversion, every spirit of rebellion, disobedience, witchcraft, infirmity, sickness, and disease that has gained access to my life and I command them to leave me now! In Jesus' name, I decree that I am free from every curse, and I am free to be all God created me to be, and to do all God has for me to do. Whomever the Son sets free is free indeed! I decree that goodness and mercy shall follow me all the days of my life and I will dwell in safety in the house of the Lord forever. Father, send Your Holy Spirit to fill every vacant place in me now. Fill me to overflowing and clothe me in power. Saturate me, God, in Your presence. Thank You that You hear my prayer and love me unconditionally. All glory and praise be Yours, Amen."

Prayer to Break Soul Ties

This time we will pray to break soul ties with people we have depended on to meet our emotional needs. I will use "my mother" as an example, but please replace "my mother" and the applicable pronouns (all underlined portions) with the name of the person and appropriate pronoun, *or* thing (it), you have wrongly attached to and depended on.

"Lord, I thank You for "<u>my mother</u>." I thank You for all "<u>she</u>" was (is) in my life and all "<u>she</u>" has done for me. Lord, I confess that I have placed "<u>my mother</u>" above and before You in my heart and I am sorry. The first affection of my heart should always be for You. You, O God, are my first love, for You loved me first, even before I was conceived. I repent, God for looking to "<u>my mother</u>" for what I should have looked to You for, for forming an ungodly covenant and union of soul with "<u>her</u>" and for breaking my covenant with You. Please forgive me God. I choose to forgive myself and I receive Your forgiveness in its fullness. Thank You, Lord. In Jesus' name, I now renounce and break the ungodly portion of my union with "<u>my mother,</u>" the unhealthy dependence on "<u>her</u>" and the ungodly covenant that resulted." (Continue below)

Applicable only to those cutting soul ties with their mom:
"I cut the umbilical cord that has spiritually remained and has kept me attached to her in an ungodly way (take a pair of scissors and cut the umbilical cord in the spirit) and I release my mother to You, God." (If your mother was controlling, forgive her here.)

Continue: "I ask, Lord, that every part of me that was tied to "<u>my mother</u>" in an ungodly way would be washed in Your blood and brought back to me. Make me whole in You, God. I call back to myself each part of my soul wrongly attached to "<u>her,</u>" and I release back to "<u>my mother</u>" every part of "<u>her</u>" wrongly attached to me. I ask You, Lord, to heal every wound in me that has caused me to be too attached to "<u>my mom</u>." I now break every curse that has been empowered because of this ungodly union. I thank You, Jesus, that You have redeemed me from every curse and that no curse has any more right to operate in my life. I bind and take authority over every spirit of idolatry, control, fear, intimidation, and witchcraft, in the name of Jesus, and I resist their maneuvers against me. I break their power in my life, and I command them to leave me now and not come back, in Jesus' name. I decree that I am free in Christ to be all God has created me to be and do all God has planned for me to do. Holy Spirit, come! I welcome You and trust You to be everything I need in this life. Help me to discern Your presence and fill me afresh. Cause me to overflow with Your abundant life. In Jesus' most glorious name, Amen."

REPRESSED EMOTIONS

There's a quote from the 2008 movie, *Fireproof*, that I will never forget: "Don't just follow your heart 'cause your heart can be deceived. You've got to lead your heart."

"Follow your heart." We hear that a lot in the world, don't we? On the surface we think it's good advice but what it's really saying is follow your feelings. Feelings of the heart can be fickle, changing frequently according to moods, not generally grounded, or rooted in truth—very much of the flesh and not the Spirit.

What happens when we don't *feel* like going to work? We still go to work, don't we? If we followed our feelings every time, we'd soon be fired. Jeremiah 17:9 tells us, the heart is full of deceit. It would be best to lead our heart in partnership with the Holy Spirit in truth and holiness.

Having said all that, let's not assume that our feelings are not important. Let's not think that our feelings should be ignored or stuffed into tiny boxes and stored away in the closets of our heart. Our hearts need to be healed by acknowledging them and being truthful about our feelings. Too often we have been taught not to express our feelings and resulting emotions. Maybe we've been told, "don't be a cry baby," "get over it," "you're too sensitive," and been shamed for the feelings we have had.

Perhaps we've buried our emotions to survive or perhaps we've wanted to appear to others as a *good* Christian or as someone who has it all together. Healing comes when we strip away the masks and admit what we *truly* feel to Jesus, in prayer. When we are willing, the Holy Spirit is so gracious to help us identify the feelings that need to be released.

Two Temples Similar Pattern

It's interesting that in 1 Corinthians 6:19 we are called a *temple* of the Holy Spirit as back in the Old Testament, there was another *temple*, tabernacle, or abiding place for God which the Israelites built. When we consider *its* pattern, we can gain some great insight on how the Holy Spirit lives in us.

In Exodus 25:8, God began to give Moses the pattern for building the tabernacle, "Have the people of Israel build me a holy sanctuary so I can live among them. You must build this Tabernacle and its furnishings exactly according to the pattern I will show you" (NLT). All the way through to Exodus 40 we see Moses taking instruction from God and the Israelites working to complete it. Finally in Exodus 40 it is completed:

> So at last Moses finished the work. Then the cloud covered the Tabernacle, and the glory of the LORD filled the Tabernacle. Moses could no longer enter the Tabernacle because the cloud had settled down over it, and the glory of the LORD filled the Tabernacle. (Exodus 40:33-35 NLT)

As soon as the work was completed, exactly how God had told them to do it, His presence came, and God dwelled among them.

The tabernacle consisted of three parts as follows: the *Outer Court*, the *Inner Court* and the *Holy of Holies* and it was in the *Holy of Holies* where God Himself dwelt. Just as the tabernacle of Moses had three parts, we too have three parts—our spirit, soul, and body. Each of our parts relates to each part of the tabernacle. The *Holy of Holies* relates to our spirit man, where the Holy Spirit comes to live in us. The *Inner Court* relates to our soul, or our heart, and the *Outer Court* relates to our body. The good news, however, is the curtain in the tabernacle of Moses, which separated the *Holy of Holies* from the Inner Court was torn in two (Matt.27:51), thereby giving us access to God. The barrier that separated us from God was removed. Through Jesus, we have been given a new opportunity to apprehend the glory of God and for the Holy Spirit to live in our entire being. The Holy Spirit does not have to stay in our spirit man as if He is confined there.

In our temple, there also need not be any division between our Holy of Holies (spirit) and our Inner Court (soul/heart). The Holy Spirit is now free to penetrate our heart and then our body with His presence and power as the blood of Jesus has eliminated our guilt. However, because we have free will, I believe we must invite the Holy Spirit to do so. We must invite the Holy Spirit to possess us, to overtake us completely in soul and body, as we put to death our fleshly desires, honor God with our body, and choose to live by the Spirit. It's worth noting though, the Holy Spirit cannot reach our Outer Court (body) without first going through our Inner Court (heart/soul). It would therefore be appropriate to ask ourselves, "Is my heart open to Him? And is my heart penetrable?" The only person preventing the Holy Spirit from entering your heart and then your body, is you.

What would prevent the Holy Spirit from entering our heart? Have you ever been hurt by someone who was supposed to love you? Have you ever been repeatedly hurt by a loved one? Have you ever decided that loving and allowing yourself to feel was too painful? Have you ever decided to shut your heart down or build a fortress around it? Beloved, if you've answered yes, it's possible the Holy Spirit is prevented from penetrating your heart because of the hard protective shell around it.

In most cases, a hard protective shell around the heart helps us to feel safe. It keeps people out, but it also keeps our emotions in, contained, suppressed, so we can stay strong, and capable, not appearing weak to anyone. The shell may have served us well. It may have kept us in a space of coping with life, but it's not going to serve us well when we're wanting to be healed by God. For some, healing won't happen until they allow their protective shell to be broken and dismantled.

Beloved, letting your defenses down is the first step to your *break*through. Yes, it might get messy, and it might be painful. It will provoke agonizing tears, but allowing the Holy Spirit in and allowing your emotions out will lead you out of captivity and into freedom. It will feel like heart *break*, but sometimes a breaking is required before God can put it back together as He wants it.

For a long time, you may have worked hard at protecting your heart from being broken, but the benefit of surrendering your heart is, "The Lord is close to the brokenhearted; he rescues those whose spirits are crushed" (Psalm 34:18 NLT) and "He heals the brokenhearted and bandages their wounds" (Psalm 147:3 NLT). Lastly, Jesus Christ, your Healer, is the fulfillment of Isaiah's prophecy found in Isaiah 61 that says, "He has sent me to bind up the brokenhearted, to proclaim liberty to captives and freedom to prisoners" (Isaiah 61:1 NASB). The Lord knew heart break was inevitable on this earth, so He provided the solution—His presence within.

I recently had the privilege of publishing a book for Dr. Douglas Carr called, *777: Seven Curses, Seven Sprinklings & Seven Blessings*. In it, Dr. Carr explains that Jesus shed His blood in seven specific places which when applied to our body and mind, allows us to invoke seven specific blessings for healing. For example, the blood shed from Jesus' hands can be applied to *our* hands to heal our physical hands or break any curse that might be operating against our success and *what we put our hands to*. The blood shed from Jesus' brow due to the crown of thorns being forced into His head, can be applied to our minds to heal our mental health, or break any curse that may be operating against our mind, possibly blocking creative ideas or God's voice. It's a powerful concept, but I bring this up now because the seventh place Dr. Carr mentions where Jesus shed His blood, was from His heart.[81]

---

[81] Dr. Douglas E. Carr, *777 Seven Curses, Seven Sprinklings & Seven Blessings: Invoking the Blood Jesus Shed in Seven Places to Break Seven Curses and Release Seven Blessings* (Sturgis: DCFreedomMinistry, 2024). Print.

John 19:31-34 tells us that the day before the Sabbath, the soldiers were ordered to break the legs of the crucified victims, including Jesus, so the bodies could be removed from the crosses. The Jewish leaders did not want these men to still be on gruesome display during their holy day. So, the soldiers broke the legs of the two thieves, but when they came to Jesus, He appeared to have already died, so instead of breaking His legs, they thrust a spear up into His side. Verse thirty-four tells us this brought a "sudden flow of blood and *water*." My research indicates the *water* would have come from the build up of fluid in His pericardium sac directly surrounding His heart[82] which confirms for us that His heart was indeed pierced. The blood that poured out that day was not just from His torn flesh but from His pierced heart. His heart was pierced and literally broken through by the spear that was thrust into His side.

The blood of Jesus is powerful and effective to heal everything we apply it to, so let's take the blood from Jesus' broken heart and apply it to our own, through prayer. And as we do, let's repent for self-protection (not letting the Holy Spirit in and not allowing ourselves to feel), cold-heartedness, hard-heartedness, and even possibly rejecting pieces of our soul or identity that have been too difficult to process (this is called dissociation). Let's ask the Lord to give us a heart of flesh,[83] a heart that is soft, warm toward others, full of love, and whole. Let's give God the Lordship of our heart.

Prayer

Read through this prayer silently first and bring your heart into agreement with it. Just saying words is powerless; we must engage our heart and pray in faith—believing what we are praying.

---

[82] https://www.compellingtruth.org/blood-water-Jesus.html

[83] "And I will give them one heart [a new heart], and put a new spirit within them. I will take from them the heart of stone, and will give them a heart of flesh [that is responsive to My touch]" (Ezekiel 11:19 AMP).

"Father God, I repent for self-protection, for not allowing the Holy Spirit in and not allowing my feelings out and I repent for being cold and hard-hearted. I also repent, Lord, for separating, rejecting, and burying pieces of my identity and soul that have been too painful to recognize—that carry too much trauma for me to process. Please forgive me, God, for walking in agreement with self-protection, hard-heartedness, cold-heartedness, rejection of self and dissociative disorders; I renounce them all now in Jesus' name. I choose to forgive myself and every person that has hurt me and caused me to be traumatized. Lord, I now accept Your forgiveness and cleansing in its fullness according to first John 1:9 and declare that I am forgiven. I ask You, Lord, to heal every wound in me that caused me to partner with these sinful ways. I ask You, God, to heal me of trauma. I come out of agreement with trauma, and I release it to You now. Lord, make me whole in You. By faith, I now take the blood that Jesus shed from His broken heart, and I apply it to my broken heart and my fractured soul, and I receive the healing the blood of Jesus carries and creates. I thank You, God, for the blood of Jesus that is powerful and effective for my healing. Thank You, God, that You are creating in me a new heart and re-uniting every piece of my soul together as one. Lord, I send the blood of Jesus up and down my bloodline to heal and cleanse the generations of the iniquity of self-protection, hard-heartedness, cold-heartedness, self-rejection, and dissociation. I submit to You, Lord, and I resist the devil according to James 4:7. I renounce, bind, and take authority, in Christ, over every demon of self-protection, self-rejection, cold-heartedness, hard-heartedness, and dissociation and I command them to go now, in Jesus' name; leave me and my generational line right now, in Jesus' mighty name. (breath deep; command them to go until you sense a release) I sever and close every entry point that gave them access and I declare these demons no longer have access to me or my children. I thank You, Jesus, that You are our Deliverer and that You sing songs of deliverance over us (Ps. 32:7, Zeph. 3:17). I receive it now, in Jesus' name. I thank You, God, that my life is hidden in You, and I ask You, God, to cause my heart to beat again—to cause my heart to love again, and trust again. Lord, put Your love for me and others in my heart; I want to love like You. Give me a soft, warm heart like Yours. Teach me God; I submit to Your ways. Lastly Father, fill me afresh with Your Holy Spirit. Fill me to overflowing and saturate me in Your Spirit and power, in Jesus' name, Amen."

Honesty and Integrity

Stuffing or hiding our *true* emotions equates to wearing a mask and does not reflect honesty or integrity. Back in chapter 5, I mentioned the miser from Proverbs 23:6-7; he is a good example of someone who does not walk in the truth of his heart or in integrity. Instead, he pretends. He says the *right* thing even though it's *not* how he truly feels. What he says does not line up with his heart. "'Eat and drink,' he says to you, but his heart is not with you" (Proverbs 23:7 NIV). The miser hides how he really feels.

God wants us to walk in truth, and He wants us to be truthful about the deep things of our heart. Integrity means to be honest, and the Bible has much to say about it. Proverbs 10:9-10 says, "He who walks in integrity walks securely, But he who perverts his ways will be found out" (NASB). Psalm 119:1 says, "Joyful are people of integrity, who follow the instructions of the LORD" (NLT). Proverbs 2:7 says, "He grants a treasure of common sense to the honest. He is a shield to those who walk with integrity" (NLT). Proverbs 11:5 says, "The godly are directed by honesty; the wicked fall beneath their load of sin" (NLT). Most striking of all is Psalm 32:1-5:

> Oh, what joy for those whose disobedience is forgiven, whose sin is put out of sight! Yes, what joy for those whose record the LORD has cleared of guilt, whose lives are lived in

complete honesty! *When I refused to confess my sin, my body wasted away*, and I groaned all day long. Day and night your hand of discipline was heavy on me. My strength evaporated like water in the summer heat. Finally, I confessed all my sins to you and stopped trying to hide my guilt. I said to myself, "I will confess my rebellion to the LORD." And you forgave me! All my guilt is gone. (NLT, emphasis added)

"Are all our feelings sin though?" you may ask. No, not all, of course, but many of the negative ones—yes. You're not going to like this, but many of the negative feelings we have are based on worship of self. (Ouch! That's a serious truth bomb, right there!)

Hmm... you may be pondering, *what does she mean by that?* Well, frustration, I think is a good example. If I'm frustrated, I am frustrated because something is not going *my* way or going how I expect, want, or need—something is more challenging than it needs to be and is testing my patience. Another example is jealousy. If I'm jealous, I feel as though someone else has more favor than me. Thirdly, if my feelings are hurt, angry, bitter, or even hateful toward someone, it's usually because someone has done something to me that I don't like; it could be something that has simply inconvenienced me, made me look bad, feel bad or it could be worse. But the point is, it's *all* about me and hanging on to those emotions is harmful to ourselves.

There are times when anger is not sinful necessarily, but again, we've already talked about the need to confess our anger to God in a timely manner to avoid it becoming sin and giving the devil a foothold.

A good example of a negative emotion not being sin is sadness. We may be sad because others have gone through tough things or injustice of some sort and being empathetic toward others is a good thing, but it all depends on what is driving the emotion. If my sadness is about me, I may need to draw some boundaries or remove myself from an abusive situation, but I will need to take it to the Lord and stop wallowing in self-pity. If it's about someone else, the Lord is probably provoking me to pray for them.

Have you ever wondered how Jesus coped emotionally with all the betrayal, rejection, humiliation, and sheer abuse He suffered? How did Jesus not become offended and how did He not have wounded feelings and emotions? If anyone has the right to have hurt feelings, it was Jesus. The answer is: He wasn't focused on Himself. His focus was always on others. This is in no way meant to cause anyone shame. We are human! It is only to reiterate the need to get our feelings out by confessing them to the Lord and shifting our focus from ourselves to others.

All the negative feelings and emotions we try to bury, make us sick. So, it's time to get a feelings jar started or a feelings journal and use it to confess our feelings to Jesus. At the end of every day, ask yourself, "How did I feel today and why?" and write it down. Tell Jesus about it while you're at it and give it to Him. Taking this inventory is so very helpful at not holding onto and storing emotional baggage. The Lord wants truth and honesty to rule our heart. Let's not hide or wear masks pretending to be okay. Let's get real friends. Let's release to the Lord everything He purchased, including our feelings and emotions.

Have you ever tried to justify your anger and offense to the Lord? I have and it didn't go very well. Why? Well, because whatever we've suffered, Jesus has suffered more. Yes, the Lord is compassionate and longsuffering—absolutely! He understands and He allows us to grieve our losses and sufferings, but there is a time when He will say, "Okay, beloved, it's time to come out of that pit. I need you to rise in my Spirit and be my witness on the earth."

I know. Many have suffered unimaginable things and that may be you. But Jesus suffered it all. The good news is "we do not have a High Priest who is unable to sympathize *and* understand our weaknesses *and* temptations (and sufferings), but One who has been tempted [knowing exactly how it feels to be human] in every respect as *we are*, *yet* without [committing any] sin" (Hebrews 4:15

AMP, round brackets mine). When we are willing, in the power of the Holy Spirit, to shift our focus from ourselves back to Jesus, we will realize our suffering doesn't compare to His. Jesus said that in this world we would have trouble, *but take heart*, "I have overcome the world" (John 16:33 NKJV).[84] In other words, "Be encouraged! I have overcome everything the world has thrown at you, and you are invited to join me in that same victory by focusing on me and not yourselves—by worshipping me and finding your identity in me" (my paraphrase). If your sufferings and grief are keeping you in a pit of despair, your focus is off. Focus on the risen Christ—the Christ Who has overcome it all and will hold the devil accountable for what he has done to you.

Jesus said in Matthew 11:28-30:

> Come to me, all of you who are weary and carry heavy burdens, and I will give you rest. Take my yoke upon you. Let me teach you, because I am humble and gentle at heart, and you will find rest for your souls. For *my yoke is easy* to bear, and the burden I give you is light. (NLT, emphasis added)

If life is hard, put the heavy burdens down and give them to Jesus. Jesus said that *His yoke is easy*. If there is not an *ease* for you in navigating life and its challenges, perhaps you're yoked to something else. Jesus broke the curse of striving. Jesus broke the curse of hard. Toxic emotions create a yoke (a connection that controls us) between us and an event or us and another person. However, these yokes can be broken by the anointing of the Holy Spirit when we confess the toxic emotions we've carried, forgive ourselves and others and exchange that false yoke for an *easy* yoke with Jesus.

---

[84] Jesus was not talking about sickness or disease as "trouble" in this verse. He was talking about being hated by the world—about suffering persecution, and injustice (eg. rejection, abandonment, abuse, and loss perhaps of loved ones, resources, jobs, opportunities, friends, etc).

Jesus was incredible. He was human, yet He had such a close relationship with His Father, He was able to derive all His worth and value from Him. *In no way did Jesus ever look to another human being for validation.* Did you hear that? Let me say it again. In *no way* did Jesus ever look to another human being for validation or love. He was completely secure in Who He was as God's Son. We should and can be the same. But, if we're honest, we're not there yet. We are still a work in progress, in the process of renewing our mind in many ways, but most importantly, about who we are to and in Christ.

If we too can get to the place where we so believe in the love of God for us and we completely trust in His acceptance of us just the way we are, we wouldn't need validation from anywhere or anyone else, and we wouldn't care if someone didn't like us or said something mean to us or about us. Our heart would be secure. We would be unoffendable.

First John 4:15-16 says, "If anyone acknowledges that Jesus is the Son of God, God lives in them and they in God. And so we know and *rely* on the love God has for us. God is love. Whoever *lives in love* lives in God, and God in them" (NIV, emphasis added). Do you *rely* on God's love? Do you live in or *constantly* abide in the love of God? Hmm… Yeah, I fall short of that too. But if we were to *rely* on God's love, and if we were to *live* in God's love, we wouldn't *need* to get love from anyone else, would we? The phrases that we sing in a popular chorus, "Christ is enough for me," and "Everything I need is in You," would be true of us. We would know that we know, we are loved all the time, and we would be able to express that love to others *despite* how they act toward us. How incredible that would be.

If we were secure in the love of God, knowing our true status as sons and daughters, we wouldn't *need* anyone else. This isn't to say we shouldn't be in relationship with anyone else, it just means our self-worth would not ride on relationship with others. We were made to love others. We were made for relationships, but not to *get* anything—only to *give*. We were made to be a blessing, to love others well, and to represent Jesus on the earth through that love.

May it be our goal to have all our needs met in Jesus Christ and not *rely* on anyone else to meet those needs. Only in our security with Christ can we truly be immune to the emotions that bind us. May we have an undisputable revelation of the love of God in its fullness and trust it to be everything we need and more, causing us to be completely free from offense in every form.

Bring us deeper into Your love, Lord, and into fellowship with You! Help us to let the feelings from the past go and bring us higher into Your love and truth. In Jesus' name. Amen.

Spend some time in prayer and let God know how you have been feeling. Be specific and allow the Holy Spirit to minister His love to you.

FALSE BURDENS AND FALSE RESPONSIBILITIES

In Romans 12:1 Paul exhorts us, "Therefore I urge you, brothers and sisters, by the mercies of God, to present your bodies as a living and holy sacrifice, acceptable to God, which is your spiritual service of worship" (NASB). Then Paul continues in verse four to expound on our different acts of service unto the Lord:

> For just as we have many parts in one body and all the body's parts do not have the same function, so we, who are many, are one body in Christ, and individually parts of one another. However, since we have gifts that differ according to the grace given to us, each of us is to use them properly: if prophecy, in proportion to one's faith; if service, in the act of serving; or the one who teaches, in the act of teaching; or the one who exhorts, in the work of exhortation; the one who gives, with generosity; the one who is in leadership, with diligence; the one who shows mercy, with cheerfulness. (Romans 12:4-8 NASB)

This passage highlights for us seven gifts of the Spirit that motivate us. They are prophecy, service, teaching, exhorting, giving, and showing mercy. We would do well to identify which of these gifts we operate in, so we can understand ourselves better. A great resource that expands on all these gifts is a book by Don and Katie Fortune, called *Discover Your God-Given Gifts*. I'd like to highlight mostly the gift of mercy and compassion in this chapter about the blockage of false responsibility as it is the person with the gift of mercy that is most likely to stumble here.

The person with the gift of mercy (very often thought of as the gift of compassion) is beautiful and has been given the amazing ability to express love and patience to those with various needs, and those who may be difficult to love. This is something that our world is in desperate need of, and I would like to say "thank you" to you if you have walked this out as the Spirit has enabled you. People with this gift may be drawn to certain vocations like pastors, missionaries, nurses, doctors, psychologists, psychiatrists, social workers and more.

According to Don and Katie Fortune, a person of mercy may have the following characteristics:

- A tremendous capacity to show love.
- Always looks for good in people.
- Senses the spiritual and emotional condition of a group or individual.
- Is attracted to people who are hurting or in distress.
- Takes action to remove hurts and relieve distress in others.
- Is more concerned for mental and emotional distress than physical distress.
- Is motivated to help people have right relationships with one another.
- Loves opportunities to give preference or place to others.
- Is careful with words and actions to avoid hurting others.
- Easily detects insecurity or wrong motives.
- Is drawn to others with the gift of compassion (mercy).
- Loves to do thoughtful things for others.
- Is trusting and tries to be trustworthy.
- Avoids conflicts and confrontations.
- Doesn't like to be rushed in a job or activity.
- Is typically cheerful and joyful.
- Is ruled by the heart rather than the head.
- Rejoices to see others blessed and grieves to see others hurt.
- Is a crusader for good causes.
- Intercedes for the hurts and problems of others.[85]

---

[85] Don & Katie Fortune, *Discover Your God-Given Gifts* (Grand Rapids: Chosen Books, 2009), 184-194. Print.

Does this sound like you?

The Holy Spirit gives these gifts and functions to us as He wills and what He gives is always perfect. What's not perfect yet, is us. And we still live in a world that is also imperfect. As a result, the unhealed parts of our heart could cause us to practice or function in our gift(s) in a wrong way. Our wounds can cause our gift to be distorted, and we can end up misusing what God has given us, many times without even being aware of it.

Don and Katie list these as potential problems for the compassion person:

- Indecisiveness.
- taking up another person's offense.
- easily hurt by others.
- empathizes too much with the suffering of others.
- affectionate nature that is often misinterpreted by the opposite sex.[86]

I would also add the following to the list above:

- Tends to see every hurting individual as their own little project to fix or save. (This makes the person of compassion the one to most likely carry false burdens and take on responsibilities that are not theirs to take.)

What are false burdens or false responsibilities? Doesn't Christ expect us to *care for* and *help* everyone? The short answer to that last question is, "No." You *individually* are not expected to care for *everyone*. (Did I just hear a sigh of relief?) The broader Church, *as a collective*, is expected to have compassion on everyone and care for those in need—never to overlook anyone, but *individually*, we are given *specific* assignments by God which may include *specific* people He wants us to care for. It is very important for us to discern who it is God has assigned to us and focus our energy and resources there. As well, it's also important to make this distinction: we are

---

[86] Fortune, *Discover Your God-Given Gifts*, 198-200. Print.

expected to have love in our hearts for everyone, but how we are to express that love to each varies. Some we are to love from a distance and some we are called to put legs to our love in closer or close proximity.

False burdens and false responsibilities are burdens and responsibilities that we have not been called by God to take on. If we are taking on responsibilities that we have not been called to take on, we are not anointed for the job. Not being anointed means we do not have the grace, strength, or the blessing from God to do it. In this case, we end up working or attempting to help others in our own strength, accumulating for ourselves dead works—works that lead to death. Remember John 15:5 Jesus says, "I am the vine, you are the branches. He who abides in Me, and I in him, bears much fruit; for without Me you can do *nothing*" (NKJV, emphasis added). When we attempt to work outside of God's will, we're hurting ourselves, and we could be hurting others. We could be getting in God's way of rescuing someone in addition to wearing ourselves right out. Wouldn't the devil just love that? He loves to wear the saints out.

I would encourage you now to begin to ask the Holy Spirit if this is an issue for you. And as you do, let's consider what might cause a person of compassion to take up burdens and responsibilities that don't belong to them.

The world, unfortunately, is a particularly challenging and harsh place for the person of compassion and mercy. Here's what Don and Katie Fortune say about it:

> "The motivational gift of compassion is potentially both the most beautiful gift of all and the most emotionally destructive. It all depends upon the degree to which the compassion person has overcome his or her own emotional wounds... Of all the recipients of gifts, the compassion child needs the most love, tenderness and adult protection. Those who receive this nurturing emerge into adulthood reasonably whole emotionally and are able to cope with

life's challenges. Those who don't often require much encouragement, counseling, deliverance and healing in order to come into their rightful inheritance of a life free of encumbrances."[87]

A person of compassion who has not been healed from their own emotional wounding as Don and Katie Fortune have noted above, can very easily make assumptions, and take it upon themselves to minister to everyone in need who comes into their life, without discerning the Lord's will or purposes. They could also find that ministering to those in need helps them to feel better about themselves, and they can end up doing it for the wrong reasons. Ministering to others can give someone who has felt worthless a sense of purpose and that feels fantastic to our flesh. In fact, it feels so good that it can even become an addiction.

Other factors can also play a part in compelling a person of compassion to over do it. Some children who have had responsibilities put on them too early (often first-born's) because of dysfunction in the home and/or have been abused, become *strong rescuers* and are compelled to rescue *everyone*—siblings, friends, and others who they meet because they have fallen into a pattern, they want to please others, or they don't want others to go through what they went through. We could call this pattern or *compulsion to rescue*, a *messiah complex*. Someone with a *messiah complex* sees it as their job to rescue or save everyone. Of course, we know in our heads that we are no one's savior, but our past wounding can cause us to believe we need to try and save or rescue everyone, none the less.

Let's talk about some real-life examples. God calls Christians to seek Him personally in their own private lives with the goal of forging a relationship of intimacy with Him. However, if a person with a *messiah complex,* steps in and solves or attempts to solve every problem a person is confronted with, they could be thwarting

---

[87] Fortune, *Discover Your God-Given Gifts*, 197. Print.

God's plan by not making it necessary for them to seek God for themselves. God is notorious for shaping our character through adversity.[88] If we make a habit of rescuing people from their adversity, again, we could be getting in God's way.

A great example of someone who God shaped through adversity is Joseph in the Old Testament. Joseph went through much as God formed his character. Joseph was thrown into a pit by his jealous brothers, sold into slavery, thrown in jail, and forgotten about for a season until he was suddenly remembered and recognized for his dream interpretation skills. It was all necessary for Joseph to be developed and matured into a man fit to fulfil the purposes God had for him. In the beginning he was proud and arrogant, but in the end, Joseph was finally able to be the leader God needed.

Here's a question: would you have rescued Joseph given the chance? Or would you have discerned God's purposes in allowing Joseph to go through all he did? Not everyone we see going through a hard time is for us to rescue! We must ask the Lord. Are there those whom you have rescued, time and time again, but they never seem to learn from their experience or rise out of their self-sabotaging ways? Perhaps it's time to break the cycle. There are some who must hear the Lord for themselves and we all must submit to God's process of forming our character and growing us into mature sons and daughters.

Is this making sense yet? Do you see yourself rescuing others? Is it a pattern in your life? Or is it indeed the Holy Spirit leading you *each time*?

One final exhortation: Do not think that *you* are anyone's answer. Jesus ultimately is the answer for each person. We are not. However, Jesus does use us for His purposes to accomplish His work. It is vital that we follow His lead.

---

[88] "And not only this, but we also celebrate in our tribulations, knowing that tribulation brings about perseverance; and perseverance, proven character; and proven character, hope;" (Romans 5:3-4 NASB).

Prayer

Let's repent for taking on false responsibility by praying something like this:

"Dear Lord, I repent for holding responsibility that was never mine to hold and hanging on to responsibility for people, past what You have ordained or called me to. I also repent for carrying burdens that are not mine to carry. (If the Lord shows you specific examples, elaborate your prayer and repent for those specific things.) I repent for getting in Your way, Lord—for rescuing those You were trying to discipline. I ask You to forgive me. Lord, I choose to forgive myself and I choose to receive Your forgiveness in its fullness. I lay down at the foot of Your cross my spouse, children, family members and friends and I choose to trust You with them. I ask You, Lord, to co-parent my children with me, to be the leader in that parenting, and to fill in all the gaps where I miss it and when my children are out of my care—when they're at school and in every place where I am not. I realize that I can't possibly control everything about their lives, and I need Your help. I lay down my spouse and my expectations of them. I choose to trust Your process with them, Lord. I choose to believe that because You love them even more than I do, that You've got them. You are changing them and working in them like only You can.

I lay down every person I have ever ministered to, and I ask You to lead me and give me discernment on who You want me to come along side and help. And who I shouldn't. I lay down every burden I have taken on that was never mine... (be specific if you can). Lord, I realize now that I am NOT responsible for: *(list things that you have felt responsible for but realize now that you are not.)* And I renounce the lie that: *my value is contingent on how many people I rescue* (add any other lies you think you have believed connected to false responsibilities. Examples may be, *I will not be loved*

279

if I don't take responsibility for my younger siblings; I will get in trouble if I don't take responsibility for my younger siblings; My younger siblings may die if I don't take responsibility for them. My own children may die if I don't control them or rescue them. I may lose my child if I don't control him/her. If these are lies that you believe, you will also need to repent for, bind, renounce, and cast out fear.)

I ask You Father to heal every wound in me that has caused me to want to rescue everyone and to take on responsibility that isn't mine. And I ask You to cleanse my bloodline, up and down, of this issue. I forgive my ancestors for operating in false responsibility and I cut off from my descendants the tendency to want to rescue others or help others outside of God's will. I declare that every curse that has been operating because of our disobedience is broken now, in Jesus' name.

I renounce false responsibility, false burdens, and control. I sever all agreement with them now and I choose to forgive myself and every other person who has partnered with me in this sin. I bind every demon associated with them. I bind the demons of false responsibility and control. I bind false burdens and I command false responsibility, false burdens, and control to leave me now in the mighty name of Jesus. (Breathe them out). I command them to leave on my breath right now (breathe deep). Thank You, Father that You are delivering me and setting me free right now, in Jesus' name.

Father, I ask You now to fill me up with Your Spirit—to baptize me afresh in Your Spirit today. I ask You to fill every place in me that has been vacated. I don't want to be empty, Lord. I want to be completely overtaken by You! Come Holy Spirit.

Thank You, Jesus. Thank You, Father. Thank You, Holy Spirit. Amen."

FALSE RELIGIONS AND SECRET SOCIETIES

Our involvement with false religion, cults, and secret societies sets us up for demonic influence and invites demons of error, deception, confusion, and antichrist to attempt to control us. It is therefore necessary to discover what exactly are false religions, cults, and secret societies, to determine if we have been involved in them.

Merriam-Webster defines a cult as "a religion regarded as unorthodox or spurious."[89] Spurious means "of falsified or erroneously attributed origin—forged," and "of a deceitful nature or quality."[90]

In *Kingdom of the Cults*, Walter Martin agrees that a cult is any religious group which differs significantly from the norm of our culture, which is vague, but defines it with a little more clarity by writing:

> "...a cult might also be defined as a group of people gathered about a specific person or person's misinterpretation of the Bible. For example, Jehovah's Witnesses are, for the most part, followers of the interpretations of Charles T. Russell and J.F. Rutherford. . . Jehovah's Witnesses today still look to the Watchtower organization and its Governing Body to understand the Bible. In fact, Jehovah's Witnesses are taught that they *cannot* understand the Bible without the organization explaining it to them."[91]

---

[89] https://www.merriam-webster.com/dictionary/cult
[90] https://www.merriam-webster.com/dictionary/spurious
[91] Walter Martin, *The Kingdom of the Cults* (Minneapolis: Bethany House Publishers, 1965, 1977, 1985, 1997), 17. Print.

John the Apostle wrote first John as a letter to many of the churches in his time. His purpose was to reassure Christians in their beliefs and to counter the false teachings circulating at the time that denied the identity of Jesus Christ as the Son of God. Here's 1 John 4:1-2:

> Dear friends, do not believe everyone who claims to speak by the Spirit. You must test them to see if the spirit they have comes from God. For there are many false prophets in the world. This is how we know if they have the Spirit of God: If a person claiming to be a prophet acknowledges that Jesus Christ came in a real body, that person has the Spirit of God. (NLT)

Jesus Himself said in Matthew 7:15-21:

> Beware of false prophets who come disguised as harmless sheep but are really vicious wolves. You can identify them by their fruit, that is, by the way they act. Can you pick grapes from thornbushes, or figs from thistles? A good tree produces good fruit, and a bad tree produces bad fruit. A good tree can't produce bad fruit, and a bad tree can't produce good fruit. So every tree that does not produce good fruit is chopped down and thrown into the fire. Yes, just as you can identify a tree by its fruit, so you can identify people by their actions. (NLT)

I believe another scripture that helps us identify false teaching is found in 1 John 1:8-10:

> If we claim we have no sin, we are only fooling ourselves and not living in the truth. But if we confess our sins to him, he is faithful and just to forgive us our sins and to cleanse us from all wickedness. If we claim we have not sinned, we are calling God a liar and showing that his word has no place in our hearts. (NLT)

As well, 2 Timothy 3:16:

> All Scripture is inspired by God and is useful to teach us what is true and to make us realize what is wrong in our lives. It corrects us when we are wrong and teaches us to do what is right. (NLT)

In summary, we can identify false religions or cults by the following characteristics:

1. They gather around another person's teachings rather than the teachings directly from the Bible; people are even told they are not able to interpret the Bible on their own and must rely on the teachings of the organization to understand the scriptures.

2. They dispute and don't recognize the true identity of Jesus Christ as divine—the only begotten Son of God, sent by The Father. As a result, they do not *worship* Jesus. They may like Jesus, trust His teachings, respect Him, but they do not *worship* Him as *divine* and are therefore misguided. (Remember Matthew 16:13-17, "When Jesus came to the region of Caesarea Philippi, he asked his disciples, "Who do people say the Son of Man is?" They replied, "Some say John the Baptist; others say Elijah; and still others, Jeremiah or one of the prophets." "But what about you?" he asked. "Who do you say I am?" Simon Peter answered, "You are the Messiah, the Son of the living God." Jesus replied, "Blessed are you, Simon son of Jonah, for this was not revealed to you by flesh and blood, but by my Father in heaven" (NIV).)

3. Their leader(s) and/or founder(s) have consistent bad fruit in their lives displayed in their actions and/or words due to a lack of character and *true* divine direction.

4. They may claim to be sinless and perfect as they are.

5. Lastly, they may not see the Bible as the infallible "Word of God" in its entirety; they want to "cherry-pick" scriptures according to which ones align with their beliefs.

It is important to note in this discussion that we are speaking of groups of religious leaders and adherents who teach a *different* gospel from the true Gospel presented in scripture, involving the distortion of *core* Christian beliefs and the person and work of Jesus. Christians don't always agree on *peripheral issues* but that does not, by any means, give us reason to accuse such as being false teachers, prophets, apostles, etc. Any Christian person or denomination that believes they already have the *full* revelation or understanding of scripture now—that they are 100% right and everyone else is wrong—is operating in arrogance, pride, and deception. We are all still learning and hearing from the Spirit the revelation of the mysteries of God.[92] Remember Jesus said in John 16:12, "There is so much more I want to tell you, but you can't bear it now" (NLT). First Corinthians 13:9-10 says, "For *we know in part* and we prophesy in part. But when that which is perfect has come, then that which is in part will be done away" (NKJV, italics mine).

2 Peter 2:1-2 says:

> But there were also false prophets in Israel, just as there will be false teachers among you. They will cleverly teach destructive heresies and even deny the Master who bought them. In this way, they will bring sudden destruction on themselves. Many will follow their evil teaching and shameful immorality. And because of these teachers, the way of truth will be slandered. In their greed they will make up clever lies to get hold of your money. But God condemned them long ago, and their destruction will not be delayed. (NLT)

Notice in the above passage, false teaching involves destructive heresies, denial of the Master (Jesus), shameful immorality, slandering of truth, and greed. Let's discern rightly the way of truth. Let's be careful who we slap slanderous labels on and be sure not

---

[92] "It is the glory of God to conceal a matter, But the glory of kings is to search out a matter" (Proverbs 25:2 NKJV). (Also: 1 Cor. 4:1, Luke 8:10, Daniel 2:47)

to touch God's anointed ministers and teachers. Just because we don't agree with someone on every point, does not make them a false teacher.

Have you ever been involved in a false religion or cult that teaches false doctrine? Some religions that are considered cults are: Jehovah's Witness, Scientology, Christian Science, Unity, Witness Lee, The Way International, Unification Church, Mormonism, Church of the Living Word, Children of God, Swedenborgians, Worldwide Church of God, Unitarianism, and New Age.[93]

I also strongly suggest breaking association and covenant with any Christian denomination holding a cessationist belief (the view that the manifestation gifts of the Holy Spirit from 1 Corinthians 12:7-11—tongues, miracles, healing, prophecy etc.—were only for the initial Apostolic age when the church was birthed and have now ceased) or an annihilationism belief (the belief that the wicked are ultimately destroyed, ceasing to exist, rather than the biblical understanding of eternal damnation). As well, I suggest renouncing Catholicism because of the many man-made, extra-biblical beliefs they have added along with the worship of Mary and saints.

Other religions teaching doctrine contrary to Christian beliefs, that may or may not be classified as "cults" are: Zen Buddhism, Hare Krishna, Baha'ism, Rosicrucian, Science of the Mind, Science of Creative Intelligence, Hinduism, Sikhism, Taoism, Shinto, Jainism, Eckankar, Roy Masters, Silva Mind Control, Father Divine, Theosophical Society, Islam, and Black Muslim.[94] If you have been involved in any of the aforementioned, don't despair, freedom is just a prayer away:

> "Lord, I confess that I have been involved in (name the false religion) but I now know that (name false religion) doesn't

---

[93] Neil T. Anderson, *Helping Others Find Freedom in Christ: Connecting People to God Through Discipleship Counseling* (Ventura: Regal Books: A Division of Gospel Light, 1995), 279. Print.

[94] Anderson, *Helping Others Find Freedom in Christ*, 279. Print.

honor You because it doesn't teach truth. God, I repent, and I ask You to forgive me for my participation in this false religion and for believing its lies. I choose to forgive myself and every person who led me into it, every person who encouraged me in it, taught me and participated with me. In Jesus' name, I now renounce the lie that (repeat the lie that you were taught and believed). (Repeat this last sentence until you have renounced all the lies the Holy Spirit brings to your remembrance.) I ask You, God, to cut off from my life every effect of these lies, in Jesus' name. I renounce and bind the spirit of (name the religion) and every spirit associated with it. I renounce and bind every lying spirit, the spirit of antichrist, deception, error, confusion, and witchcraft in Jesus' name, and I command all of them to leave me now. Spirit of (name the religion), spirit of lying, spirit of antichrist, deception, error, confusion, and witchcraft, come up and out, in Jesus' name! Go to the feet of Jesus and never come back. (Blow them out of your mouth in faith, if there is no other obvious manifestation like coughing.) Thank You, God, for Your forgiveness and grace in my life and I recognize You, Lord, as supreme. I give You complete control. I say that every curse empowered through false teaching is now broken off my life and I am free in Christ to experience His love, joy, peace, and blessings. Holy Spirit come and fill me afresh, in Jesus' name. Amen"

Secret Societies

Another area we must consider are secret societies like Freemasonry (also considered a cult by many), Eastern Star (women's division of Freemasonry), Job's Daughter, Shriners, The Orange Order (Orangemen), Knights of Columbus, all fraternities/sororities (example: Yale's Skull & Bones, Yale's Scroll and Key, U. of Virginia's Seven Society etc.), Hermetic Order of the Golden Dawn, Knights Templar, Bohemian Club, Sons of Liberty,

Odd Fellows, Bilderberg Group, Ku Klux Klan, Rosicrucians, The Black Hand and more.

There is always a spiritual element to secret societies that will distort truth and the worship of God. Through initiation ceremonies and oaths, participants are always, very subtly and deceptively led to worship false gods, the organization, and the leaders of it. Participants being initiated into the organization are usually required to take oaths of secrecy. Some societies require them to promise secrecy and lead participants to curse specific parts of their own bodies, including internal organs and reproductive organs as well as those of their family members, should they fail to comply. It sounds crazy and it's hard to believe, but these oaths are always on the "downlow" and are never talked about or admitted to. If a participant were ever asked about it, they would always deny it. No one would openly admit to this type of confession or oath taking, but it absolutely does happen. You may not have been involved in Freemasonry yourself, but your ancestors may have been, in which case, it is still very important to pray release from their demonic influence as the curses resulting from Freemasonry pass through the generations to at least four generations deep.

There is an excellent teaching by Linda Heidler from a conference that was held in February of 2015 at Apostle Chuck Pierce's church, Glory of Zion, called, "Reversing the Effects of Freemasonry." Go to YouTube to view the full teaching so that you are informed. The link is https://www.youtube.com/watch?v=8Z-D8bY6rS8 (go ahead and advance the video past the worship segment if you so desire). This link may only be available for a time. Hopefully you can catch it. Here is the prayer she prays at the end of the video to lead you into freedom from Freemasonry and ALL its effects:

"Lord, I come to You in the authority of Jesus, and I renounce all involvement with witchcraft and Freemasonry in my family right now and I stand before You, God, as one who wants my soul, mind, will, emotions, strength, and body, totally submitted and committed to You. I stand before You, God, as Your daughter/son—as one who has been bought by Your blood, who has been set apart for You and by You. Lord, where my true identity in You was exchanged for a false identity, or where I allowed a false identity to be imposed on me and where my true authority in You was stolen and replaced by false authority, I repent of it and renounce it now and I say, "give it back!" Right now, I take back my God-given identity that He created for me, and I take back the God-given authority that He has invested in me as His child and co-heir. Lord, where I have relinquished my God-given value or where it was stripped away from me, where I have been subjected to a value system that required me to perform and word hard in order to prove my worth or to feel like I was worth anything at all, I renounce it and I break away from that system right now; that is not the truth of God. I do not agree with it anymore. I reject the belief that I have to work, strive or prove my worth in order to be loved and I declare that my worth comes from God, and I am worthy of love simply because He made me. I take back my God-given, unique, intrinsic value and worth right now in Jesus' name. I throw out that slipshod slipper and I put on what God has given me. I declare that my feet are shod with the shoes of the gospel of peace and that I am prepared to share that peace wherever I go. I declare that I am sure footed, and that God has given me hinds' feet—feet that are able to walk in high places without intimidation or fear—feet that are swift, agile, and nimble in order to navigate any terrain and escape any trap. I declare that I am able to leap and run into my destiny with God and when I see the vision, I am going to run for it and not be worried about being tripped up by any slipshod slipper. Right now, I pull off that hoodwink and I take back my mind, my eyes, my ears, and my mouth. I now open my eyes, ears, and mouth and I declare that I am free to think, see, hear, and speak the way God wants me to. My spiritual senses are completely open to discern what God wants me to discern. I grab hold of my access to the mind of Christ and the wisdom of God, and I am going to expect and allow God to transform and conform my mind to the mind of Christ without hindrance. I am ripping off this noose from around my neck that has caused me to be in bondage and under the control of a freemason spirit; I am not going to be led around by any false worship system or spirit anymore. I declare that my heart and soul are now free to follow the leading of the Holy Spirit and that ugly spirit that opposes and hates the Holy Spirit is not going to have any influence or control over me anymore. I take away that dagger from my chest, and I decide right now that I will no longer guard my emotions or be fearful of expressing myself. I choose to release my emotions, and I declare that I am going to know the joy of the Lord and the joy of my salvation. I am going to know the compassion of Jesus; I'm going to know the love of God like I've never known it before. Where I have been blocked from knowing the love that God has for me, I'm not going to be blocked anymore. I am going to freely receive the love of God. I repent and renounce the words spoken by my family member before me, when they said they were "seeking the light of Freemasonry." Right now, I pull that dark cover off my spirit and I take back my spirit that was made to commune with my Heavenly Father, to commune with the Holy Spirit—that was made to receive revelation from Him. I take back my spirit and declare that it is free to commune with God and receive from Him and I ask You, Lord, for new levels of communion and revelation. Right now, I renounce and break all of the oaths and vows and curses spoken against my body, and I take back the health that You pre-ordained and purchased for me, God. I take back the strength in my body that You want me to have. Your Word says that Your Spirit living inside of me quickens my mortal body and causes me to be in health. Lord, I know that my body is important to You as it is Your temple, so I refuse to have my body infested with sickness, disease, weakness, or infirmity. I take back what You have given to me and what is rightfully mine, in Jesus' name.

I declare that I have repented of all participation in the ceremonies of Freemasonry. I have renounced the spiritual transactions that took place in those ceremonies. I have reclaimed my God given identity, worth, and destiny. I have reclaimed my soul, mind, emotions, will, and senses. I have reclaimed my physical body. I have reclaimed my spirit. I have broken all covenant agreements with the false religious system of Freemasonry.

I now submit myself, body, soul, and spirit to the living God, the God of Israel, Maker of heaven and earth. I fully enter into covenant with Him. I now position myself in active resistance to the devil. According to the Word of God: Submit to God, resist the devil, and he must flee (James 4:7)! I claim my right to every blessing of God in place of the curses that have been affecting my life. The Word of God says that the blessing of God will overtake me. Healing, prosperity, favor, protection, power, wisdom, and all the blessings of God are now free to come on me and my children. I am unhindered by any connection to false worship. I now freely enter into a new level of worship of the true and living God and of Jesus, His only Son with all my heart, soul, mind, and strength. I WILL go to new realms of worship in the Spirit and will join with angels in worshipping You, Lord. I will fulfill the destiny for which I was created. I will storm the gates of hell and prevail. Hallelujah! Amen."[95]

---

[95] Linda Heidler, *Reversing the Effects of Freemasonry*, YouTube. https://www.youtube.com/watch?v=8Z-D8bY6rS8.

I would also add:

"I choose to forgive every ancestor who participated in Freemasonry or any other secret society; I forgive them for every curse and oath they spoke against me, my body, and my children and their bodies. I forgive them for activating curses against us and I forgive every person who deceived them, leading them into the secret society, and leading them while in it. I choose to forgive every person who led their initiation ceremony and I pray also for their families as well—that they would be set free from Freemasonry too, in Jesus' name. Amen"

FINAL THOUGHTS

Wow! It's been a wild ride, I know. I pray you are not shell shocked by all the issues we are called to work through. Do not be discouraged! This is a process, and you can revisit this book any time. Thanks for sticking with it my friend. I deeply respect your willingness to allow the Holy Spirit to lead you through some tough terrain.

Eternal life is a gift. Romans 6:23 says, "For the wages of sin is death, but the gift of God is eternal life in Christ Jesus our Lord" (NIV). It is not something that can be earned or bought. It is free, and it is from the Lord.

Imagine for a moment that salvation is a gift wrapped in shiny silver paper with a beautiful ribbon and bow. In order for that gift to be yours, you must accept it, receive it, and take into your hands. Once it's yours, you have a choice. You can choose to simply admire the pretty wrapping and display it on a shelf or you can open it. If you don't open it, you will never know what *all* is inside.

Many Christians don't open the gift. They receive it but they don't open it and realize all the contents of the gift—all that it means for them. They think the gift is having an eternal home in heaven when they leave this earth, but what they don't know or believe is that it's so much more than that.

Second Corinthians 8:9 says, "You know the generous grace of our Lord Jesus Christ. Though he was rich, yet for your sakes he became poor, so that by his poverty he could make you rich" (NLT). In this passage, Paul is encouraging the Corinthians to be generous in their giving but at the same time he illustrates for us a miracle that occurred at the cross—the miracle of exchange. Paul highlights the exchange of our poverty for His riches and many other verses in the Bible tell us of other things that Jesus has exchanged with us. We have received His righteousness in exchange for our guilt and sin.

We have received His health in exchange for our sickness. We have received His life in exchange for our death. We have received His spiritually alive nature for our fallen, dead one—and we could go on. The key to an exchange though is the release of the old. We could not receive true life if we weren't willing to give up our old life, which in reality is death, and we wouldn't be able to receive freedom if we didn't give up our sin and bondage.

Have you ever heard the analogy of the eagle that was raised in a cage? The eagle had the wings and the ability to fly—the ability to soar at great heights, but since it was raised in a cage, it was familiar with the cage. Even though the door was open, it didn't venture out. The eagle stayed in captivity even when it had the option to be free.

Have we gotten used to our captivity? Are we sometimes like that eagle that won't pursue or choose freedom? I think sometimes we are. I think our mindsets and wounded soul condition become familiar, like old slippers that we've worn forever, that have molded to our feet; they "feel" right, and they "feel" comfortable even though the foam on the bottom has worn out and flattened completely. New slippers would be better, but we prefer the old ones that we know—the ones we have become attached to. "I don't need to change. I'm fine," we say to ourselves as we obstinately refuse refining. "There's nothing wrong with this cage. I have food. I have air. I'm surviving just fine the way I am." Although this may be true, simply surviving is not what we are meant to do. We are meant to thrive! We are meant to soar! Yes, it takes some work. It takes some grit, but it is better to reach for the high call of God on our life than to just sit in complacency. God calls us higher.

I pray you are willing to reach for the higher places in God to experience His goodness and healing. I pray that you will run the good race and fulfill your destiny in Christ. May the mercy and goodness of God be made manifest before you, behind you, beside you, and all around you. May His healing come upon you powerfully and lift you up into a revelation of heaven on earth. And I pray that at the end of your life, when you are received into Glory, you will hear, "Well done, good and faithful servant" and that you will be received with shouts and cheers from all the saints.

All glory to God for His magnificent, amazing power which He has made available to us, His children—those who trust in Him completely, fully, and eternally. Thanks for allowing me to speak into your life.

Blessings upon blessings be yours in Christ Jesus! Amen.

APPENDIX A

Healing Scriptures

Psalm 23
Exodus 15:26
Exodus 23:24-26
Romans 10:17
Isaiah 55:6-12
2 Samuel 22
Psalm 103:1-4
Psalm 91
Psalm 121
Psalm 107:19-20
Psalm 34:19
Psalm 118:14-17
Isaiah 53:1-6
Matthew 13:10-15
Mark 11:22-25
Matthew 8:14-17
Isaiah 54:4-10, 13-17
Isaiah 57:18-19
1 Peter 2:21-25
Proverbs 4:20-27
Proverbs 3:5-8
Proverbs 12:28
Proverbs 16:24
Mark 5:25-34
Mark 9:23
Romans 8:31-39
Psalm 41:1-3

1 Corinthians 1:30
2 Corinthians 5:21
Matthew 5 :17-18
John 14:27
John 16:33
1 John 4:1-4
John 10:7-10
John 6:63
1 John 5:1-5
1 John 5:18
Colossians 2:9-10
Colossians 2:13-15
Galatians 3:13-14
Romans 8:1-2
Romans 8:11-15
Romans 5:17
Romans 6:10-14
2 Corinthians 5:17
Colossians 1:13-14
Colossians 1:21-22
James 4:7-10
James 1:17-25
John 14:12-14
Romans 12:1-2
Matthew 16:13-19
Revelation 12:11

APPENDIX B

Occult, Pagan, witchcraft practices for which we need to repent:

- horoscopes, getting a psychic reading, practicing divination (operating as a psychic), reading Tarot cards, palm reading, tea leaf reading, astrology / Zodiac signs, chakra reading, coffee ground reading, channeling, clairvoyance, putting faith in charms / crystals or oils, enchantments, extrasensory perception, fortune-telling, grave soaking, casting hexes, idol worship, casting incantations and/or spells, practicing magic, operating as a medium or going to a medium, nature worship, necromancy, omens, Ouija Board, parapsychology, psychokinesis, sacrifices in all forms, séances, sending energy, sorcery, spirit guides, tag locking, telepathy, transcendental meditation, witchcraft, wizardry, manifesting, numerology, astral projection, shape-shifting, automatic writing, table lifting, levitation, anthroposophy, animism, blood pacts, voodoo, fetishism, chasing ghosts, Wicca, Kabbalah, spiritism (being a Spiritist/talking to the dead), Theosophy, New age.

Alternative healing modalities that open us up to demons (because they look to and engage spiritual power from a source other than God or they have originated in a false religion or the practice of "spiritism") for which we need to repent:

- Reiki, Acupuncture, Dry-needling, Hypnosis, Chiropractic[96], Yoga, energy healing.

---

[96] Chiropractic began in 1895 with Daniel David Palmer who was a spiritist (someone who talks to the dead). Wikipedia says, "As an active spiritist D. D. Palmer said he "received chiropractic from the other world" from a deceased medical physician."

A Note on Yoga

Yoga originated with the spiritual practices in Hinduism and Buddhism. *Yoga* means "yolk" or "union." The poses in Yoga are named after and represent Hindu and Yogic deities [false gods or what we call demons]. Here's a quote from a website about yoga: "As a way of connecting to, revering and paying respect to deities, many yoga postures represent not just what the deity looks like, but also everything they stand for. As we practice the posture, we put our focus on the energy and essence of the deity and look to embody their qualities."[97] Here's the definition of Yoga from Wikipedia: "Yoga is a group of physical, mental, and spiritual practices or disciplines that originated in ancient India, aimed at controlling body and mind to attain various *salvation goals*, as practiced in the Hindu, Jain, and Buddhist traditions." Salvation goals? We've already attained salvation. Let's not mess with it by playing with false gods. God has already told us that He is the only true God and legitimate source of spiritual power. We need to believe Him.

All yoga fruit comes from the ancient yoga tree with the original roots; It doesn't matter how you attempt to alter the fruit or polish it up, all yoga fruit comes from that ancient tree of deception.

Prayer to Come out of Agreement with Yoga

"Father, I confess that I have participated in Yoga. I repent. Please forgive me. Forgive me for paying homage to and worshipping false gods through the movements of my body. I repent for using my body as an instrument of unrighteousness. I didn't know what I was doing; I was deceived.

I choose to forgive myself, every Yoga instructor, and every person who participated with me or led me into it. I receive Your forgiveness, Lord.

---

[97] [https://www.ekhartyoga.com/articles/practice/6-sacred-yoga-poses]

I renounce Yoga, idolatry and false worship. I bind and renounce every deity associated with Yoga including Lakshmi, Saraswati, Durga, Hanuman, Dancing Shiva, Chakrasamvara, Hevajra, Kalachakra, Krishna, Radha, Shiva, Ganesha, Vishnu, Brahma, Kali, Parvati, Mahakala, and Tara. I bind and renounce the eight limbs of Yoga, and the Kundalini spirit. I renounce every Yoga pose and move I have done. I ask You, Lord, to deliver me from each one right now. I command every one of these false gods and their demons to leave me right now, in Jesus' name! Go! Leave me now and go to the feet of Jesus. (Breathe. Continue to command them to go until you sense that you are free. Envision them leaving upon your natural breathing.) Thank You, Jesus. Fill me with Your Spirit afresh. In Jesus' name, amen."

ABOUT THE AUTHOR

Barbara is an author, spiritual mentor, and pastor at heart, who has been passionately pursuing Jesus and the Kingdom of God for more than 30 years. With the Lord moving powerfully in her, she has experienced victory over barrenness, physical issues, and emotional strongholds that have threatened to control her life and is now imparting the same to others. Her passion is to share the love and power of God to heal from the inside out, through prayer and deliverance with all who will receive.

With a solid foundation on the Bible, the infallible Word of God and established fruit in her life, Barbara moves in the gifts of healing, discerning of spirits and prophecy for the encouragement of all and for the equipping of the Saints.

Barbara is aligned with Apostle Barbara Yoder of Michigan and Patricia King's Women in Ministry Network.

Barbara's other books are available on Amazon:

1. *Key to Fertility: Re-Writing Your Stories for Success in Conceiving and Birthing Babies*
2. *Barren No More: Prayer Strategy for Every Believer Experiencing Fertility Challenges*
3. *Sweet Sorrow - Releasing Your Son to His Bride: What Every Mother Needs to Know*
4. *Identity Theft: Coming Back to the Perfect Intentions of God for My Life, coming soon.*

Suggested Reading:
Victory Over the Darkness by Neil T. Anderson, *Prayers that Rout Demons* by John Eckhardt, *The Bait of Satan* by John Bevere, and *Destroying the Spirit of Rejection* by John Eckhardt

BIBLIOGRAPHY

Anderson, Neil T. *Helping Others Find Freedom in Christ*. Ventura, California: Regal Books, 1995.

Anderson, Neil T. *Victory Over the Darkness*. Bloomington, Minnesota: Bethany House, 2014.

Bevere, John. *The Holy Spirit – An Introduction*. Palmer Lake, Colorado: Messenger International, 2013.

Carr, Dr. Douglas E. *Free Indeed from Root Spirits*. Sturgis, Michigan: DCFreedomMinistry, 2014.

Carr, Dr. Douglas E. *Patterns of Perversity: Freedom from Iniquity*. Sturgis, Michigan: DCFreedomMinistry, 2022.

Carr, Dr. Douglas E. *777: 7 Curses, 7 Sprinklings & 7 Blessings*. Sturgis, Michigan: DCFreedomMinistry, 2024.

Dedmon, Kevin. *The Ultimate Treasure Hunt*. Shippensburg, Pennsylvania: Destiny Image Publishers, 2007.

Idleman, Kyle. *gods At War: The Battle for Your Heart That Will Define Your Life*. Louisville, Kentucky: City on a Hill Productions, 2012. DVD.

Malone, Dr. Henry. *Shadow Boxing*. Lewisville, Texas: Vision Life, 1999.

Martin, Walter. *The Kingdom of the Cults.* Minneapolis, Minnesota: Bethany House Publishers, 1965, 1977, 1985, 1997.

Pierce, Chuck D. *God's Now Time for Your Life*. Ventura, California: Regal Books, 2005.

Sheets, Dutch. *Authority in Prayer: Praying with Power and Purpose*. Minneapolis, Minnesota: Bethany House, 2006.

Sheets, Dutch. *Intercessory Prayer*. Ventura, California: Regal Books, 1996.

Ward Heflin, Ruth. *Glory: Experiencing the Atmosphere of Heaven*. Hagerstown, Maryland: McDougal Publishing, 1990, 2000.

Wilson, Darren. *Father of Lights*. WP Films, 2012. DVD.